Agent-Based Models in Economics

In contrast to mainstream economics, complexity theory conceives the economy as a complex system of heterogeneous interacting agents characterised by limited information and bounded rationality. Agent-based models (ABMs) are the analytical and computational tools developed by the proponents of this emerging methodology. Aimed at students and scholars of contemporary economics, this book includes a comprehensive toolkit for agent-based computational economics, now quickly becoming the new way to study evolving economic systems. Leading scholars in the field explain how ABMs can be applied fruitfully to many real-world economic examples, and represent a great advancement over mainstream approaches. The essays discuss the methodological bases of agent-based approaches and demonstrate step-by-step how to build, simulate and analyse ABMs, and how to validate their outputs empirically using the data. The contributors also present a wide set of model applications to key economic topics, including the business cycle, labour markets and economic growth.

DOMENICO DELLI GATTI is Economics Professor at Catholic University, Milan, Department of Economics and Finance. He is Director of the Complexity Lab in Economics. His research interests focus on the role of financial factors (firms' and banks' financial fragility) in business fluctuations. Together with Mauro Gallegati he has provided important contributions to agent based macroeconomics (e.g., the book Macroeconomics from the Bottom Up). He has published extensively in high ranking journals and is editor of the *Journal of Economic Interaction and Coordination*.

GIORGIO FAGIOLO is Professor of Economics at the Institute of Economics, Scuola Superiore Sant'Anna, Pisa. His research interests include agent-based computational economics; empirics and theory of economic networks; and the statistical properties of microeconomic and macroeconomic dynamics. His papers have been published in numerous journals including *Science*, the *Journal of Economic Geography*, and the *Journal of Applied Econometrics*.

MAURO GALLEGATI is Professor of Economics at the Università Politecnica delle Marche, Ancona, and he has been a visiting professor in several Universities, including Stanford, MIT and Columbia. He has published journal papers in numerous subject areas including agent based economics, complexity, economic history, nonlinear mathematics, and econophysics, and he sits on the editorial board of several economic journals and book series.

MATTEO RICHIARDI is Senior Research Officer at the Institute for New Economic Thinking, Martin Oxford School, University of Oxford; an assistant professor at the University of Torino, an associate member of Nuffield College, Oxford; and an affiliate of Collegio Carlo Alberto, Torino. An internationally recognised scholar in both agent-based and dynamic microsimulation modelling, he has also worked as a consultant on labour market policies for the World Bank. He is Chief Editor of the *International Journal of Microsimulation*, and project leader of JAS-mine, an open source simulation platform for discrete event simulations (www.jas-mine.net).

ALBERTO RUSSO is Assistant Professor of Economics at the Università Politecnica delle Marche, Ancona. His research interests include agent based modelling and complexity economics, inequality and macroeconomic dynamics, and financial fragility and systemic risk. He has published in such recognized journals as *International Journal of Forecasting*, the *Journal of Economic Behaviour and Organization*, and the *Journal of Economic Dynamics and Control*. He also serves as guest editor and referee for several international journals.

Agent-Based Models in Economics
A Toolkit

Edited by

DOMENICO DELLI GATTI
Catholic University of the Sacred Heart

GIORGIO FAGIOLO
Sant'Anna School of Advanced Studies

MAURO GALLEGATI
Marche Polytechnic University

MATTEO RICHIARDI
University of Torino

ALBERTO RUSSO
Marche Polytechnic University

CAMBRIDGE
UNIVERSITY PRESS

University Printing House, Cambridge CB2 8BS, United Kingdom

One Liberty Plaza, 20th Floor, New York, NY 10006, USA

477 Williamstown Road, Port Melbourne, VIC 3207, Australia

314-321, 3rd Floor, Plot 3, Splendor Forum, Jasola District Centre, New Delhi - 110025, India

79 Anson Road, #06-04/06, Singapore 079906

Cambridge University Press is part of the University of Cambridge.

It furthers the University's mission by disseminating knowledge in the pursuit of
education, learning and research at the highest international levels of excellence.

www.cambridge.org
Information on this title: www.cambridge.org/9781108414999
DOI: 10.1017/9781108227278

© Cambridge University Press 2018

First published 2018

A catalogue record for this publication is available from the British Library

Library of Congress Cataloging in Publication data
Names: Delli Gatti, Domenico, editor.
Title: Agent-based models in economics : a toolkit / edited by
Domenico Delli Gatti [and four others].
Description: Cambridge, United Kingdom ; New York, NY :
Cambridge University Press, [2017] | Includes bibliographical references and index.
Identifiers: LCCN 2017042298 | ISBN 9781108414999 (Hardback : alk. paper) |
ISBN 9781108400046 (Paperback : alk. paper)
Subjects: LCSH: Econometric models. | Economics–Mathematical models.
Classification: LCC HB141 .A3185 2017 | DDC 330.01/5195–dc23
LC record available at https://lccn.loc.gov/2017042298

ISBN 978-1-108-41499-9 Hardback
ISBN 978-1-108-40004-6 Paperback

To our heterogeneous most relevant ones.

An important scientific innovation rarely makes its way by
gradually winning over and converting its opponents:
What does happen is that the opponents gradually die out.

(Max Planck)

Contents

Figures

Tables

Contributors

Domenico Delli Gatti (Catholic University of the Sacred Heart, Milan, Italy) is Professor of Economics at Catholic University of the Sacred Heart, from which he received his PhD in 1987. His research interests focus on the role of financial factors (firms' and banks' financial fragility) in business fluctuations, a field he started exploring in collaboration with Hyman Minsky in the late 1980s and revisited in a new light due to the research work carried out with Joe Stiglitz and Bruce Greenwald since the 1990s. He has been a visiting scholar to several universities, including Stanford, Massachusetts Institute of Technology and Columbia. He was previously the editor of the *Journal of Economic Behavior and Organization* and is currently the editor of the *Journal of Economic Interaction and Coordination*. Recently he has devoted his research effort to two areas of research: the first one concerns the properties of multi-agent models characterised by "financial frictions"; the second area concerns the properties of networks in borrowing-lending relationships.

Giorgio Fagiolo (Sant'Anna School of Advanced Studies, Pisa, Italy) is Full Professor of Economics at Sant'Anna School of Advanced Studies, where he holds a tenured position in the Institute of Economics. He holds a bachelor's degree in mathematical statistics from the Sapienza University of Rome and a PhD in economics from the European University Institute (Florence, Italy). His main areas of scientific interest include agent-based computational economics, complex networks, evolutionary games, industrial dynamics and economic methodology (with particular emphasis on the scientific status of agent-based computational economics, empirical validation of economic models and their policy-related implications). His papers have been published in Science, *Journal of Economic Geography, Journal of Applied*

Econometrics, PLOS ONE, Journal of Economics Dynamics and Control, Computational Economics, New Journal of Physics, Physical Review E, Journal of Economic Behavior and Organization, Journal of Artificial Societies and Social Simulations, Global Environmental Change, and Macroeconomic Dynamics – among others.

Mauro Gallegati (Marche Polytechnic University, Ancona, Italy) obtained his PhD in Economics in 1989 from the University of Ancona with a thesis on financial fragility, supervised by Hyman Minsky. He is currently Professor of Economics at the Marche Polytechnic University. He has been a visiting professor at several universities including Stanford, Massachusetts Institute of Technology and Columbia. He is on the editorial board of several economic journals and book series. His research includes business fluctuations, nonlinear dynamics, models of financial fragility and heterogeneous interacting agents. He is well known from his widely cited work with Bruce Greenwald and Joseph E. Stiglitz, developing theory of asymmetric information and heterogeneous agents and their applications. He has published papers in the top journals on economics, economic history, history of economic analysis, nonlinear mathematics, applied economics, complexity and econophysics.

Matteo Richiardi (University of Turin, Italy) is a senior research officer at the Institute for New Economic Thinking, Oxford Martin School, University of Oxford; assistant professor at the University of Turin; associate member of Nuffield College, Oxford; and affiliate of Collegio Carlo Alberto, Turin. He received an MSc in economics from University College London, and a PhD in economics from the University of Turin. He is habilitated to full professor in Italy. He has also worked as a consultant on labour market policies for the World Bank. Richiardi is an internationally recognised scholar in both agent-based and dynamic microsimulation modelling. His work involves both methodological research on estimation and validation techniques, applications to the analysis of distributional outcomes and the functioning of the labour market and welfare systems. He is the chief editor of the *International Journal of Microsimulation*, and project leader of JAS-mine, an open-source simulation platform for discrete event simulations (www.jas-mine.net).

Alberto Russo (Marche Polytechnic University, Ancona, Italy) has been Assistant Professor of Economics at Marche Polytechnic University since December 2008. He obtained his PhD in economics from the University of

Pisa in 2005. He was a post-doc research fellow at the Scuola Normale
Superiore di Pisa from 2005 to 2007. His main research interests are
agent-based modelling and complexity economics, inequality and
macroeconomic dynamics, financial fragility and systemic risk, social classes
and distribution and experimental economics. He has published in recognised
journals, such as *International Journal of Forecasting, Journal of Economic
Behavior and Organization, Journal of Economic Dynamics and Control,
Journal of Economic Issues, Journal of Evolutionary Economics,
Macroeconomic Dynamics, Metroeconomica*, among others. He serves as
guest editor, as well as referee, for international journals, organizes
international conferences and collaborates on Italian and European research
projects.

Preface

As Schumpeter pointed out long ago, conceptual frameworks, models and policy prescriptions are embedded in the economist's 'preanalytic vision' of the economy. And preanalytic visions have been, and still are, very different in the profession.

Nowadays the majority of the profession embraces the *neoclassical approach* to economic behaviour, according to which agents are endowed with substantial rationality, adopt optimal rules and interact indirectly through the price vector on markets which are continuously in equilibrium. This approach has been extraordinarily fruitful, as it has allowed economists to build models that can be solved analytically and yield clear-cut policy implications. The obvious case in point is Walras's theory of General Equilibrium, beautifully outlined in his *Elements d'Economie Politique*, and elegantly extended and refined by Arrow and Debreu. Moreover, the approach has been remarkably flexible. Appropriately designed variants of the neoclassical approach have been applied to economies characterised by imperfect competition, imperfect information, strategic interaction, and heterogeneous agents. The most insightful of these theoretical developments have been incorporated in micro-founded macroeconomic models of the *New Neoclassical Synthesis* that have been all the rage during the years of the Great Moderation.

However, the capability of the neoclassical approach to encompass and explain all the complex details of economic life has reached a limit. For instance, it is now abundantly clear that the neoclassical approach is not well-suited to describe the Global Financial Crisis and the Great Recession. In models that follow the New Neoclassical Synthesis, in fact, a great recession may be explained only by a large aggregate negative shock, whose probability is extremely low (i.e., it is an extreme and rare event). This mechanism does not clarify much of the crisis and does not help to devise appropriate remedies.

The current predicament, both in the real world and in the public debate, resembles the early 1930s. The way out of the Great Depression required a new economic theory and the Second World War.[1] Luckily, in order to escape the current predicament, we can dispense at least with the latter. We still need, however, to reshape the way in which we think about the economy.

For several years now, a *complexity approach* has been developed which conceives the economy as a complex system of heterogeneous interacting agents characterised by limited information and bounded rationality. In this view, a 'crisis' is a macroscopic phenomenon which spontaneously emerges from the web of microscopic interactions. *Agent-Based Models (ABMs)* are the analytical and computational tools necessary to explore the properties of a complex economy.

Agent-based macroeconomics is still in its infancy, but it is undoubtedly a very promising line of research. So far only a small minority in the economic profession has adopted this approach. This may be due to the wait-and-see attitude of those who want to see the approach well established in the profession before embracing it. The hesitation, however, may also come from methodological conservatism. For instance, while in other disciplines the explanatory power of computer simulations is increasingly recognized, most economists remain dismissive of any scientific work that is not based on strict mathematical proof.[2] With the passing of years, however, agent-based (AB) tools have been refined. This book is a guide to the main issues which an interested reader may encounter when approaching this field. We hope this will help in nudging a new generation of curious minds to explore the fascinating field of complexity.

We thank for comments, criticisms and insightful conversations Tiziana Assenza, Leonardo Bargigli, Alessandro Caiani, Alberto Cardaci, Ermanno Catullo, Eugenio Caverzasi, Annarita Colasante, Giovanni Dosi, Lisa Gianmoena, Federico Giri, Jakob Grazzini, Bruce Greenwald, Ruggero Grilli, Alan Kirman, Roberto Leombruni, Simone Landini, Domenico Massaro, Mauro Napoletano, Antonio Palestrini, Luca Riccetti, Andrea Roventini, Joe Stiglitz, Leigh Tesfatstion.

This book benefited from funding from the European Community's Seventh Framework Programme (FP7/2007–2013), INET, CRISIS, NESS, and MATHEMACS.

---

[1] The unemployment rate, which peaked at 1/4 of the labour force during the Great Depression, went back to the long-run 'normal' of around 1/20 only after the end of the war. The huge increase in government spending due to the war effort helped to absorb the unemployment generated by the Great Depression.

[2] A recent intriguing line of research aims at providing analytical solutions to multi-agent systems adopting the apparatus of statistical mechanics, e.g., the Fokker-Planck equations. See, for instance, M. Aoki (2011), Di Guilmi (2016).

1

Introduction

Domenico Delli Gatti and Mauro Gallegati

1.1 Hard Times for Dr Pangloss

High and persistent unemployment, over-indebtedness and financial instability, bankruptcies, domino effects and the spreading of systemic risk: these phenomena have taken center stage in light of the Global Financial Crisis.

By construction, the *Neoclassical approach* is much better suited to study the features of the world of Dr Pangloss (Buiter, 1980) than the intricacies of a complex, financially sophisticated economy. This point is well taken in the introduction of a seminal paper by Bernanke, Gertler and Gilchrist published well before the Global Financial Crisis: 'How does one go about incorporating financial distress and similar concepts into macroeconomics? While it seems that there has always been an empirical case for including credit-market factors in the mainstream model, early writers found it difficult to bring such apparently diverse and chaotic phenomena into their formal analyses. As a result, advocacy of a role for these factors in aggregate dynamics fell for the most part to economists outside the US academic mainstream, such as Hyman Minsky, and to some forecasters and financial market practitioners.' (Bernanke et al., 1999, p. 1344).

This candid admission by three of the most distinguished macroeconomics (one of them destined to be Chairman of the Federal Reserve for eight long and turbulent years) – which, incidentally, provides a long overdue implicit tribute to Hyman Minsky – also provides the research question for a model of the *financial accelerator* which has started a non-negligible body of literature in contemporary macroeconomics.

In order to put this development in macroeconomic thinking into context, it is necessary to recall that any mainstream macroeconomic model is based on a Dynamic Stochastic General Equilibrium (DSGE) skeleton, which can support either a Real Business Cycle (RBC) model or a New Keynesian (NK) model.

The latter differs from the former because of the presence of *imperfections*, the most important being imperfect competition and nominal rigidity. The structural form of the standard NK-DSGE framework boils down to a three-equation model consisting of an optimising IS equation, an NK Phillips curve and a monetary policy rule based on changes in the interest rate.

The NK-DSGE framework is, of course, too simple and therefore inadequate to analyse the emergence of a financial crisis and a major recession for the very good reason that neither asset prices nor measures of agents, financial fragility show up anywhere in the model. In order to make the model operational from this viewpoint, *financial frictions* have been incorporated into the basic model in one way or another.

In the last decade we have witnessed an explosion of models with these types of frictions. The story that can be attached to this literature, however, can be told in simple terms. A negative shock triggers a recession and yields a reduction of firms' internally generated funds. Borrowers need more funds, but lenders are less willing to supply loans as the value of firms' collateral is also going down. Hence, firms might be forced to scale activity down. This in turn will lead to lower cash flow, and to a *further deceleration* of activity.

The financial accelerator provides a mechanism of *amplification* of an aggregate shock (i.e., a positive feedback or a self-reinforcing mechanism) based on financial factors. By construction, however, it cannot be a model of the *origin* of a financial crisis and the ensuing recession.

As in all DSGE models, in fact, in models characterised by financial frictions a fluctuation is also determined by an aggregate shock (an impulse) and is channeled to the economy by a propagation mechanism. Moreover, the stability of the steady state makes fluctuations persistent but relatively short lived. Therefore, a great recession may be explained only by a sizable aggregate negative shock and is bound to disappear relatively soon. Recent models incorporating financial frictions trace back the great recession to a major negative shock (possibly of a new type: an 'investment shock', a 'financial shock' instead of the usual Total Factor Productivity shock) which spreads through the economy and becomes persistent because of the financial amplification, but is temporary so that the economy goes back to equilibrium in due time.

This view of the Global Financial Crisis is not convincing. It does not provide a plausible theory of its origin, since the crisis was not the consequence of a global shock, but originated from a small segment of the US financial system (the subprime loans market) and spread to the entire US financial system and to the world economy. Moreover, it does not provide an appropriate characterisation of the actual recovery, which has been unusually long and painful.[1] In fact, during the recession, quantitative forecasts of future GDP growth (also at a very short-time horizon) generated by these models systematically overestimated actual GDP growth.

The financial accelerator story is intriguing, but is not enough to characterise a major crisis. Models with financial frictions yield interesting results, but their scope is necessarily limited because of the built-in features of the DSGE framework. This framework, in fact, abstracts from the complex web of financial and real relationships among heterogeneous agents that characterise modern financially sophisticated economies and are at the root of the spreading of financial fragility economywide. Contemporary macroeconomics, in other words, has assumed away most of the features of the economy which are relevant today.

1.2 The Complexity View

For several years now, a different approach has been developed which conceives the macroeconomy as a *complex system* of heterogeneous agents characterised by bounded rationality, endowed with a limited and incomplete information set, interacting directly and indirectly with other agents and the environment.

In a complex economy, an idiosyncratic shock – i.e., a shock to a specific agent – can well be the source of an epidemic diffusion of financial distress. In other words, idiosyncratic shocks do not cancel out in the aggregate, especially if the macroeconomy is characterised by an underlying network structure and the idiosyncratic shocks hit crucial nodes of the network. Therefore a recession may not be caused only by an aggregate shock.

To be specific, in a credit network, the financial accelerator can lead to an avalanche of bankruptcies due to the positive feedback of the bankruptcy of a single agent on the net worth of the 'neighbours' linked to the bankrupt agent by credit relationship. This is, of course, ruled out by construction in a framework with a representative firm and a representative bank.

In order to deal with these issues, one has to start with a population of heterogeneous agents. *Heterogeneity*, therefore, is key in modelling the phenomena which we want to investigate.

---

[1] The idea of a 'secular stagnation' pioneered by L. Summers, which is gaining ground in the profession, is based exactly on the unusual length and painfulness of the recovery from the Great Recession.

1.3 Heterogeneity in a Neoclassical World

The way in which financial frictions have been incorporated in current macroeconomic models provides an example of a recurrent pattern in the development of contemporary macroeconomics. Research issues brought to the fore by new macroeconomic facts are incorporated into an analytical edifice based on neoclassical foundations by means of appropriate twists of some assumptions or by additional assumptions, as epicycles in Ptolemaic astronomy. This is the way in which 'normal science' (in Kuhn's wording) adjusts to real macroeconomic developments. In this way, there is nothing truly new under the sun.[2]

Heterogeneity has been incorporated in Neoclassical models since the early 1990s. This is an impressive achievement, as the Neoclassical approach is utterly unsuitable for the study of this issue. In a Neoclassical Representative Agent-Rational Expectations world, equilibrium prices depend on a relatively small number of state variables and shocks. Forming Rational Expectations of future prices in such an environment is a daunting but not impossible task, as the Representative Agent in the model has the same information of the modeller herself, the 'true' model of the economy included (at least in reduced form).

Things are much more complicated in a multiagent setting. In this case, equilibrium prices are in principle a function of the entire distribution of agents (e.g., households' wealth). Hence, to form expectations, agents need to know the entire distribution at each point in time, i.e., the law of motion of this distribution. An impossible task. This is the well known 'curse of dimensionality'.[3] Neoclassical Heterogeneous Agents Models have been developed in order to study the causes and consequences of income and wealth inequality in a DSGE framework.[4]

These papers by Imrohoroglu, Hugget, Aiyagari essentially relax only the Representative Agent assumption (and only as far as households are concerned), but generally retain all the other conceptual building blocks of

---

[2] As Max Planck put it: 'Normal science does not aim at novelties of fact or theory and, when successful, finds none.'

[3] One possible way is to keep the number of agents low, i.e., to reduce the dimensionality of the problem (two types of agents). An example, among many, is the NK-DSGE framework with Limited Asset Market Participation, where households can be either free to access financial markets or financially constrained. In the latter case, households cannot smooth consumption by borrowing and lending.

[4] These models are also known as Bewley models (according to the terminology proposed by Ljungqvist, 2004) or Standard Incomplete Markets models (Heathcote, 2009). Notice that Heterogeneous Agents and Incomplete Market go hand-in-hand, for reasons which will become clear momentarily.

DSGE models (intertemporal optimization, continuous market clearing and general equilibrium).[5]

In Aiyagari (1994) households are heterogeneous because of idiosyncratic shocks to earnings. If the markets were complete, these shocks would be insurable and therefore they would not impinge on average or aggregate consumption (they would wash out in the aggregate).[6] Under these circumstances, the long-run or 'equilibrium' distribution of wealth would be both indeterminate and irrelevant (because any distribution of wealth would yield the same average behaviour).

If markets were incomplete, on the contrary, the possibility to insure against idiosyncratic risk would be limited and therefore: (1) idiosyncratic risk would impact on consumption (and macroeconomic performance), (2) the equilibrium distribution of wealth would be determinate. In Aiyagari's model particularly, inequality yields precautionary savings which impact positively – through investment – on growth.

Research in this field has been extended in at least three directions: (1) the analysis of other sources of heterogeneity (besides idiosyncratic shocks to earnings), e.g., innate characteristics; (2) the analysis of additional ways to insure idiosyncratic shocks; (3) the impact on aggregate fluctuations (see Heathcote, 2009). Focusing on the third line, we will single out the pioneering paper by Krusell and Smith (Krusell and Smith, 1998) as typical of the approach.

Krusell and Smith circumvent the curse of dimensionality in a very smart way. They summarise the shape of the agents' distribution by means of a finite number of its moments. In this way they can abstract from the actual distribution and be as precise as they wish in describing its shape: the larger the number of moments considered, the more granular the description of the distribution. For simplicity, they use only two moments: The first moment (mean) captures the central tendency of the distribution; the second moment (variance) captures the dispersion, one aspect of the degree of heterogeneity characterising the distribution. When dispersion is low, the mean of the distribution is almost sufficient to describe the distribution itself. Therefore

---

[5] See Rios-Rull (1995) for a review of early work in this area.
[6] Completeness and homothetic preferences imply a linear relationship between consumption and wealth at the individual level, i.e., Engel curves are linear. In this case, perfect approximation applies: average consumption will be a linear function of average wealth. Only the first moment of the distribution of wealth is necessary to determine average (and aggregate) consumption. Heterogeneity, as captured by the variance and higher moments of the distribution, is irrelevant. Of course this is no longer true if the relationship between consumption and wealth at the individual level is nonlinear. If the relationship were concave, for instance, an increase in the dispersion of wealth would lead to lower consumption on average – thanks to Jensen inequality – even if the mean were preserved.

higher moments of the distribution can be safely ignored and one can think of the economy as if it were a Representative Agent world, identified with the Average Agent.

Agents in a Krusell-Smith economy are 'near rational' as they optimise using only the moments of the distribution. Forming near rational expectations of future prices in such an environment is a daunting but not impossible task, as equilibrium prices are functions only of the moments of the distribution instead of the entire distribution.

In this model there is *approximate aggregation*: 'in equilibrium all aggregate variables ... can be almost perfectly described as a function of two simple statistics: the mean of the wealth distribution and the aggregate productivity shock' (Krusell and Smith, 1998, p. 869). Using only these measures, near-rational agents are able to minimise the forecast errors (therefore higher moments of the distribution do not affect the decision of the agents).

Moreover, Krusell and Smith show through simulations that macroeconomic time series generated by the model are almost indistinguishable from those generated by a Representative Agent model. Hence macroeconomic fluctuation can be sufficiently described by fluctuation of the mean; higher moments of the distribution do not add much to the picture. In other words, taking heterogeneity on board does not add much to the accuracy of the model. Only the first moment of the distribution has macroeconomic consequences. In a sense, this is a very smart way of resurrecting the moribund Representative Agent and the macroeconomic literature based on it.

However, as shown by Heathcote (2009), with reference to fiscal shocks, there are indeed real-world circumstances in which heterogeneity has important macroeconomic consequences, even in Neoclassical multiagent models.

1.4 Agent-Based Models (ABMs)

The research agenda of the Neoclassical multiagent literature is very specific, dictated by the self-imposed guidelines on the way in which economic theorising should take form in the Neoclassical approach. Heterogeneity, therefore, is key in these models, but is dealt with in a restricted, disciplined environment. This may be considered a virtue of the approach, but can also be a limitation as issues and problems which are indeed important 'out there' in the real world are left out of the admissible set of issues and problems to be dealt with. *Agent Based Models* (ABMs) have a completely different origin and a much more flexible agenda. ABMs are the analytical and computational tools developed by an interdisciplinary network of scientists – physicists, economists, computer scientists – to explore the properties of *Complex Adaptive Systems* (CAS), i.e., 'systems comprising large numbers of coupled elements the properties of which are modifiable as a result of environmental interactions ... In general CAS are highly nonlinear and are organised on many spatial and temporal scales' (1st workshop on CAS, Santa Fe, 1986).

In ABMs a multitude of objects, which are heterogeneous under different profiles, interact with each other and the environment. The objects are autonomous, i.e., there is no centralised (top-down) coordinating or controlling mechanism. Therefore, ABMs cannot be solved analytically. The output of the model must be computed and consists of simulated time series.

Agent-based Computational Economics (ACE) is the application of agent-based (AB) modelling to economics or: 'The computational study of economic processes modelled as dynamic systems of interacting agents' (Tesfatsion and Judd, 2006, p. 832). The economy, in fact, can be conceived of as a complex adaptive system.

Behavioural equations may or may not be derived from optimization. AB modellers generally prefer to assume that agents are characterised by bounded rationality; they are 'not global optimisers, they use simple rules (rules of thumb) based on local information' (Epstein, 2006a, p. 1588).[7]

No equilibrium condition is required (out-of-equilibrium dynamics). This is, in a sense, a consequence of the assumption according to which there is no top-down coordinating mechanism in ABMs. The Walrasian auctioneer, who is gently nudging the agents towards an equilibrium position, is indeed a metaphor of such a top-down coordinating mechanism. AB modellers, in fact, generally prefer to assume that markets are systematically in disequilibrium. In principle, however, at least some markets may converge to a statistical equilibrium.

ABMs are built from the bottom-up. At the micro-level, the behaviour of heterogeneous agents is captured by simple, often empirically based heuristics which allow for adaptation, i.e., gradual change over time in response to changing circumstances. Aggregate variables are determined by means of summation or averaging across the population of heterogeneous agents. Instead of untying the Gordian knot of aggregation, in ABMs this is cut by allowing the computational tool to do the job. Due to interaction and nonlinearities, statistical regularities emerge at the macroscopic level that cannot be inferred from the primitives of individuals. These *emergent properties* are at the core of macroeconomics in a complex setting. Generally, aggregate variables in

---

[7] In principle, however, behavioural rules can be either grounded in bounded rationality (rules of thumb) or can be derived from specific optimization problems (optimal rules).

macroeconomic ABMs (e.g., GDP) show a tendency to self-organise towards a stable aggregate configuration occasionally punctuated by bursts of rapid change. The self-organisation of the macroeconomy can be represented by a *statistical equilibrium* in which the aggregate spontaneous order is compatible with individual disequilibrium. The equilibrium of a system no longer requires that every single element be in equilibrium by itself, but rather that the statistical distributions describing aggregate phenomena be stable, i.e., in 'a state of macroscopic equilibrium maintained by a large number of transitions in opposite directions' (Feller, 1957, p. 356). This is not general equilibrium in the standard meaning, i.e., a state in which demand equals supply in each and every market.

In a macroeconomic ABM – i.e., an ABM applied to the macroeconomy – a 'crisis', i.e., a deep downturn followed by a long and painful recovery, is a macroscopic phenomenon which spontaneously emerges from the web of microscopic interactions. In a macro ABM, in other words, big shocks are not necessary to explain big recessions, an appealing property indeed in light of the Global Financial Crisis.

The real-world phenomena that are conceived of as rare 'pathologies' in the Neoclassical view – high and persistent unemployment, over-indebtedness and financial instability, bankruptcies, domino effects and the spreading of systemic risk – turn out to be the spontaneous emerging macroscopic consequence of complex interactions in a multiagent framework with heterogeneous agents.

1.5 Plan of the Book

The main aim of this book is to provide an introduction to Agent-Based Modelling methodology with an emphasis on its application to macroeconomics.

The book is organised as follows. In Chapter 2 we answer the most basic questions: What is an ABM? When is it necessary and/or appropiate to build such a model? The chapter ends with a succinct overview of a very early example of ABM: Schelling's model of racial segregation.

In Chapter 3 we provide a formal characterisation of an ABM as a recursive model. We put ABMs in the wider context of simulation models and introduce notation and key concepts to describe the agents' state and behavioural rules in ABMs in rigorous terms.

Chapter 4 is devoted to a general overview of rationality, the determination of behavioural rules and expectation formation in contemporary macroeconomics, from Keynesian aggregative models to macroeconomic ABMs passing through monetarist, New Classical and New Keynesian models. This survey allows us to put the AB methodology into context and paves the way to the more detailed analysis of behavioural rules and learning processes in Chapter 5.

Chapter 5, in fact, digs deeper into the definition and description of the agent's rationality and learning processes. Where do behavioural rules come from? Agents in real economies are intentional subjects. In order to decide on a line of action (a behavioural rule), in fact, they must form mental representations of their environment and of the behaviour of other agents. Behavioural rules in the real world, therefore, must be related to the cognitive processes that guide actions. Learning is a key ingredient of these cognitive processes.

Chapter 6 deals with the issue of interaction, which is key in ABMs. In a sense, the chapter is an introductory overview of network theory, a rapidly expanding field both in mainstream and complexity theory. ABMs, in fact, are often based on an underlying network structure, e.g., of trading relationships, credit relationships, supply chain, etc.

Chapter 7 explores the research outcome of an ABM, i.e., the model behaviour. The AB researcher, in fact, sets up the 'rules of the game' – i.e., she builds the model – but does not know in advance the implications of those rules, e.g., the statistical structure of the output of simulations. The chapter presents techniques to gain understanding about the model behaviour – the Data Generating Process implicit in the ABM – which are quite underexplored in the AB literature. In a model which requires simulations, only inductive knowledge about its behaviour can be gained, by repeatedly running the model under different samples from the parameter space.

Chapter 8 is devoted to the empirical validation of ABMs. Empirically validating an ABM means, broadly speaking, 'taking the model to the data', essentially in the form of empirical and/or experimental data. Validation may concern the model inputs and/or outputs. Input validation is essentially the assessment of the 'realism' of the assumptions on which the model rests while output validation is the assessment of the capability of the model to replicate in artificial or simulated data the stylised facts of economic reality under consideration. Output validation is a joint test on the structure of the model and the values of the parameters. This means that input and output validation are connected.

Chapters 9 deals with the issue of estimation of ABM parameters, an intriguing new field which aims to align the empirical validation techniques of ABMs to that of standard macroeconomic models where estimation tools are readily available and relatively easy to implement.

2

Agent-Based Computational Economics: What, Why, When

Matteo Richiardi

2.1 Introduction

What are agent-based (AB) models? In a nutshell, they are models (i.e., abstract representations of the reality) in which (i) a multitude of objects interact with each other and with the environment, (ii) the objects are autonomous (i.e., there is no central, or "top-down," control over their behavior and, more generally, on the dynamics of the system)[1], and (iii) the outcome of their interaction is numerically computed. Since the objects are autonomous, they are called agents. The application of agent-based modeling to economics is called Agent-Based Computational Economics (ACE). As Leigh Tesfatsion – one of the leading researchers in the field and the "mother" of the ACE acronym – defines it, ACE is

> the computational study of economic processes modeled as dynamic systems of interacting agents (Tesfatsion, 2006).

In other terms, AB models are the tool traditionally employed by ACE researchers to study economies as complex evolving systems, that is systems composed by many interacting units evolving through time.

None of the features above, in isolation, define the methodology: the micro-perspective implied by (i) and (ii) is roughly the same as the one adopted, for instance, by game theory, where strategic interaction is investigated analytically (though in game theory the number of individuals who populate the models is generally very small). The computational approach, instead,

---

[1] The Walrasian auctioneer, for instance, is a top-down device for ensuring market clearing. Another example of top-down control is the consistency-of-expectations requirement typically introduced by the modeler in order to allow for a meaningful equilibrium in neoclassical models. More on this point on Section 2.2 below.

is typical of Computational General Equilibrium or Stock-Flow Consistent models, which are, however, based on aggregate representations of the system.

In this introductory chapter we describe the features of AB models (Section 2.2), offering an overview of their historical development (Section 2.3), discussing when they can be fruitfully employed and how they can be combined with more traditional approaches (Section 2.4). As an example, we describe one of the first and most prominent AB models, Thomas Schelling's Segregation model (Section 2.5). Conclusions follow.

2.2 Features of Agent-Based Models

The basic units of AB models are the "agents." In economics, agents can be anything from individuals to social groups – like families or firms. They may also be more complicated organizations (banks for instance), or even industries or countries. Agents can be composed by other agents: the only requirement being that they are perceived as a unit from the outside, and that they *do* something – that is they have the ability to *act* – and possibly *react* to external stimuli and *interact* with the environment and with other agents.

The environment, which may include physical entities (like infrastructures, geographical locations, etc.) and institutions (like markets, regulatory systems, etc.) can also be modeled in terms of agents (a central bank, the order book of a stock exchange, etc.), whenever the conditions outlined above are met. If not, it should be thought of simply as a set of variables (say "weather" or "business confidence") characterizing the system as a whole or one of its parts. These variables may be common knowledge among the agents or communicated throughout the system by some specific agent – say the statistical office – at specific times. From what we have said so far, it should be clear that aggregate variables like consumption, savings, investment and disposable income, which are the prime units of analysis of Keynesian macroeconomics, cannot be modeled as agents in an AB framework as they are computed by aggregating microeconomic agent quantities; the same applies to the fictitious representation of a representative agent (RA), a cornerstone of neoclassical economics. Therefore, ACE can in principle provide sound microfoundations for traditional Keynesian macroeconomics, and sound aggregate results for the neoclassical analysis based on individual optimization. The direct modeling of a demand or a supply curve is also forbidden in an agent-based setting: rather, these aggregate functions may (or may not) emerge as the outcome of the decisions of the individual agents.

2.2.1 Scope of Agent-Based Models

AB models are in general developed to analyze the effects of *interaction*. What do we exactly mean by interaction? An interaction between agents in a real-world economy may take many different forms. It may represent a physical exchange of commodities, but it may also be a direct exchange of information or knowledge, or even an expectation relationship (agent A thinks that agent B is relevant for the consequences of her actions, and therefore forms an expectation over agent B's future actions). Notice that such a general definition of interactions encompasses the traditional notion of externalities in economics, which is one of the possible causes for market failures. The AB approach, contrary to the standard approach to economics, does not treat externalities as a perversion of an economic system, but it acknowledges their central role in shaping social dynamics. As we shall show in more detail throughout this chapter, the fact that agents directly interact in nontrivial ways is often central to understand how and why economies behave as we observe them to do in reality.

In general, common AB research questions are related to how the aggregate behavior of a system is affected by differences in individual behavior, individual characteristics, norms and institutions, etc. The focus of interest is generally *explanation* and *replication*, rather than *prediction* and *control* (Epstein, 2008). In other terms, much more effort has been historically put in describing reality like it is, and possibly explaining why it is like we observe it, rather than understanding how it will be and what we need to do to make it like we would like it to be.

AB models are typically general (dis)equilibrium models: both the supply side and the demand side of a market are explicitly modeled, and the feedback between the different sides/level of analysis (micro and macro, for instance) constitute the main object of interest. However, unlike what happens in the standard general equilibrium model, there is no top-down restriction preventing the economy to always fluctuate out-of-equilibrium. In fact, equilibrium in its traditional meaning is not a requirement in AB modeling, and if any type of equilibria emerges, it must be an endogenous outcome generated by the interactions among the agents. For example, in general equilibrium models, the aggregate supply-demand equivalence is posited as an assumption. In equivalent AB models of market dynamics, one would typically observe an evolving relationship between aggregate supply and demand, which may not always be perfectly balanced, but nonetheless may tell us something about the endogenous re-equilibrating ability of the economy.

All that accounts for the complexity of AB models and requires that individual behavior is kept as simple as possible to avoid the risk of having an excessively rich model which would then hamper interpretation and analysis.[2] These common characteristics are a distinctive feature of AB models and distinguish the methodology from other techniques that share the same basic ingredients – once again, micro-foundations and a computational approach. In particular, they discriminate between AB models and *microsimulation*, a technique used to investigate the effects of individual heterogeneity, often in one-sided models of a market (labor supply for example), mainly for prediction or policy analysis.

2.2.2 The Whole and Its Parts

Having agents as the unit of analysis, AB modeling is deeply rooted in *methodological individualism*. This doctrine was introduced as a methodological precept for the social sciences by Max Weber, most importantly in the first chapter of Economy and Society – although the term was already present in Schumpeter.[3] Methodological individualism amounts to the claim that social phenomena must be explained by showing how they result from individual actions, which in turn must be explained through reference to the intentional states that motivate the individual actors.[4] However, the term still bears some ambivalence over whether explanations should be in terms of individuals alone, or in terms of individuals plus their interaction (Hodgson, 2007). In the first meaning, methodological individualism suggests that the "whole" is nothing but the "sum of its parts," a position that has been labeled *reductionism* (Jones, 2000). This interpretation implies that the aggregate behavior can be derived observing the behavior of a single agent, a position that is clearly incompatible with the AB modeling approach. On the other hand, reductionism is implicit in the RA paradigm, which claims that the whole society can be analyzed in terms of the behavior of a single, representative individual.

The opposite view is *holism*, the idea that the properties of a given system cannot be determined or explained by the sum of its component parts alone; rather, the system as a whole determines in important ways how the parts behave.[5] As such, holism is closely related to *organicism*, introduced as a biological doctrine stressing the importance of the organization, rather than

---

2 A 1:1 map of reality being not only almost impossible to build, but also by far useless.
3 See Weber (1968) and Schumpeter (1909).
4 The use of methodological individualism in Economics was championed by the Austrian school of Economics in the twentieth century, of which Friederich von Hayek was one of the main exponent (von Hayek, 1948). The legacy of Hayek to agent-based modeling and the complex system approach (see, for instance, von Hayek, 1967) has been amply recognized (Rosser, 1999; Vaughn, 1999; Koppl, 2000; Vriend, 2002; Rosser, 2010).
5 The general principle of holism was concisely summarized by Aristotle in his Metaphysics: "The whole is more than the sum of its parts."

the composition of organisms.[6] This view has gained renewed popularity as a new science of Complexity – which, as we will discuss in the next section, is to a large extent responsible for the introduction of AB models in the study of social and biological systems – developed in the last decades of the twentieth century.

So, where does AB modeling stand in this debate? As already noted, AB models are characterized by the fact that aggregate outcomes (the "whole") are computed as the sum of individual characteristics (its "parts"). However, aggregate behavior can often be recognized as distinct from the behavior of the comprising agents, leading to the discovery of unexpected ("emergent") properties. In this sense, the whole is more than – and different from – the sum of its parts. As the Nobel prize-winning physicist Philiph Anderson concisely expressed, "More is different" (Anderson, 1972). It might even be the case that the whole appears to act *as if* it followed a distinct logic, with own goals and means, as in the case of a cartel of firms that act in order to influence the market price of a good. From the outside, the whole appears no different from a new agent type. A new entity is born, the computational experiment has been successful in "growing artificial societies from the bottom up."[7] Epstein (2006b, p. 66) explains the point with the following analogy:

> Suppose we know all of the underlying components of a system and all of the rules by which these components interact – does it then follow that we understand the system? Perhaps not. For example, if we know the color, shape and location of every piece of glass in a stained glass window, do we necessarily know what figure will emerge from their conglomeration? While clearly all the information is there, we may not be able to imagine what the completed window looks like just from reading about each piece and its location. We may need to "assemble" the window in some form before any kind of image can emerge. We might get a good idea of the window by using a crude line drawing, or perhaps a more elaborate full-color diagram will be required. The level of necessary detail will be linked to some inherent characteristics of the actual image. In some cases, the easiest way to "know" the window is to assemble the entire thing piece by piece.

2.2.3 The Dual Problem of the Micro-Macro Relationship

As we have seen, AB modeling allows us to investigate the interplay occurring at two different scales of a given system: the micro structure and the macro structure. This investigation may occur in two directions: (i) to find the

---

[6] William Emerson Ritter coined the term in 1919.
[7] As in the title of the well-known book by Epstein and Axtell (1996).

aggregate implications of given individual behaviors and interaction structures, and (ii) to find the conditions at the micro level that give rise to some observed macro phenomena. We refer to these two perspectives as the *dual problem* of the micro-macro relation. Both share the same approach: "If you didn't grow it, you didn't explain it" (Epstein, 1999), which motivates the definition of ACE as *generative social science*.

Of course, AB modeling is by no means the only way to study the dual problem of the micro-macro relation. However, taking into account the interaction of a multitude of (heterogeneous) agents of possibly different types easily becomes analytically intractable, and the traditional approach of simplifying everything may – as it should be clear from the discussion above – "throw the baby out with the wash water." On the contrary, AB models only require to "wait and see" the unveiling of the consequences of the assumptions, and leave much more freedom than conventional economics in the specifications of the assumptions.

Because of this focus on the theoretical links between micro and macro, the typical AB model is a relatively small "toy" model, where only the essential features for some interesting aggregate properties to emerge from the rules of micro interaction are included, possibly at the expenses of realism.[8] However, in recent years, larger AB models are starting to appear, claiming a richer empirical content. These models explicitly aim at replacing dynamic stochastic general equilibrium (DSGE) as the workhorse at the core of macroeconomics, and constitute at present the biggest challenge for AB research.[9]

2.2.4 Adaptive vs. Rational Expectations

The generative approach of AB modeling has one crucial theoretical impli-cation, which accounts for the main divergence with neoclassical models: *rational expectations* (RE) are banned.

The assumption of RE – which was introduced in economics by Muth (1961) – states that agents' predictions of the future value of economically relevant variables are not systematically wrong, because all errors are random. This amounts to say that RE are model-consistent: all agents in the model are able to solve the model and behave in a mutually consistent way so that outcomes meet expectations, on average; no one regrets his decision rule, though many may be disappointed by the outcome.[10] Thus, RE lead naturally

---

[8] As exemplified by the Schelling's segregation model described later in the chapter.
[9] See Dawid et al. (2013) and Caballero (2010).
[10] The strongest version of RE leads to the efficient-market hypothesis, which asserts that financial markets are "informationally efficient" and no arbitrage opportunities can arise.

to Nash-type equilibria concepts: given an equilibrium outcome, no (rational) individual would unilaterally depart.

Appealing as it seems, RE have a number of drawbacks and limitations. First, their application to macro models with representative agents is theoretically flawed as it suffers from the usual aggregation problem: even if all individuals have RE, the representative household describing these behaviors may exhibit behavior that is not rational.[11] But, admittedly, this is a problem of RA, not of RE. However, even in a truly microfounded model with perfect knowledge, RE outcomes might easily be non-computable: agents have to anticipate the outcome and conform to it in advance; therefore, the system "jumps" to the equilibrium. In the best case, off-equilibrium trajectories converge to the equilibrium path. However, strong hypotheses are needed for such convergence properties to hold, and these are not warranted by the assumptions made at the micro level. The existence of an RE Nash equilibrium (or of some refinements thereof) does not imply that such an equilibrium is attainable, not to say that it can be attained on reasonable time scales or at reasonable computing costs. As Duncan Foley summarizes:

> The theories of computability and computational complexity suggest that there are two inherent limitations to the rational choice paradigm. One limitation stems from the possibility that the agent's problem is in fact undecidable, so that no computational procedure exists which for all inputs will give her the needed answer in finite time. A second limitation is posed by computational complexity in that even if her problem is decidable, the computational cost of solving it may in many situations be so large as to overwhelm any possible gains from the optimal choice of action" (Albin, 1998).

By converse, in AB models – much as in the real world – agents are characterized by *bounded rationality* and hold *adaptive expectations* (Conlisk, 1996; Gigerenzer and Selten, 2001a). They have to *learn* from their experience and possibly from other agents. They are goal seekers and they can be forward looking, but their ability to infer the rules of the game in order to form expectations is constrained by what they know about the model they inhabit, which is typically limited and may change over time. Moreover, their computing ability is also constrained. They therefore have to use simple rules based on local information (Edmonds, 1999; Manson, 2006; Pyka and Fagiolo, 2007; Hommes, 2009).

How does individual and social learning affect the behavior of a system? An extreme viewpoint is that evolutionary mechanisms will result in surviving individuals with high levels of rationality, or those who will behave *as if*

---

[11]   See Janssen (1993).

they were fully rational. Professional billiard players might not be able to assess numerically the angles and distances of the balls, compute the optimum directions of travel, and hit the balls at the exact point and with the strength indicated by the formulas. However, if they were not able to reach essentially the same result, they would not in fact be expert billiard players: they behave as if they knew the math, and the same math can be used by some external observer to describe and predict their action (Friedman, 1953).

However, it is not true that individual rationality always leads to individually optimal outcomes, nor that competitive pressure is able to compensate for lack of individual rationality. The winner curse exemplifies: in a common-value auction with incomplete information, the auctioned item is worth roughly the same to all bidders, who differ only by their respective estimates of the market value. The winner is the bidder with the highest bid, which reflects the highest estimate. If we assume that the average estimate is accurate, then the highest bidder overestimates the item's value: thus, the auction's winner is likely to overpay.

It is also not true that a sub-optimal individual behavior necessarily leads to inefficiencies. For instance, it is generally acknowledged that freeways cannot sustain a flux of more than 2,000 vehicles per hour per lane. However, urban freeways are able to carry about 2,500–3,000 vehicles per hour per lane, because drivers "learn" that in order to go faster they have to restrain from passing slower vehicles (Richiardi, 2005).

The same holds with social outcomes. While neoclassical modeling implicitly assumes that "the invisible hand requires rational fingers" (Epstein, 2006b, p. 26), AB models allow us to investigate how different types of fingers work, from the dumbest to the more expert.

Note that while it is easy to implement adaptive expectations in a computer simulation, it is very cumbersome to simulate agents with rational expectations (the opposite is true in analytical models), as this involves solving the problem of the agents simultaneously, while the computer is essentially a sequential machine.[12] It could be argued that the same holds for real agents.

2.2.5 Additional Features of Agent-Based Models

We have so far introduced the three fundamental characteristics of AB models: there are agents that play the role of actors, there is no script or *deus ex-machina*[13] and the story is played "live" (computed).

---

[12] See Chapter 5 on AB models as recursive systems.
[13] In the Greek theater, a mechanism was used to drop one or more divinities on the stage to solve complicated situations, in which there was no apparent way out.

However, there are a number of characteristics that are often found in AB models, and may motivate their use. Following Epstein (1999; 2006a), we can include:

- *Heterogeneity.* While in analytical models there is a big advantage in reducing the ways in which individuals differ, the computational burden of an AB model does not change at all if different values of the parameters (preferences, endowments, location, social contacts, abilities, etc.) are specified for different individuals. Normally, this is done by choosing a distribution for each relevant parameter, and this simply implies that a few parameters (those governing the distribution) are added to the model.
- *Explicit space.* This can be seen as specification of the previous point: individuals often differ in the physical place where they are located, and/or in the neighbors with whom they can or have to interact (which define the network structure of the model).
- *Local interaction.* Again, this can be seen as a specification of the network structure connecting the agents. Analytical models often assume either global interaction (as in Walrasian markets), or very simple local interaction. AB models allow for much richer specifications.
- *Scalability.* AB models can be easily scaled up. This is different from analytical models, where solutions can generally be found either for very few or very many agents. For example, in physics, planetary motion can be analytically handled only with one, two, three or infinitely many planets. Similarly, in economics, analytical models exist for monopolies, duopolies and perfect competition. However, there are many examples where the scaling up of a system (by increasing the number of agents or the number of choices) might end up in a very different behavior: for instance, when a phase transition occurs at some threshold. The identification of these qualitative change in behavior or, by converse, of scaling regularities (scaling laws) might be important in understanding a dynamical system. In an AB model, the only constraint for scaling up a model is computing time. This should not be downplayed, and great care should be taken that the model remains of tractable computational complexity; but as computing power constantly increases, the issue is in principle of limited importance.[14]

---

[14] By tractable computational complexity we generally mean models that can be computed in polynomial time, $O(n^k)$, where k is a nonnegative integer and n is the complexity of the input. Indeed, according to the Cobham-Edmonds thesis, computational problems can be feasibly computed on some computational device only if they can be computed in polynomial time; that is, if they lie in the complexity class $\mathbb{P}$. However, the size of the exponent k and of the input n does matter: when n is large, even $O(n^3)$ algorithms are often impractical.

• *Nonequilibrium dynamics*. AB models are (stochastic) recursive models, in which the state of the system at time $t + 1$ is computed (or probabilistically evaluated) starting from the state at time t. Hence, they allow the investigation of what happens all along the route, not only at the start and at the end of the journey.

The latter point is of great importance and must be elaborated upon. W. Brian Arthur (2006) offered a beautiful and concise statement of its relevance for economic theory:

> Standard neoclassical economics asks what agents' actions, strategies, or expectations are in equilibrium with (consistent with) the outcome or pattern these behaviors aggregatively create. Agent-based computational economics enables us to ask a wider question: how agents' actions, strategies or expectations might react to – might endogenously change with – the pattern they create. In other words, it enables us to examine how the economy behaves out of equilibrium, when it is not at a steady state.

> This out-of-equilibrium approach is not a minor adjunct to standard economic theory; it is economics done in a more general way. [...] The static equilibrium approach suffers two characteristic indeterminacies: it cannot easily resolve among multiple equilibria; nor can it easily model individuals' choices of expectations. Both problems are ones of formation (of an equilibrium and of an "ecology" of expectations, respectively), and when analyzed in formation – that is, out of equilibrium – these anomalies disappear.

Of course, the fact that AB models can be investigated out of equilibrium does not mean that equilibrium analysis is not relevant for AB models. Think of equilibrium as some sort of "constant" behavior, either at the micro or at the macro level: a regularity that the model is able to produce, under some circumstances. Admittedly, this is a very loose definition of equilibrium, and we will come back to it in Chapter 5. What is sufficient to say here is that the characterization of such regularities is an inescapable requirement for the understanding of the behavior of a system. Moreover, a regularity needs not to be *absorbing* (once there, the model displays it forever since); it may be *transient*, and vanish after some time, possibly when some other condition is met. These transient regularities might characterize the adjustment phases, or – in Artur's parlance – the nonequilibrium properties of the system. What we believe is important to stress is that a model without regularities is *useless*: we don't really need a formal apparatus to say that anything can happen. We can go further, claiming that a model without regularities is *impossible*: a model that has no properties does not exist (even pure white noise can be formally characterized). In this sense, equilibrium analysis is not marginalized by AB modeling. But the point remains that in AB modeling, we can let the properties of the system manifest themselves and study their dynamic unfolding.

2.3 The Development of ACE

The roots of AB modeling can be traced down to the study of cellular automata.[15] AB models further developed within the evolutionary economics approach and the so-called Santa Fe perspective on the study of complex systems, though an overlooked antecedent, is to be found in the dynamic microsimulation literature.

2.3.1 Evolutionary Roots

From a historical point of view, the first attempts to introduce in the study of economic dynamics thinking concepts like bounded rationality, adaptive expectations, disequilibrium, local interactions and so on, come from what we now label "evolutionary economics" (Dosi and Nelson, 1994). Evolutionary economics employs metaphors and notions from evolutionary biology to describe the dynamics of firms, markets and economies over time. Central to this approach are the notions of *selection* (only the best firms survive competition), *variety* over which selection operates (firms are heterogeneous in their knowledge bases and cognitive repertoires, such as behavioral and learning rules), *novelty* (firms endogenously introduce innovations) and *interaction* (firms exchange information and knowledge).

The seminal book by Nelson and Winter (1982) was a landmark achievement in this respect, as it presented a series of stylized models of industry dynamics very much in the spirit of what we now call AB models. These models describe the evolution of industries characterized by boundedly rational firms and analyzed by means of simulations, in line with the suggestions of Herbert Simon (1981).

The book emphasized the role of *routines* and *heuristics*. These behavioral rules need to be *robust* in the sense that they can be used repeatedly and successfully in similar circumstances, but *simple* enough to be developed by real world agents without the computational abilities and mental sophistication of rational profit maximizers neoclassical agents. Despite their simplicity, heuristics and routines can be applied to solve, in intelligent ways, the complex

---

[15] See von Neumann and Burks (1966); Gardner (1970); and, for a first application to social issues, Schelling (1969).

problems faced everyday by real world organizations. Just as a Rubik's cube solver decomposes the problem of getting a cube with each face consisting of one color in smaller but simpler tasks (getting a single face with one color, then adding another face with another color and so on), firms facing complex problems (introducing an innovation, coping with turbulent markets, etc.) try to decompose them in smaller tasks and goals to which they apply some preexisting routine. In other words, problems that, like the Rubik's cube, are extremely difficult (if not impossible) to solve in a one-shot way, are typically decomposed in easily recognizable sub-modules to which there is already a solution. Efficiency is traded off for feasibility: rationality, in many difficult and interesting cases, may not be an intelligent way to cope with a problem (Dosi et al., 2005).

Evolutionary economics can be seen as one of the first, most important, antecedents of the ACE approach. ACE is in some sense a more general perspective, as it is not necessarily linked with the idea of selection typical of the evolutionary camp. This has restricted the applicability of evolutionary models to situations where selection is an issue, primarily industry and firm dynamics. The demand side of the markets were instead less prone to be modeled via the variety-selection metaphor (consumers are not selected on the base of what they choose to consume).

2.3.2 The Santa Fe Perspective: The Economy as an Evolving Complex System

The development of AB computational economics is closely linked with the work conducted at the Santa Fe Institute, a private, not-for-profit, independent research and education center founded in 1984 in Santa Fe, New Mexico. The purpose of the Institute has been, since its foundation, to "foster multidisciplinary collaboration in pursuit of understanding the common themes that arise in natural, artificial, and social systems." This unified view is the dominant theme of what has been called the new *science of complexity* (Figure 2.1).[16]

---

[16] See also, among many others, (Edmonds, 1999; Phelan, 2001; Chu et al., 2003) and especially the popular books by James Gleick (1987) and Mitchell Waldrop (1992). A rather critical view of the research on complex systems undertaken at the Santa Fe Institute through the mid-1990s can be found in the writings of the science journalist John Horgan (1995, 1997). A very good account of the relationships between complexity theory, cybernetics, catastrophe theory and chaos theory (the four Cs) and their implications for economic theory, can be found in Rosser (1999).

BULLETIN OF THE SANTA FE INSTITUTE, VOL.1 NO.1

PREVIEW OF WORKSHOP ON COMPLEX ADAPTIVE SYSTEMS

Jack Cowan and Marcus Feldman

Twenty-five scientists, from fields as diverse as population biology, theoretical physics, psychology, computer science, mathematics, and political science, will discuss interdisciplinary aspects
of complex adaptive systems in a two-week Santa Fe Institute workshop organized by Santa Fe Institute Trustees Jack Cowan (Chicago)
and Marcus Feldman (Stanford). The workshop will be at the School
for American Research from July 28 to August 9. It has been made
possible by a substantial grant from the Alfred P. Sloan Foundation.

Complex adaptive systems are systems comprising large numbers of
coupled elements the properties of which are modifiable as a result of environmental interactions. To put it another way, complex adaptive systems process information, and can modify their
internal organization in response to such information. In general, complex adaptive systems are highly nonlinear and are organized on many spatial and temporal scales. Their investigation is
important for an understanding of many physical, biological, and
social phenomena and for the design and construction of new instruments, especially computers and robots. The theory of evolution provides a good example of how these problems originate in
natural science. The theory is concerned with adaptive changes
over time in the distribution of phenotypes within one or more
populations.

Figure 2.1 Excerpt from the *Bulletin of the Santa Fe Institute*, Vol. 1, No. 1,
June 1986.

For what concerns economics, the main outcomes of the research project
conducted at the Santa Fe Institute were three books, all bearing the title
The economy as an evolving complex system (Anderson et al., 1988; Arthur
et al., 1997; Blume and Durlauf, 2006). From the preface of the 1997 volume,
edited by W. Brian Arthur, Steven Durlauf and David Lane:

> In September 1987 twenty people came together at the Santa Fe Institute to talk
> about "the economy as a evolving, complex system". Ten were theoretical
> economists, invited by Kenneth J. Arrow, and ten were physicists, biologists and
> computer scientists, invited by Philip W. Anderson. The meeting was motivated by
> the hope that new ideas bubbling in the natural sciences, loosely tied together under
> the rubric of "the sciences of complexity", might stimulate new ways of thinking
> about economic problems.
>
> [...] But just what is the complexity perspective in economics? That is not an
> easy question to answer. [...] Looking back over the developments in the past
> decade, and of the papers produced by the program, we believe that a coherent
> perspective – sometimes called the "Santa Fe approach" – has emerged within
> economics (Arthur et al., 1997).

Arthur goes on in describing the main characteristics of the Santa Fe approach.[17] These were identified in models having cognitive foundations, structural foundations, no global controller, and exhibiting continual adaptation, perpetual novelty and out-of-equilibrium dynamics (Arthur, 1990).

Two main reasons can help explaining why the Santa Fe approach gained some visibility outside the restricted group of people interested in the complexity theory (perhaps contributing in this way to mount what Horgan [1995, 1997] called an "intellectual fad"). Together, they offered an appealing suggestion of both what to do and how to do it. The first reason was the ability to present the complexity paradigm as a unitary perspective. This unitary vision stressed in particular the existence of feedbacks between *functionalities* and *objectives*: individual objectives determine to some extent the use and modification of existing functionalities, but functionalities direct to some extent the choice of individual objectives. It is this analytical focus that proved to be valuable in disciplines as diverse as the social sciences, the biological sciences and even architecture. The second reason has to do with the creation of a specific simulation platform that allowed relatively inexperienced researchers to build their own "toy" models that, thanks to the enormous and sustained increase in commonly available computing power, could run quickly even on small PCs. This simulation platform was called SWARM (Askenazi et al., 1996), and consisted of a series of libraries that implemented many of the functionalities and technicalities needed to build an agent-based simulation, using the schedule of the events, the passing of time and graphical widgets to monitor the simulation. In addition to offering a practical tool to write agent-based simulations, the SWARM approach proposed a protocol in simulation design, which the SWARM libraries exemplified.

Ten years and two volumes later, Blume and Durlauf summarize this intellectual Odyssey as follows:

> On some levels, there has been great success. Much of the original motivation [...] revolved around the belief that economic research could benefit from an injection of new mathematical models and new substantive perspectives on human behavior. [...] At the same time [...] some of the early aspirations were not met. The models presented here do not represent any sort of rejection of neoclassical economics. One reason for this is related to the misunderstanding of many non-economists about the nature of economic theory; simply put, the theory was able to absorb SFI-type advances without changing its fundamental nature. Put differently, economic theory has an immense number of strengths

---

[17] Although this perspective is associated with the Santa Fe Institute, it was initiated in Europe by chemists and physicists concerned with emergent structures and disequilibrium dynamics (more precisely, in Brussels by the group of Nobel prizewinning physical chemist Ilya Progogine and in Stuttgart by the group of the theoretical physicist Hermann Haken) – see Haken, 1983; Prigogine and Stengers, 1984; Nicolis and Prigogine, 1989.

that have been complemented and thereby enriched by the SFI approach.
Hence, relative to the halcyon period of the 1980s, this SFI volume is more
modest in its claims, but we think much stronger in its achievements
(Blume and Durlauf, 2006).

2.3.3 AB Models as Dynamic Microsimulations

An earlier antecedent of AB modeling can be identified in the dynamic
microsimulation (DMS) literature, and in particular in two almost forgot-
ten works: Barbara Bergmann's microsimulation of the US economy and
Gunnar Eliasson's microsimulation of the Swedish economy (Bergmann,
1974; Eliasson et al., 1976; Bergmann et al., 1977; Eliasson, 1977). For the
connections between AB modeling and DMS see Richiardi (2013).

Broadly defined, microsimulation is a methodology used in a large variety
of scientific fields to simulate the states and behaviors of different units –
individuals, households, firms, etc. – as they evolve in a given environment –
a market, a state, an institution. Very often it is motivated by a policy interest,
so that narrower definitions are generally provided.[18]

The field of microsimulation originates from the work of Guy Orcutt in
the late 1950s (Orcutt, 1957; Orcutt et al., 1961). Orcutt was concerned that
macroeconomic models of his time had little to say about the impact of
government policy on things like income distribution or poverty, because these
models were predicting highly aggregated outputs while lacking sufficiently
detailed information of the underlying micro relationships, in terms of the
behavior and interaction of the elemental decision-making units. However, if
a nonlinear relationship exists between an output Y and inputs X, the average
value of Y will indeed depend on the whole distribution of X, not only on the
average value of X.

Orcutt's revolutionary contribution consisted in his advocacy for a new
type of modeling which uses as representative distributions of individuals,
households or firms inputs, and puts emphasis on their heterogeneous decision-
making, as in the real world. In so doing, not only is the average value of
Y correctly computed, but its entire distribution can be analyzed. In Orcutt's
words, "This new type of model consists of various sorts of interacting units
which receive inputs and generate outputs. The outputs of each unit are, in part,
functionally related to prior events and, in part, the result of a series of random
drawings from discrete probability distributions."

---

[18] For instance, Martini and Trivellato (1997, p. 85) define microsimulation models as "computer
programs that simulate aggregate and distributional effects of a policy, by implementing the
provisions of the policy on a representative sample of individuals and families, and then
summing up the results across individual units."

As defined, DMS appears very similar to AB modeling. The main differences can be traced down to the following (i), microsimulations are more policy-oriented, while AB models are more theory-oriented and (ii) microsimulations generally rely on a partial equilibrium approach, while AB models are most often closed models.

Bergmann and Eliasson questioned the second tenet, and introduced two basic innovations with respect to the DMS literature that was emerging at the time – and in which they were firmly grounded: in their macro models with production, investment and consumption (Eliasson also had a demographic module) they explicitly considered the interaction between the supply and demand for labor, and they modeled the behavior of firms and workers in a structural sense. On the other hand, the standard approach to microsimulation – or, as Guy Orcutt called it, the "microanalytic approach for modeling national economies" (1990) – was based on the use of what he considered as a-theoretical conditional probability functions, whose change over time, in a recursive framework, describe the evolution of the different processes that were included in the model. This is akin to reduced-form modeling, where each process is analyzed conditional on the past determination of all other processes, including the lagged outcome of the process itself.

Bergmann and Eliasson had a complete and structural, although relatively simple, model of the economy, which were calibrated to replicate many features of the U.S. and Swedish economy, respectively. However, their approach passed relatively unnoticed in the DMS literature, which evolved along the lines identified by Orcutt mainly as reduced form, probabilistic partial equilibrium models, with limited interaction between the micro unit of analysis and with abundant use of external coordination devices in terms of alignment to exogenously identified control totals. On the contrary, the AB approach emerged with a focus on general equilibrium feedbacks and interaction, at the expenses of richer empirical grounding. Hence, the work of Bergmann and Eliasson could be interpreted as a bridge between the (older) DMS literature and the (newer) AB modeling literature, though this intellectual debt goes relatively unnoticed among AB practitioners.

2.3.4 The Experimental Machine

Crucial for the development of agent-based modeling has been the increasing availability of computing power, which allowed to run even complicated simulations on small PCs.[19]

---

[19] This is summarized by the empirical law of a twofold increase in performance every two years. It is worth remembering that some of the brightest minds of their time – gathered together around physicists Robert Oppenheimer under the Manhattan project, the World War II U.S.

Together with continuous hardware improvements came software development. Aside traditional programming (in Fortran, C++, etc.) three different approaches emerged. The first one relies on general-purpose mathematical software, like MATHEMATICA, MATLAB or MATCAD. The second one, exemplified by the STARLOGO/NETLOGO experience, is based on the idea of an agent-based specific language (Resnick, 1994). The third one represents a protocol in the design process, implemented as agent-based specific libraries in standard programming languages (like Java).[20] The ancestor of these agent-based tools is SWARM. The principles of the SWARM approach are:

- the use of *object-oriented programming* language, with different objects (and object types) being a natural counterpart for different agents (and agent types);
- a *separate implementation* of the model and the tools used for monitoring and conducting experiments on the model (the so called "Observer");
- an architecture that allows nesting models one into another, in order to build a *hierarchy* of "swarms" – a swarm being a group of objects and a schedule of actions that the objects execute. One swarm can thus contain lower-level swarms whose schedules are integrated into the higher-level schedule.

While in the revolutionary days of the Santa Fe Institute, the third approach appeared to be the most promising, a more anarchic attitude (Feyerabend, 1975) has now emerged among practitioners.

Finally, despite the fact that AB models are most often computer models and that the methodology could not develop in the absence of cheap and easy-to-handle personal computers, it is beneficial to remember that one of the most well-known agent-based models, the pioneering work on spatial segregation by the Nobel laureate Thomas Schelling, did not make use of computers at all (Schelling, 1971). As Schelling recalls, he had the original idea while seating on an airplane, and investigated it with paper and pencil. When he arrived home, he explained to his son the rules of the game and got him to move zincs and coppers from the child's own collection on a checkerboard, looking for the results. "The dynamics were sufficiently intriguing to keep my twelve-year-old engaged" (Schelling, 2006).

Army project at Los Alamos aimed at developing the atomic bomb – were reported to spend half of their time and effort in order to find smarter algorithms and save precious computing time on the huge but slow machines available (Gleick, 1992).

[20] This allows the possibility to integrate tools developed as separate libraries by third parties (for graphical visualization, statistical analysis, database management, etc.).

2.4 Why Agents

Although ACE developed together with the Santa Fe approach, its applicability is by no way limited to the analysis of complex systems. Abstracting from the characteristics of the system being modeled, ACE proves valuable in two cases:

- to get a quick intuition of the dynamics that the system is able to produce and
- to thoroughly investigate models that are not susceptible of a more traditional analysis, or are susceptible of a more traditional analysis only at too a high cost.

Often, an AB model can be quickly implemented, and it can be used not differently from scrap paper. It allows to experiment with hypothesis and assumptions, and gives a hint to which results can be proved. It often suggests the refinements that might eventually lead to a fully algebraic solution of the model.

However, it might turn out that an analytical solution is not even necessary or not feasible. It is possible to identify three distinct uses of agent-based models in the social sciences, apart from the scrap-paper method described above. These uses can be ranked according to their auxiliary nature, with respect to analytical modeling (Axtell, 2000).[21]

The first use is *numerical computation of analytical models*. Note with Axtell that

> [t]here are a variety of ways in which formal models resist full analysis. Indeed, it is seemingly only in *very* restrictive circumstances that one ever has a model that is completely soluble, in the sense that everything of importance about it can be obtained solely from analytical manipulations.

Situations that resort to numerical computation and may prove useful include (a) when a model is not analytically soluble for some relevant variable, (b) when a model is stochastic, and the empirical distribution of some relevant variable needs to be compared with the theoretical one, of which often few moments can be analytically derived, and (c) when a model is solved for the equilibrium, but the out-of-equilibrium dynamics are not known. In particular, with reference to the last point, it may happen that multiple equilibria exist, and that the equilibrium or (at least some of) the equilibria are unstable, that they are realized only in the very long run. Conversely, it may happen that equilibria exist but are not computable.[22] Finally, it may be the case that the equilibrium

---

[21] The categories identified below correspond only partially to Axtell's.
[22] Axtell provides references and examples for each case.

is less important than the out-of-equilibrium fluctuations or extreme events. Clearly, agent-based simulations are not the only way to perform numerical computations of a given analytical model. However, they may prove effective and simple to implement, especially for models with micro-foundations.

The second use is *testing the robustness of analytical models* with respect to departures from some of the assumptions. Assumptions may relate to the behavior of the agents, or to the structure of the model. Note that, in general, as the assumptions are relaxed or altered, an analytical solution becomes very improbable (otherwise, the possibility of changing them could have been easily incorporated in the original work, leading to a more general model). One important feature of ACE is that in considering departures from the assumptions of the reference model, a number of different alternatives can be investigated, thus offering intuition toward a further generalization of the model itself.

The first two uses of ACE models are *complementary* to mathematical analysis. The third use is a *substitute*, going beyond the existence of an analytical reference model. It provides *stand-alone simulation models* for (a) problems that are analytically intractable or (b) problems for which an analytical solution bears no advantage. The latter may happen when negative results are involved, for instance. A simulation may be enough to show that some institution or norm does not work in the intended way. Analytical intractability may arise when more complicated assumptions are needed, or when the researcher wants to investigate the overall effect of a number of mechanisms (each possibly already analytically understood in simpler models) at work at the same time.

It must be added that developing AB models as substitutes for mathematical analysis in economics is also a way to propose an alternative to the standard mainstream (neoclassical) paradigm. Neoclassical models are indeed firmly rooted in the presumption that any meaningful economic model must start from a set of unavoidable assumptions that represent the core of the paradigm. These, in a nutshell, are: (i) agents are fully-rational with unbounded computational skills; (ii) equilibrium is defined by rational expectations at the individual level, and by a no-arbitrage condition at the aggregate level, and (iii) interactions and heterogeneity, to a first approximation, only add noise to the underlying economic dynamics. These assumptions allow one to safely employ models with a representative individual replacing a wealth of heterogeneous agents, and focus on simple setups concerning interactions and externalities (for instance, competitive markets where firms do not interact with anyone else or strategic situations where everyone interacts with everyone else). Notice that this set of core assumptions are typically not sufficient to get analytical solutions from a neoclassical model (other, ever stronger assumptions are necessary), but they help a lot in simplifying the framework: in fact removing each of them generates a lot of problems as far as analytical tractability of neoclassical models is concerned. Therefore, studying complementary models in an ACE perspective also means to provide a valid scientific alternative paradigm to neoclassical economics, one firmly rooted instead on concepts like bounded rationality, direct interactions, disequilibrium, etc.

As will become clearer, these departures from the benchmark assumption traditionally used in neoclassical models are also more in line with what experimental and empirical data tell us about the way real-world economic agents (all of us) behave and interact in everyday life. Interpreted in the light of empirical and experimental evidence, assumptions like full rationality are clearly at odds with reality. Under that perspective, ACE can be seen as a substitute to standard neoclassical approaches to economics that tries to build more reasonable models based on reality to better address its behavior, a new approach that rejects the idea that good models can be built using false assumptions and trying instead to explore models based on assumptions more in line with what we know about how real-world agents behave and interact.

2.5 An *Ante Litteram* Agent-Based Model: Thomas Schelling's Segregation Model

One of the early and most well known examples of an AB model is the segregation model proposed by Thomas Schelling, who received the 2005 Nobel prize for his studies in game theory (Schelling, 1969, 1971). To correctly assess the importance of the model, it must be evaluated against the social and historical background of the time. Up to the end of the 1960s, racial segregation was institutionalized in the United States. Racial laws required that public schools, public places and public transportation, like trains and buses, had separate facilities for whites and blacks. Residential segregation was also prescribed in some states, although it is now widely recognized that it mainly came about through organized, mostly private efforts to ghettoize blacks in the early twentieth century – particularly the years between the world wars. But if the social attitude was the strongest force in producing residential segregation, the Civil Rights movement of the 1960s greatly contributed to a change of climate, with the white population exhibiting increasing levels of tolerance. Eventually, the movement gained enough strength to achieve its main objective: the abolition of the racial laws. This was sealed in the Civil Rights Act of 1968 which, among many other things, outlawed a wide range of discriminatory conduct in housing markets. Hence, both the general public attitude and the law changed dramatically during the 1960s. As a consequence, many observers predicted a rapid decline in housing segregation. The decline, however, was almost imperceptible. The question then was why this happened. Schelling's segregation model brought an answer, suggesting that small differences in tolerance level or initial location could trigger high level of segregation even without formal (legal) constraints, and even for decent levels of overall tolerance. In the model, whites and blacks are (randomly) located over a grid, each individual occupying one cell. As a consequence, each individual has at most eight neighbours (Moore neighborhood) located on adjacent cells. Preferences over residential patterns are represented as the maximum quota of racially different neighbors that an individual tolerates. For simplicity, we can assume that preferences are identical: a unique number defines the level of tolerance in the population. For example, if the tolerance level is 50% and an individual has only five neighbors, he would be satisfied if no more than two of his neighbors are racially different. If an individual is not satisfied by his current location, he tries to move to a different location where he is satisfied.

The mechanism that generates segregation is the following: Since individuals are initially located randomly on the grid, by chance there will be someone who is not satisfied. His decision to move creates two externalities: one in the location of origin and the other in the location of destination. For example, suppose a white individual decides to move because there are too many black people around. As he leaves, the ethnic composition of his neighborhood is affected (there is one less white). This increases the possibility that another white individual, who was previously satisfied, becomes eager to move. A similar situation occurs in the area of destination. The arrival of a white individual affects the ethnic composition of the neighborhood, possibly causing some black individual to become unsatisfied. Thus, a small nonhomogeneity in the initial residential pattern triggers a chain effect that eventually leads to high levels of segregation. This mechanism is reinforced when preferences are not homogeneous in the population.

Figure 2.2, which shows the NETLOGO implementation of the Schelling model, is an example.[23] The left panel depicts the initial residential pattern, for a population of 2,000 individuals, evenly divided between "green" and "red," living on a 51 × 51 cells torus (hence the population density is 76.9%). Two values for the tolerance threshold are tested: in the first configuration, tolerance is extremely high (70%), while in the second it is significantly lower

---

[23] Wilensky (1998), who introduced only minor changes with respect to the original version.

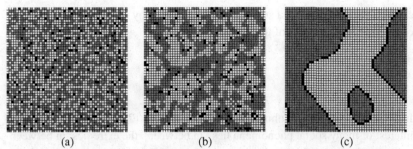

(a)   (b)   (c)

A cell is either empty (black) or occupied by a gray or white individual. (a) Initial (random) pattern. The average share of racially similar neighbors is roughly 50%. With a tolerance level of 70%, around 15% of the individuals are not satisfied. With a tolerance level of 40%, around 70% of the individuals are not satisfied. (b) Tolerance level = 70%. Final pattern: the average share of racially similar neighbors is around 75%; everyone is satisfied. (c) Tolerance level = 40%. Final pattern: the average share of racially similar neighbors is around 99%; everyone is satisfied.

Figure 2.2 NETLOGO implementation of Schelling's segregation model.

(30%) – although at a level that would still be considered decent by many commentators. The initial residential pattern (obviously) shows no levels of segregation: every individual has on average 50% of neighbors of a different race. However, after just a few periods the equilibrium configurations of the middle (for a tolerance level of 70%) and right (for tolerance level of 30%) panels are obtained. The level of segregation is high: more than three quarters of neighbors are on average of the same racial group, even when individuals are actually happy to live in a neighborhood dominated by a different racial group. Moreover, most people live in perfectly homogeneous clusters, with different ethnic clusters being often physically separated from each other (by "no man's lands"). Only the relative mix brought by confining clusters keeps down the measure of overall segregation in the middle panel. Should the overall composition of the population be biased in favour of one ethnic group, we would clearly recognize the formation of ghettos.

Note that the formation of racially homogeneous ethnic clusters and ghettos is an emergent property of the system, which could hardly be deduced by looking at individual behavior alone without considering the effects of interaction. Actually, it can be shown that no matter the shape of individual preferences, the resulting aggregate pattern is always one in which segregation occurs. Moreover, the clusters themselves could be considered as the elementary unit of analysis at a different, more aggregate level, and their behavior – whether they shrink, expand, merge or vanish – studied with respect to some exogenous changes in the environment. Not only a *property*, a statistical regularity, has emerged, but also a whole new *entity* can be recognized. However, this new entity is nothing else but a subjective interpretation by some external observer of an emergent property of the system.

2.6 Conclusions

In their brilliant book, John Miller and Scott Page (2006) maintain that the interest of many social phenomena lies "in between" the extremes: in between various scientific fields, in between the few (often just one or two) and the infinitely many agents of neoclassical models, in between the continuous and the discrete, in between the micro and the macro. They argue that the science of complex systems, and in particular the use of computational models, is the most appropriate approach to the investigation of these phenomena.

In this short introduction, we have discussed why this might be the case. We have described the main features of ACE, and showed how it can be a valid methodology for the investigation of social phenomena. The use of AB models can complement the traditional tools, or can provide a valid alternative. Although the agent-based methodology is used in disciplines as different as biology, medicine, natural resources management and sociology, its potential for economics is still deeply undervalued. We therefore conclude with J. Doyne Farmer and Duncan Foley that "[t]he economy needs agent-based modelling" (Farmer and Foley, 2009). The rest of the book is devoted on how to develop and analyze such models.

3

Agent-Based Models as Recursive Systems

Matteo Richiardi

3.1 Introduction

A rather common misunderstanding about simulations is that they are not as sound as mathematical models. Computer simulations are, according to a popular view, characterised by an intermediate level of abstraction: they are more abstract than verbal descriptions but less abstract than 'pure' mathematics. This is nonsense. Simulations *do* consist of a well-defined (although not concise) set of functions, which relate inputs to outputs. These functions describe a fully recursive system and unambiguously define its macro dynamics. In this respect, AB models are no different from any other model: they are logical theorems saying that, given the environment and the rules described by the model, outputs necessarily follow from inputs. As in any other model, they provide sufficiency theorems: the environment and the rules are sufficient conditions to obtain the results, given the inputs. The resort to computer simulations is only an efficient way – given some conditions – to obtain the results.

In this chapter we offer a characterisation of AB models as recursive models. The chapter has a simple structure: Section 3.2 places AB modelling in the wider context of simulation models; Section 3.3 introduces the notation and the key concepts; finally, Section 3.4 concludes elaborating on what constitutes a proof in an AB setting.

3.2 Discrete-Event vs. Continuous Simulations and the Management of Time

Computer-based simulations face the problem of reproducing real-life phenomena, many of which are temporally continuous processes, using discrete microprocessors. The abstract representation of a continuous phenomenon in a simulation model requires that all events be presented in discrete terms. However, there are different ways of simulating a discrete system.

In *Discrete Event Simulations* (DES) entities are thought of as moving between different states as time passes. The entities enter the system and visit some of the states (not necessarily only once) before leaving the system. This can be contrasted with *System Dynamics* (SD), or *continuous simulation modelling*, a technique created during the mid-1950s by Jay Forrester at the Massachusetts Institute of Technology (Forrester, 1971), which characterises a system in terms of ordinary differential equations (ODEs). SD takes a slightly different approach to DES, focusing more on flows around networks than on the individual behaviour of entities. In SD, three main objects are considered: stocks, flows and delays. Stocks are basic stores of objects, as the number of unemployed workers. Flows define the movement of items between different stocks in the system and out/into the system itself, as, for example, the rates in and out of employment and the fraction of workers that enter and exit the labour force in a given timeframe (e.g., a week). Finally, there may be delays between measurement and action upon that measurement, for instance if it takes some time before unemployed workers become discouraged and decide to leave the labour force. An SD model is a network of stocks, flows and delays.

Note that in DES, inherently continuous processes, as the increase in human capital due to being in education, must be discretised (for instance by modelling degree completion: the level of human capital increases only upon obtaining the degree). On the other hand, a continuous approximation must be taken for inherently discrete events in SD, as in the labour example above: if there are many workers, the fact that any individual can be in only one state (either employed or unemployed) does not affect the smoothness of the aggregate flows. The discrete nature of digital computers however requires to take a further approximation, simulating to any degree of accuracy the differential equations with the corresponding difference equations, by considering increasingly smaller time frames.

Where do AB models lie in this taxonomy? AB models are in essence discrete event simulations. Although there are authors in the simulation literature stressing the difference between AB models and DES (for instance, see Siebers et al., 2010), these differences appear to be related more to the modelling specification and the purpose of the analysis than to the technical implementation. The theory of discrete event simulations originated in the Operation Research (OR) literature, a discipline concerned with system optimization where decision problems are broken down into basic components and then solved in defined steps by mathematical analysis. Discrete event

Table 3.1 *Discrete Event Simulations (DES) vs. Agent-Based (AB) models.*

Discrete-event simulations	Agent-based models
Process oriented (top-down modelling approach); the focus is on modelling the system in detail, not the entities.	Individual based (bottom-up modelling approach); the focus is on modelling the entities and interactions between them.
One thread of control (centralised).	Each agent has its own thread of control (decentralised).
Passive entities, i.e., something is done to the entities while they move through the system; intelligence (e.g., decision-making) is modelled as part in the system.	Active entities, i.e., the entities themselves, can take on the initiative to do something; intelligence is represented within each individual entity.
Queues are a key element.	No concept of queues.
Flow of entities through a system; macro behaviour is modelled.	No concept of flows; macro behaviour is not modelled, it emerges from the micro decisions of the individual agents.
Input distributions are often based on collect/measured (objective) data.	Input distributions are often based on theories or subjective data.

Source: Siebers et al. (2010).

simulations are therefore often understood as top-down exercises: the object of interest is a specific process (e.g., the functioning of an emergency room), which is analysed in terms of its constituent sub-processes. The difference in perspective can be seen in Table 3.1, which describes the main attributes of the two techniques according to Siebers et al. (2010).

Apart from these differences in use, AB modelling and DES share the same structure: in both cases, models consist of a set of entities that interact with each other in an environment. This leads researchers within the OR literature itself to recognise that the two methodologies 'are like England and America – separated by a common language.' (Brailsford, 2014, p. 3).

Note that the recognition of the atomistic (i.e., discrete, at a microscopic level) nature of most processes implies that any SD system admits a DES/AB representation (Macal, 2010). Every well formulated continuous simulation model has an equivalent formulation as a discrete event simulation. However, in some cases this may not be convenient, as AB models are a lot more time consuming to build and run.

Within the literature on DES, an important distinction concerns the treatment of time. Discrete-time simulations break up time into regular time slices

Δt (steps) and the simulator calculates the variation of state variables for all the elements of the simulated model between one point in time and the following. Nothing is known about the order of the events that happen within each time period: discrete events (marriage, job loss, etc.) could have happened at any moment in Δt, while inherently continuous events (ageing, wealth accumulation, etc.) are best thought to progress linearly between one point in time and the following one.

By converse, discrete-time simulations are characterised by irregular time frames that are punctuated by the occurrence of discrete events (jumps). Between consecutive events, no change in the system is assumed to occur; thus the simulation can directly jump in time from one event to the next.

Note the distinction between treatment of *events* and treatment of *time*. Irrespective of time being sampled at regular or irregular intervals, an AB model is always a discrete event simulation.

In both continuous and discrete time, discrete event simulations and AB models can be understood as a *recursive system* (Figure 3.1). A recursive system is one in which the output is dependent on one or more of its past outputs. If the system is 'memoryless', meaning that the probability distribution of the next state depends only on the current state and not on the sequence of events that preceded it, the system is a *Markov chain*: 'the future depends on the past only through the present'. Note that it is always possible to redefine the state space by taking into account all relevant past states, so that the identification of Markov chains and recursive systems is complete. For instance, suppose that the transitions between employment (E) and unemployment (U) depend on the current state, $s_0 = \{U, E\}$, and the state in the previous period, $s_{-1} = \{U, E\}$. We can redefine the state space as $s = \{(U, U), (U, E), (E, U), (E, E)\}$, where each possible state is a combination of the current and the previous state, (s_0, s_{-1}), obtaining a Markov chain. Hence, AB models *are* Markov chains (Izquierdo et al., 2009). Further, AB models can also be seen as *dynamical systems* (Hinkelmann et al., 2011) – systems where a function describes the time evolution of the system in the state space (Luenberger, 1979). Markov chains are naturally related to linear dynamical systems, since the state transition probabilities of Markov chains evolve as a linear dynamical system (Attal, 2010).

Markov chains are important because, if some conditions hold, it is possible to characterise a stationary distribution of the states by looking only at the transition matrix between states. Unfortunately, the applicability of Markov chain theory to AB modelling is limited. This is because the state space of an AB model can grow enormous, so that the transition matrix often does not

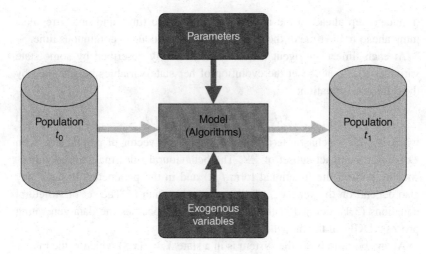

Figure 3.1 The recursive nature of AB models.

have an analytical representation and it might well be time inhomogenous, that is the probability of a transition from one state to another state might change over time.

The recursive nature of AB models has one important computational consequence. As Barbara Bergmann put it:

> The elimination of simultaneous equations allows us to get results from a simulation model without having to go through a process of solution. (Bergmann, 1990)

It is the recursive structure of the simulation that allows computability. This is to be contrasted with the fixed-point structure of rational expectations models (see Chapter 4), which makes computability much harder. Moreover, recursivity has not only an instrumental value in modelling complex system; it also reflects an intrinsic characteristics of reality:

> The world is essentially recursive: response follows stimulus, however short the lag. (Watts, 1991)

3.3 The Structure of an AB Model

In this section, we offer a formal characterisation of AB models as recursive systems. Our analysis applies both to models set in discrete time, and to models set in continuous time; the only differences the interpretation of $t + 1$: one (regular) step ahead to the next period in discrete time, and one (irregular) jump ahead to the time of the next event in event queue in continuous time.

At each time t, an agent i, $i \in 1 \ldots n$, is fully described by some state variables $x_{i,t} \in \Re^k$.[1] Let the evolution of her state variables be specified by the difference equation:

$$x_{i,t+1} = f_i(x_{i,t}, x_{-i,t}, \theta_i, \xi_{i,t}) \tag{3.1}$$

where $\xi_{i,t}$ are stochastic terms, and $\theta_i \in \Theta$ is a vector of parameters, with Θ being a compact subset of $\mathbb{R}^Q$. The behavioural rules may be individual-specific both in the functional form $f_i(.)$ and in the parameters θ_i, and may also depend on the state x_{-i} of all agents other than i.[2] The set of structural equations (3.1), defined at the individual level, specifies the data-generating process (DGP) of the model.

At any point in time, the system is in a state $X_t = (x_{i,t})$ which is the matrix of all individual states. By replacing Equation 3.1 in the definition above, we obtain

$$X_{t+1} = F(X_t, \theta, \Xi_t) \tag{3.2}$$

where Ξ_t is a matrix containing all stochastic elements at time t. Equation 3.2 defines the *transition equation* of the system.

Note that in optimal control theory it is distinguished between *state* and *control* variables, where the latter are characterised by two qualifiers:

1. Control variables are subject to the optimiser's choice.
2. They have an effect on the value of the state variable of interest.

In AB models however, because agents do not engage in mathematical optimisation (see Chapter 5), there is no real need to distinguish between state and control variables. Each individual variable evolves according to a rule, or law of motion, f_i. Some of them are simple accounting identities: for instance, wealth at time $t + 1$ is equal to wealth at time t plus income minus consumption, and it is not a direct object of choice for the individual. But control variables, as consumption in the earlier example, are also determined in an algorithmic way in AB models: for instance, consumption might evolve as a constant fraction of income or be influenced by neighbours and friends,

---

[1] Categorical variables can be indexed with integer values (e.g., 0 for unemployed, 1 for employed).

[2] Here, and in the following, we use 'behavioural rules' and similar terms in a loose sense that encompasses the actual intentional behaviours of individuals as well as other factors such as technology, etc.

so the only difference is that its law of motion is subject to more assumptions than the law of motions of wealth.

To elaborate on the point, optimization requires solving something like:

$$\min_{c_t} C(c_{i,t}, s_{i,t}, \theta_i^c) \tag{3.3}$$

$$s.t.$$

$$s_{i,t} = s(s_{i,t-1}, s_{-i,t-1}, c_{i,t}, \theta_i^s) \tag{3.4}$$

where c are control variables, s are state variables, C is an objective function and the constraint Equation 3.4 is the law of motion of the state variables.[3] This introduces a natural distinction between c and s. The solution of the optimization problem leads to a law of motion for the control variables,

$$c_{i,t} = c(S_{t-1}, \theta_i) \tag{3.5}$$

where S is the collection of all state variables of all individuals. This can then be plugged back into the law of motion of the state variables in Equation 3.4:

$$s_{i,t} = \tilde{s}(S_{t-1}, \theta_i) \tag{3.4'}$$

The two classes of law of motions, Equation 3.4' and Equation 3.5 have the same form. Because in AB modelling we generally do not explicit the individual optimisation problem, we can simply refer to both state and control variables as 'state variables' $x_i = [s_i, c_i]$, subject to the general law of motion (3.1).

Often, we are interested in some aggregate (observable) statistics of our economy. A vector of aggregate variables y_t is defined as a function over the state of the system, that is a projection from X to y:

$$y_t = m(X_t, \kappa_t) \tag{3.6}$$

where κ_t are extra random terms that accounts for measurement errors and other shocks to the observables, if any. This is the measurement equation, which together with the transition equation forms the state-space representation of the system. The question is whether it is possible to solve Equation 3.6 for each t, regardless of the specification adopted for $f_i(.)$, and the answer is that a solution can always be found by backward iteration, which traces the stochastic evolution of y_t back to the initial state of the system and the values of the parameters. Expliciting this relationship is complicated because of the random terms Ξ and κ that enter at every stage. As the behavioural rules f_i and the measurement function m need not to be linear, these random terms cannot

---

[3] For the sake of clarity, we omit expliciting the stochastic terms.

be netted out by taking expectations. Therefore, the only way to analyse the mapping of $(X_0, \boldsymbol{\theta})$ into $\boldsymbol{y}_t$ is by means of Monte Carlo analysis, by simulating the model for different initial states and values of the parameters, and repeating each simulation experiment many times to obtain a distribution of $\boldsymbol{y}_t$.

However, because digital computers are deterministic machines, it is possible to further pin down the formalization above.[4] In a digital computer random terms are not truly random: they are generated by an algorithm that produces sequences of numbers that resemble the properties of random numbers. Accordingly, these numbers are referred to as *pseudo-random*, and the algorithm is called *random number generator*. Each sequence is identified by a seed – which for the sake of simplicity is often called *random seed* (causing some confusion: random seeds are not *random*).[5] Specifying the random seed guarantees the reproducibility of the results.[6] Therefore, the random terms $\boldsymbol{\Xi}$ and $\boldsymbol{\kappa}$ are a deterministic function of the random seed s, and equations (3.2)–(3.6) reduce to:

$$X_{t+1} = F(X_t, \boldsymbol{\theta}, s) \tag{3.2$'$}$$

$$y_t = m(X_t, s) \tag{3.6$'$}$$

The random seed can be thought of as a latent parameter, lacking a 'natural' counterpart. Alternatively, and more conveniently, it can be considered as a further initial condition: $Z_0 = \{X_0, s\}$. By iteratively substituting X_{t+1} with X_t using (3.2$'$), we get:

$$X_t = F(F(\cdots F(Z_0, \boldsymbol{\theta}) \cdots))$$
$$= F^t(Z_0, \boldsymbol{\theta}) \tag{3.2$''$}$$
$$y_t = m\big(F^t(Z_0, \boldsymbol{\theta})\big)$$
$$= g_t(Z_0, \boldsymbol{\theta}) \tag{3.6$''$}$$

The law of motion Equation 3.6 uniquely relates the value of $\boldsymbol{y}$ at any time t to the initial conditions of the system and to the values of the parameters, and is

---

[4] *Analog computers* exist in which continuously variable physical quantities, such as electrical potential, fluid pressure or mechanical motion, are used to represent (analogously) the quantities in the problem to be solved. Answers to the problem are obtained by measuring the variables in the analog model. Analog computers are not deterministic, as physical quantities cannot be measured with absolute precision. Though digital computing has taken the lead, analog computers have been widely used in simulating the operation of aircraft, nuclear power plants and industrial chemical processes.

[5] If there are more than one random number generators, we can think of s as the seed of an additional random number generator determining the seeds of the different generators used in the model.

[6] When the random seed is not specified, it is generally taken from some environmental variable (as the computer clock), which guarantees that it is different for every simulation run.

known as the *input-output transformation* (IOT) function. The word 'function' is appropriate here, as any particular input given to the computer model will lead to only one output (different inputs might lead to the same output, though).

This is a convenient mathematical representation, and will be used in Chapter 7 for discussing the properties of AB models. However, from a practical point of view it is still true that knowledge of the IOT function must be obtained by Monte Carlo analysis, by simulating the model for different initial states, parameter values and random seeds.

Given this framework, it is easy to discuss the alleged differences in terms of 'mathematical soundness' between analytical models and computer simulations. In analytical models, the behavioural rules Equation 3.1 typically have a simple structure, with either limited or global interaction, and heterogeneity is kept to a minimum. Functional forms are often linear (or linearised). Aggregation is performed on selected variables by taking expectations over the stochastic elements, which are conveniently specified. On the contrary, an AB model poses little restrictions on the specification of Equation 3.1, but this freedom comes at two prices: (i) the modeller has to exert self-discipline in order to stick with the KISS (keep it simple, stupid) principle and connect with the existing literature and (ii) the equation for the macro dynamics Equation 3.6 can easily grow enormous, hindering any attempt at symbolic manipulation. Nevertheless, the functions Equation 3.6 are completely specified. It is thus possible to explore their local behaviour by analysing the artificial time series produced by the simulation.

3.4 Obtaining Results in AB Models

The input-output transformation function Equation 3.6 is the basic object of interest to derive results in an AB setting. Because it has no analytical formulation, it has to be analysed by means of simulations. By performing *sensitivity analyis* of the model outcomes with respect to the parameters and initial conditions, we can recover the shape of the IOT function, either locally or globally. Sensitivity analysis is discussed at length in Chapter 7, while Chapter 9 deals with making use of the IOT function for estimating the model parameters.

We now assume our veil of ignorance about the IOT function is finally lifted, and elaborate on how we can use it to increase our knowledge of the real world. However, it should be clear that AB models differ from analytical models only because of this veil of ignorance around the IOT function, which is sometimes so dark as to make the whole model appear as a 'black box'.

Hence, our discussion below is a methodological conclusion that applies to any type of model. We will revert to the specificities of AB model in the last paragraph.

When we fix the random seed, the IOT function is a deterministic mapping of inputs (parameters and the initial state of the system) into outputs, hence it identifies sufficient conditions for whatever dynamics emerge. Given the assumptions embedded in the model specification, those values of the parameters and initial conditions are sufficient to generate the observed dynamics in the simulated data. Performing Monte Carlo simulations with different random seeds allows to make probabilistic statements about the likelihood of getting an outcome, given the inputs.

If the simulated dynamics bear some resemblance o the real data, then we stumbled upon a possible explanation of the phenomenon of interest. However, there might be other explanations, either within the model itself (other combinations of inputs leading to the same outcomes, an instance of *equifinality* or *non-identification*), or outside the model, when other assumptions and model specifications are made. But if the researcher is confident enough that the assumptions are valid (see Chapter 8), then the model offers a likely explanation.

This form of logical reasoning is called abduction, or 'inference to the best explanation'. Let the observed circumstances be denoted with b, while a is an hypothetical explanation. Abduction means guessing a from b because a implies b. The American philosopher Charles Sanders Peirce (1839–1914) first introduced the concept of abduction using precisely the term guessing. To abduce a from b two steps are involved: determining that a is sufficient, even if not necessary, for b; and arguing that a is indeed an *economical* explanation for b, the KISS principle.

Models (including simulation models) can also be used in a *deductive* way, when fed with real (observed) input. Then, given the assumptions made, outputs will necessarily follow: if we observe a, the model predicts that b will happen (with some probability distribution if the random feed is not fixed).

In both cases the connection between inputs and outputs is the IOT function, the black box through which only *inductive* evidence based on the simulated data can be obtained. The proof of the results thus lies in the code, rather than in mathematical reasoning as in analytical models. This is why it is fundamental, in AB models, to write the simulation code in a clear and transparent way, document it and make it public. Also, supporting evidence for the working of the 'black box', the shape of the inferred IOT function should be provided, either in terms of analytical results for simple cases or in terms of intuition explaining why the simulated results are obtained.

4

Rationality, Behavior, and Expectations

Domenico Delli Gatti

4.1 Introduction

In order to achieve her goals, an agent must decide a line of action (a behavioral rule). Mental representations of the environment and of the behavior of other agents are key in taking this decision. The availability of an adequate and appropriate information set and of cognitive capabilities to process information, in turn, are key in forming these mental models. In a context characterized by uncertainty, one of the most important cognitive process is expectation formation. In this chapter we overview the way in which rationality, behavioral rules and expectation formation are connected in modern macroeconomics.

In Section 4.2 we set the stage by discussing (optimal) decision-making in an environment of full rationality and certainty. From Section 4.3 on, we discuss the consequences of uncertainty – in its wide range of specifications – and expectation on individual decision making and on macroeconomic performance.

Section 4.3 is devoted to the theory of choice in the presence of measurable uncertainty (risk). Uncertainty is measurable when agents are able to attach probabilities to uncertain events. In this setting the probability distribution of the variable of interest replaces the true value of the variable (which is available only in the case of certainty) in the information set of the agent. We will provide simple examples of choice in the case of risk neutrality (Subsection 4.3.1) and risk aversion (Subsection 4.3.2). Moreover, we will discuss choice in a multi-period setting (Subsection 4.3.3).

We will show that it is straightforward, and extremely useful, to extend the notion of measurable uncertainty discussed in Subsections 4.3.1 and 4.3.2 to the multi-period setting. Also in a multi-period context, in fact, the true values of the variables of interest are replaced by probability distributions.

The Rational approach to Expectation formation (RE) is the natural candidate to model expectations in such a setting. In fact we introduce a Linear
Stochastic Difference Equation at this early stage of the analysis.

We illustrate its solution by means of a graphical tool which exploits the
two-way relationship between current and expected value of a variable of
interest. The true (or actual or current) value of variable x is a function of
the expectation of the same variable x^e, in symbols $x = f(x^e)$ (represented
by the True Value, or TV, schedule). On the other hand, the Expectation of
the variable is a function of the current value: $x^e = g(x)$ (represented by the
EXpectations, or EX, schedule). The intersection of these two schedules yields
consistency (equilibrium) between actual and expected values.

This equilibrium yields correct (and model-consistent) expectations only
when the Expectation schedule coincides with the 45-degree line: $x^e = x$. In
this case, the RE equilibrium (in the absence of shocks) can be characterized
as a fixed point of map f.

Section 4.4 introduces heuristics to form expectations, with special reference
to the adaptive expectation formation mechanism.

Section 4.5 is an overview of macroeconomic thought from the viewpoint
of expectation formation. Using variants of the same basic macroeconomic
framework, we will survey models of the Neoclassical-Keynesian Synthesis, of
the Monetarist School, of the New Classical Macroeconomics and of the New
Neoclassical Synthesis. We will provide the solution of these macroeconomic
models with adaptive and/or rational expectation. We will also discuss the
effect of shocks with simple examples. We will use the graphical apparatus,
based on the TV and EX schedules, introduced in Subsection 4.3.3.

Section 4.6 touches upon the criticisms and objections to rational expectations and paves the way to the thorough discussion of these issues which will
be carried out in Chapter 5.

In Section 4.7 we present a conceptual framework to discuss the macro-
conomic role of heterogeneous expectations. In this case, the TV and EX
schedules are functions of average expectations, i.e., of the mean of individual
heterogeneous expectations.

Section 4.8 presents some ideas and an example on heterogeneous expectations in macroeconomic ABMs. Section 4.9 concludes the chapter.

4.2 Certainty

Neoclassical choice theory assumes that agents are endowed with *full or substantial rationality*, which allows to solve a well-defined (usually constrained)

optimization problem. In its simplest and clearest form, full rationality is characterized by the following assumptions: (i) agents have an objective function which associates an index of individual well-being (e.g., utility for the agent, profit for the firm) to each and every possible choice (consumption for the agent, production for the firm); (ii) agents have constraints (the budget constraint for the agent, the production function for the firm); (iii) agents have an information set which contains all the items necessary to the definition of the objective function and the constraints (prices of consumption goods and income for the agent; costs of inputs, the sale price[1] and the resources to be devoted to production for the firm); (iv) agents have the cognitive capabilities to carry on the task of finding an optimum of the objective function under constraints. In the absence of uncertainty – i.e., when all the necessary information is available – and in the absence of cognitive limitations, agents can therefore define a fully optimal behavioral rule.

For instance, in a competitive setting, the manager of a firm sets the quantity q to be produced by solving the following optimization problem:

$$\max \pi = Pq - Wn$$
$$s.t. \quad q = n^\alpha$$

where π represents profit (the objective function), P the price, W the (nominal) wage, n employment. The constraint is represented by the well-behaved production function $q = n^\alpha$ with $0 < \alpha < 1$. The information set consists of α, W, P. It is easy to see that in a competitive setting, the manager maximizes profits by choosing $q*$ such that the selling price P is equal to the marginal cost of production: $c(q)$ where $c(q) = \frac{W}{\alpha} q^{\frac{1-\alpha}{\alpha}}$. Hence

$$q^* = \left(\frac{\alpha P}{W}\right)^{\frac{\alpha}{1-\alpha}} \tag{4.1}$$

Equation 4.1 is the (optimal) behavioral rule adopted by the firm.

4.3 Uncertainty

It may well happen that some of the variables of interest are *uncertain*, i.e., unknown at the time a decision has to be taken. In our example, this is for instance the case when the selling price is unknown (for any reasons).

---

[1] The price is a piece of information for the firm in perfect competition, when the firm is a price taker; it is a choice variable in imperfect competition, when the firm has market power.

The information set is not complete. Therefore a fully optimal behavioral rule is not within the reach of the firm.

Following a well-known taxonomy proposed by Knight (1921), we distinguish between

- measurable or tractable uncertainty (also known as "risk"): in this case, agents are able to attach probabilities to uncertain events (e.g., "states of the world"); and
- untractable or "true" uncertainty: in this case, agents either do not know the states of the world or they are incapable of associating probabilities to them. As Keynes (1937) put it: they "simply don't know."

Uncertainty is measurable when the agent knows the set of all possible states of the world, the value that the variable of interest will assume in each state and the associated probability. In a sense *risk* setting the true value of the variable is replaced by the true *probability distribution* of the variable in the information set of the agent. Of course, all the states of the world must be known, i.e., there should be complete information as to the support of the probability distribution. Moreover, there should be a unique, "true" probability distribution.

4.3.1 Risk Neutrality

For instance, in our example, the manager can still make an optimal choice if the following pieces of information are available: (i) all the states of the world (to simplify matters, suppose there are only two states: the good one, characterized by "high" demand, and the bad one with "low" demand),[2] (ii) the selling price in each state of the world (P_H and P_L respectively, with $P_H > P_L$), (iii) the probability associated to each state of the world (p_H and $p_L = 1 - p_H$ respectively). If the manager is endowed with this information, she may compute the *expected* selling price $E(P) = P_L + p_H(P_H - P_L)$.

In the presence of uncertainty, it is crucial for the agent to form *expectations*, i.e., to figure out unknown aspects of the environment or of the behavior of other agents which are relevant for the achievement of her objective. Hence, in the design of agents' behavior, we must take into consideration the expectation formation mechanism.

An agent is *risk neutral* if, in the presence of (measurable) uncertainty, she will maximize the *expected value* of the uncertain payoff.

---

[2] This setting can be easily generalized to any number of states of the world.

In our example, if the manager is risk neutral, she will maximize expected profits, i.e., the difference between expected sales proceeds and current costs. Expected sales proceeds, in turn, will be equal to the product of the expected selling price and the quantity (to be decided by the firm). In the presence of uncertainty, therefore, the optimization problem of the risk neutral firm in a competitive setting must be redesigned as follows:

$$\max E(\pi) = E(P)q - Wn$$
$$s.t. \quad q = n^{\alpha}$$

$E(\pi)$ represents expected profit (the objective function). The information set consists of α, W and the *probability distribution* of the selling price (P_H with probability p_H and P_L with probability $1 - p_H$).

The manager maximizes expected profits by choosing q^* such that the expected selling price $E(P)$ is equal to the marginal cost of production $c(q)$. Hence,

$$q^* = \left(\frac{\alpha E(P)}{W}\right)^{\frac{\alpha}{1-\alpha}} \tag{4.2}$$

Equation 4.2 is the (optimal) behavioral rule adopted by the firm in the presence of measurable uncertainty. In other words, an optimal choice can still be made if the agent knows the probability distribution of the variable which is uncertain. This probability distribution plays a role in the optimal behavioral rule: the rule changes if the distribution changes (i.e., if the support or the PDF of the distribution changes). For instance, the scale of activity will increase if the probability that the firm associates with a high aggregate demand (p_H) goes up.

4.3.2 Risk Aversion

An agent is *risk averse* if, in the presence of uncertainty, she will maximize the *expected utility* of the uncertain payoff. We will discuss this issue in a simple Diamond and Dybvig (1983) setting.

Consider an agent who must choose in t how much to consume in $t + 1$ and in $t + 2$. For simplicity, suppose the agent can be of two types: (1) an "early consumer" who wants to consume c_1 in $t + 1$ (for example, because she will need medical treatment), or (2) a "late consumer" who can wait until period $t + 2$ to consume c_2. Utility, as usual, is increasing with consumption and concave: $u'(c_i) > 0$ and $u''(c_i) < 0$, $i = 1, 2$. Suppose, moreover, that the agent is endowed with one unit of wealth, which may be invested in t in (i) a liquid asset with gross return equal to 1 in any future period or (ii) an illiquid asset with gross return equal to $R > 1$ in $t+2$. By assumption, if the investment in the illiquid asset is liquidated prematurely (i.e., in $t + 1$) it will go wasted, i.e., the return on the illiquid asset in $t + 1$ is zero.

If the agent knew her type (i.e., in the absence of uncertainty), she would maximize her utility by investing her wealth entirely (1) in the liquid asset if an early consumer (so that $c_1 = 1$) or (2) in the illiquid asset if a late consumer (so that $c_2 = R$). Denoting with θ the fraction of wealth invested in the liquid asset, the fully optimal portfolio choice would be $\theta^* = 1$ when the agent is an early consumer and $\theta^* = 0$ when the agent is a late consumer.

Suppose now that the agent is uncertain about her type, which will be revealed by nature only in $t + 1$. The agent will be an "early consumer" if she will need medical treatment, a circumstance which is unknown in t and will materialize only in $t+1$. The information set is not complete: the piece of information concerning the type of the agent is not available at the moment the agent has to make a decision.[3] Therefore, a fully optimal behavioral rule is not possible. The agent, however, can still make an optimal choice if the following pieces of information are available: (i) all the states of the world in $t + 1$ (in our simple example there are only state 1 in which the agent needs to consume in $t + 1$ and state 2 in which she can wait until $t + 2$), (ii) the preferences over consumption in each state of the world represented by the well-behaved utility functions $u(c_1)$ and $u(c_2)$, and (iii) the probability associated to each state of the world (p_1 and $p_2 = 1 - p_1$).[4]

Using this information, the agent can compute the *expected utility* in t as the weighted average of the utility of consumption as an early consumer and the utility of consumption as a late consumer, where the weights are the probabilities of the two states of the world:

$$E(U) = u(c_1)p_1 + u(c_2)p_2 \qquad (4.3)$$

This is a Von Neumann-Morgestern utility function. Let's specify $u(.)$ as a CRRA[5] utility function: $u(c_i) = \frac{c_i^{1-\sigma}}{1-\sigma}; i = 1, 2$, where σ is the (relative) risk aversion coefficient.

The risk averse agent will choose in t – i.e., before the type will be revealed – c_1 and c_2 in order to maximize her expected utility under the constraint

[3]   In other words, the agent does not know whether she will need medical treatment or not in $t + 1$.

[4] p_1 is the probability of being an early consumer, i.e., in our example, of requiring medical treatment in $t + 1$. Since the endowment has already been invested in t, p_1 can also be conceived as the probability of a "liquidity shock" i.e., a shock which requires the liquidation of wealth. Thanks to the law of large numbers, p_1 (p_2) is also the fraction of early (late) consumers in the population.

[5]   The acronym CRRA stands for Constant Relative Risk Aversion.

represented by the composition of her wealth in terms of liquid and illiquid assets. If the agent turns out to be an early consumer, she will consume only the fraction of wealth invested in the liquid asset θ (so that $c_1 = \theta$); if she turns out to be a late consumer, in addition to θ, she will consume also the wealth invested in the non-liquid asset, augmented by the rate of return, $(1 - \theta)R$. Hence the problem of the agent is:

$$\max_{c_1, c_2} E(U) = \frac{c_1^{1-\sigma}}{1 - \sigma} p_1 + \frac{c_2^{1-\sigma}}{1 - \sigma} p_2$$

$$s.t. \quad c_1 = \theta$$

$$c_2 = \theta + (1 - \theta)R = R - r\theta$$

where $r = R - 1$. The elements of the information set are: σ, R and the probabilities p_1 and p_2.

Substituting the constraints in the objective function, the optimal choice of consumption translates into an optimal portfolio decision, i.e., the determination of the optimal fraction of the endowment to be invested in the liquid asset:

$$\max_{\theta} E(U) = \frac{\theta^{1-\sigma}}{1 - \sigma} p_1 + \frac{[\theta + (1 - \theta)R]^{1-\sigma}}{1 - \sigma} p_2$$

Solving for θ we get:

$$\theta^* = R \left[r + \left(\frac{r(1 - p_1)}{p_1} \right)^{1/\sigma} \right]^{-1} \tag{4.4}$$

In the special case $\sigma = 1$ (i.e., with log utility), the optimal portfolio choice boils down to:

$$\theta^* = c_1^* = \frac{R}{r} p_1 \tag{4.5}$$

so that $c_2^* = R - r\theta^* = R(1 - p_1)$.

From the discussion above, it is clear that an optimal choice can still be made if the agent knows the *probability distribution* of the types. The optimal behavioral rule changes if the distribution changes. For instance, the fraction of wealth invested in the liquid asset increases if the probability of being an early consumer (p_1) goes up. This is, in a nutshell the methodology assumed in the theory of choice in the presence of *risk*, i.e., subjective expected utility theory (Savage, 1954).

4.3.3 Optimal Choice in a Multi-Period Setting

In a dynamic context – i.e., when the time horizon of the optimizing agent consists of more than one period – the agent must solve an *intertemporal* optimization problem. This means she must decide a sequence of optimal values for the choice variables over a specified multi-period time span. For the sake of discussion, in the following we suppose this time-horizon is infinite, i.e., agents are infinitely lived.[6] As an example, let's consider an agent who must decide the optimal consumption plan over an infinite time horizon.

In a multi-period setting, it is straightforward to assume that there is uncertainty over the future states of the world.[7] Therefore, the infinitely lived agent must choose the consumption plan which maximizes expected lifetime utility (ELU), $E_t \sum_{s=0}^{\infty} \beta^s u(c_{t+s})$ – i.e., the expected sum of "felicity functions" $u(c_{t+s}); s = 0, 1, 2 \ldots$ discounted using the factor β.[8] The maximization of ELU is subject to a sequence of budget constraints, one for each period over the same time span.

The budget constraint in each period states that the uses of resources in a certain period must be smaller or equal to the resources available to the agent. In the simplest case, the agent has a certain amount of an asset b_{t-1} (in real terms) which yields a return in one period so that the resources available in t are $R_{t-1} b_{t-1}$ where R is the gross real interest rate. These resources are used to consume and accumulate assets. The budget constraint in t therefore is $c_t + b_t \leq R_{t-1} b_{t-1}$.[9]

Assuming that utility is CRRA, the intertemporal optimization problem of the agent consists in choosing a plan for consumption and asset holdings over an infinite time horizon such that

$$\max E_t \sum_{s=0}^{\infty} \beta^s \frac{c_{t+s}^{1-\sigma}}{1-\sigma}$$

$$s.t. \quad c_{t+s} + b_{t+s} \leq R_{t+s-1} b_{t+s-1} \quad s = 0, 1, \ldots$$

---

[6] Of course there can also be the dynamic case in which the time horizon is finite. The most obvious category of models of this type is the "overlapping generations" model in which there are only two periods, youth and old age. We will not treat this case here.

[7] The absence of uncertainty in a multi-period setting characterizes the "perfect foresight" scenario: all the future state variables are known with certainty. We will not deal with this scenario here.

[8] The felicity function $U(x_{1t}, x_{2t}, \ldots)$ or period utility function represents the preferences of the agent in period t. The arguments of the felicity function in period $t = 1, 2, \ldots$ are the goods in the same period ($x_{it}, i = 1, 2, \ldots, N$).

[9] The future values of the state variables must also be subject to an expectation. The expected (in t) budget constraint for t+s is: $E_t(c_{t+s} + b_{t+s}) \leq E_t(R_{t+s-1} b_{t+s-1})$.

Consolidating the first order conditions for a maximum with respect to c and b one gets the consumption Euler equation:

$$c_{t+s} = (\beta R_{t+s})^{-1/\sigma} E_t c_{t+s+1} \quad s = 0, 1, \ldots \tag{4.6}$$

Imposing the usual stationarity condition in Equation 4.6 we get the steady state of the real interest rate $R^* = 1/\beta$. In words: in the steady state, the real interest rate is equal to the rate of time preference of the agent.

We can linearize the expression above around the steady state. Denoting with x_{t+s} the percentage deviation of consumption from its steady state in period $t + s$ (i.e., $x_{t+s} := \frac{c_{t+s} - c^*}{c^*}$) and with $\mathcal{R}_{t+s}$, the percentage deviation of the real interest rate from its steady state in period $t + s$ (i.e., $\mathcal{R}_{t+s} := \frac{R_{t+s} - R^*}{R^*}$). Focusing on $s = 1$, we can write:

$$x_t = -\frac{1}{\sigma}\mathcal{R}_t + E_t x_{t+1} \tag{4.7}$$

Notice that, in the simplest case, in which there is no investment, from the aggregate resource constraint it follows that output is equal to consumption. Hence the percentage deviation of consumption from its steady state is equal to the percentage deviation of output/income from its steady state, a measure of the *output gap*.

In order to illustrate the role of expectation formation in this setting in the simplest possible way, let's assume that the real interest rate is a stochastic variable described by the following auto-regressive process:

$$R_t = (1 - \rho)R^* + \rho R_{t-1} + R^* \epsilon_t \tag{4.8}$$

where $0 < \rho < 1$ and ϵ_t is a white noise stochastic disturbance (i.e., a random variable with zero mean and constant and finite variance).[10]

From Equation 4.8 it follows that the deviation of the real interest rate from the steady state is governed by the following law of motion

$$\mathcal{R}_t = \rho \mathcal{R}_{t-1} + \epsilon_t \tag{4.9}$$

Suppose the real interest rate were equal to the rate of time preference in the past. A shock in period T, ϵ_T, generates a departure of the real interest rate from the rate of time preference, $\mathcal{R}_T = \epsilon_T$. Since $\rho < 1$, over time the auto-regressive process represented by Equation 4.9 will gradually drive the real interest rate back to its steady state R^*.

---

[10] This assumption is not meant to be realistic. It plays the pedagogical role of allowing us to introduce rational expectations at a very early stage of the exposition (see Section 4.3.3). For a more realistic model of the real interest rate see below, Section 4.5.

Since $\mathcal{R}$ is stochastic (by assumption), Equation 4.7 can be conceived as the semi-reduced form of a macroeconomic model which determines the current output gap as a function of the expected future output gap (which will be endogenized in the next section) and an exogenous shock.

A Foretaste of Rational Expectation

Equation 4.7 is a linear stochastic difference equation (LSDE). According to Equation 4.7 the actual or true value of the state variable x_t is linearly related to the expected (in t) value of x_{t+1} and to the shock $\mathcal{R}_t$. For each possible realization of the shock, Equation 4.7 can be represented as a straight line on the $(E_t x_{t+1}, x_t)$ plane, which we will label the true value (TV) schedule.[11] The 45-degree line on this plane is the fulfilled expectations (FE) schedule.

This is the first time we encounter these terms. The terminology and the graphical apparatus will be used time and time again in the present chapter to illustrate the different ways in which expectations may be formed and their consenquences for macroeconomic performance.

The decision-making process will be complete only when expectations are also endogenously determined. The obvious way to endogenize expectations consists in solving Equation 4.7 under Rational Expectations (RE). Rational or model-consistent expectations, introduced by Muth (1961) and popularized by Lucas and Sargent in the 1970s, are mathematical expectations, conditioned on the agents' information set, of the variables of interest. RE are based on the assumption that agents know the underling "true" economic model so that they can anticipate the evolution of the variables to be forecast. In fact, we will assume that agents know both the LSDE Equation 4.7 and the stochastic process Equation 4.9. In other words, the information set available to the private sector consists of the "true" model of the economy (at least in reduced form) and the parameters characterizing the distribution of $\mathcal{R}$.

In the absence of shocks, Equation 4.7 boils down to $x_t = E_t x_{t+1}$. This is represented by the straight line labelled $TV(0)$ in Figure 4.1. In this particular setting, $TV(0)$ coincides with the 45-degree line.

We will solve Equation 4.7 using the method of "undetermined coefficients." One reasonable guess is that x_t is a linear function of the random variable $\mathcal{R}_t$ (i.e., $x_t = \alpha \mathcal{R}_t$) where α is an undetermined coefficient. If the coefficient can be determined (as a polynomial of the parameters showing up in the

---

[11] Using the jargon of the adaptive learning literature (see Chapter 5) Equation 4.7 can be conceived as the *Actual Law of Motion* of the state variable.

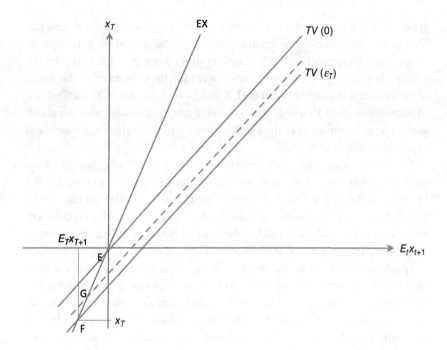

Figure 4.1 RE solution of Equation 4.7.

information set), then the guess is verified. It is easy to show that the guess is indeed verified.[12] The solution of the LSDE is

$$x_t = -\frac{1}{\sigma(1-\rho)}\mathcal{R}_t \qquad (4.10)$$

Notice that from the guess follows that $E_t x_{t+1} = \rho x_t$. This is the equation of the EXpectation schedule (EX) in Figure 4.1. Graphically the solution of the LSDE can be found at the intersection of the TV and EX schedules. In the absence of shocks, from Equation 4.10 $x = 0$ follows. In fact, the intersection of the EX and $TV(0)$ schedules is the origin of the axes (point E). Notice that, by construction, expectations are fulfilled in E (the FE schedule coincides with $TV(0)$).[13]

Suppose the economy has settled in the origin and has not experienced a shock for a long time. Suppose now a shock ϵ_T occurs in period T which

---

[12] From the guess follows that $E_t x_{t+1} = \alpha E_t \mathcal{R}_{t+1}$. From (4.9) follows that $E_t \mathcal{R}_{t+1} = \rho \mathcal{R}_t$. Hence $E_t x_{t+1} = \alpha \rho \mathcal{R}_t = \rho x_t$. Substituting this expression in (4.7) we can infer that the guess is verified with $\alpha = -\frac{1}{\sigma(1-\rho)}$.

[13] In the absence of shocks, the economy is in the steady state: $x_{t+1} = x_t$. In equilibrium (point E): $x_t = E_t x_{t+1} =$. Therefore expectations are fulfilled: $x_{t+1} = E_t x_{t+1}$.

generates a departure of the real interest rate from the rate of time preference, $\mathcal{R}_T = \epsilon_T$, and therefore a departure of consumption (and output) from its steady state. Graphically, the TV schedule shifts down (see $TV(\epsilon_T)$). The RE solution is $x_T = -\frac{1}{\sigma(1-\rho)}\epsilon_T$, which can be read as the coordinate on the y-axis of the intersection point between the EX and $TV(\epsilon_T)$ schedules. The aftershock equilibrium is point F, which does not belong to the FE schedule. In point F there is a recession – due to the sudden increase of the real interest rate – and expectations are not fulfilled.

The auto-regressive process represented by Equation 4.9 will gradually drive the real interest rate and consumption back to their steady states (point E). For instance, in period $T + 1$ the TV schedule moves up (see the dotted line), and a new (transitory) RE solution will materialize (i.e., point G). This process will go on until the TV schedule reaches the original position: $TV(0)$. At the end of the process, the economy will go back to E.

The departure of output and the interest rate from the steady state is temporary. Due to the auto-regressive nature of the shock, however, the return to the steady state takes time, i.e., the shock is characterized by some persistence. After the shock, an echo of the shock will remain in the macrosystem in each time period, which will become fainter and fainter over time. The initial recession will be replaced by smaller and smaller recessions until the output gap is closed.

In the end, in the presence of RE, in equilibrium endogenous variables are random processes, because they are (generally linear) functions of the random exogenous processes which drive their dynamics. The stochasticity of the exogenous variables is the source of uncertainty.[14] If the agent knows (i) the model of the economy, (ii) all the possible states of the world, (iii) the value of the random variable(s) of interest (the realization) in each state of the world, and (iv) the probability associated to each state of the world, then she can compute the RE equilibrium. In a nutshell, to compute the RE equilibrium the agent needs "only" the model of the economy (at least in reduced form) and the probability distribution(s) of the variable(s) of interest.

It is easy to show that in a RE context, forecast errors are white noise, i.e., their average is zero (this is the *unbiasedness* property of RE). In fact, from Equation 4.10 it follows that the error the agent makes in forecasting the output gap $e^x_{t+1} := x_{t+1} - E_t x_{t+1}$ is proportional to the error made in forecasting the interest rate $e^R_{t+1} := \mathcal{R}_{t+1} - E_t \mathcal{R}_{t+1}$:

---

[14] In the perfect foresight case, i.e. in the absence of uncertainty, the agent knows, in each period $t + s$, the realization of the stochastic variable R_{t+s}. Therefore (4.7) becomes $x_t = -\frac{1}{\sigma}\mathcal{R}_t + x_{t+1}$ i.e., the output gap is a random walk with a stochastic drift.

$$e_{t+1}^x = -\frac{1}{\sigma(1-\rho)} (\mathcal{R}_{t+1} - E_t \mathcal{R}_{t+1}) = -\frac{1}{\sigma(1-\rho)} e_{t+1}^R \qquad (4.11)$$

From (4.9) follows that $e_{t+1}^R = \epsilon_{t+1}$. Hence $e_{t+1}^x = -\frac{1}{\sigma(1-\rho)}\epsilon_{t+1}$. In the end therefore:

$$E_t e_{t+1}^x = -\frac{1}{\sigma(1-\rho)} E_t \epsilon_{t+1} = 0 \qquad (4.12)$$

Since expectations formed rationally are unbiased, in such a world people do not make *systematic* mistakes.

Notice that in the multi-period setting with rational expectations, we have made the same assumption as in the static case in the presence of measurable uncertainty (risk). In both settings, in fact, the true values of the (exogenous) variables of interest are replaced by probability distributions. The RE approach to expectation formation is the natural – i.e., most straightforward – way to model expectations in a dynamic probabilistic (risky) setting in which uncertainty may be reduced to the knowledge of a probability distribution. We will meet this notion again in the overview of macroeconomic thinking in Section 4.5.

4.4 Adaptation in Expectation Formation

In rational choice theory, behavioral rules derive from (constrained) optimization. From the economist's viewpoint, this neoclassical view of human decision-making has the advantage of drastically reducing the number of scientifically admissible behavioral rules: rules that do not derive from "first principles" can and must be discarded.[15] The main criticism to this approach is that the cognitive capabilities implicitly required to properly optimize do not seem to be within the reach of real human subjects.[16]

The neoclassical view of human decision-making has been challenged by Herbert Simon, who has pioneered a line of research on the psychological foundations of actual economic behavior which is now burgeoning under the general heading of *behavioral economics*. We will elaborate on this in Chapter 5.

---

[15] Notice, however, that there are many functional forms of the objective function and many different ways of specifying the constraints. Therefore, the neoclassical approach can generate many alternative behavioral rules for the same agent and the same problem depending upon the specific functional form of the objective function and the number and type of constraints.

[16] The neoclassical approach can be defended on the basis of the as-if argument put forward by Friedman. According to this argument, the realism of assumptions is not necessary for a model to be valid, the truly important criterion for validity being whether the model performs well or not in terms of forecasting capability. This argument has been and still is fiercely debated. Methodologically, we do not agree with it.

In Simon's view, human beings are characterized by *bounded rationality* because their cognitive ability is limited, both in collecting and in processing the relevant information. Following Keynes and Knight, we can trace back bounded rationality to a condition of *true uncertainty* – i.e., a scenario in which agents don't have a clue as to the probabilities of unknown states of the world.

In the presence of bounded rationality, agents adapt to the environment and to the other agents' behavior. *Adaptation* is the process of adjusting to changing external circumstances by following quick, computation-saving *heuristics*. In this context, expectations may well be incorrect and errors may be systematic.

The adaptive mechanism to form expectations (AE) – also known as the *error-learning hypothesis* – can be conceived of as a heuristic to form expectations when the information and cognitive capabilities necessary to solve optimization problems in the presence of uncertainty are not available to the agent. In the AE scheme, an agent updates her expectation of a certain variable in the future (say period $t + 1$) by a factor which is proportional to her forecast error in the current period. Using the symbols introduced in the previous section, the AE scheme can be represented as follows:

$$x^e_{t+1} = x^e_t + \rho e^x_t = x^e_t + \rho(x_t - x^e_t) \qquad (4.13)$$

where x^e_{t+1} is the (nonrational) expectation formed in t of the variable x in $t+1$ and ρ is a positive parameter, smaller or equal to one.

In the history of macroeconomics, adaptive expectations have been proposed well before the RE revolution. In fact, the adaptive scheme was introduced in the 1950s by Cagan and Friedman to study hyperinflations and then adopted by Friedman in the debate on the Phillips curve in the 1960s.

Adaptive expectations have been heavily criticized in the 1970s. RE theorists, in fact, held that people cannot be so stupid as to make systematic mistakes. For a decade or so, this assumption has gone unchallenged and RE have been all the rage. Nowadays, however, there is a large literature which departs more or less boldly from the RE assumption to account for the fact – which has been corroborated by plenty of experimental evidence – according to which people cannot be so smart as not to make errors on average. Adaptive expectations, therefore are currently experiencing a comeback in the light of the criticisms raised against the RE hypothesis (more on this in Chapter 5).

4.5 Riding at Full Gallop through the History of Macroeconomics

In this section we will briefly overview the development of macroeconomic thought in order to bring to the fore the role of models of expectation formation.

4.5.1 The Neoclassical-Keynesian Synthesis

We start from the workhorse of the Neoclassical-Keynesian Synthesis – i.e., the IS-LM-Phillips curve (PC) framework – which can be conceived as the mainstream macroeconomic model in the 1950s and 1960s. In this framework, expectations do not play a role. The central role of expectations will be brought to the fore by Friedman's criticism of the Phillips curve. The development of ideas on expectation formation, therefore, can be most clearly described as a sequence of variants of this framework in which expectations are incorporated in different ways.

The IS-LM-PC framework consists of the following equations:

$$x_t = -\frac{1}{\sigma}(i_t - \pi_t)$$

$$\mu = -\frac{1}{\phi}i_t + m(x_t + \pi_t)$$

$$\pi_t = kx_t$$

The first equation is the IS function. The output gap x is decreasing with the real interest $r = i - \pi$, where i is the nominal interest rate and π is inflation; σ is a positive parameter.[17] The second equation is the LM function. Money demand (on the RHS of the equation) is increasing with nominal income (in growth rates), i.e., $x + \pi$ and decreasing with the nominal interest rate; ϕ, m are positive parameters. We assume $\phi > 1$. Money supply (LHS) grows at the exogenous rate μ. The third equation is the Phillips curve, which associates inflation positively to the output gap; k is a positive parameter.[18] The Phillips curve can be conceived as a Keynesian aggregate supply (AS) curve on the (x, π) plane. It incorporates *nominal rigidity*.[19]

---

[17] The IS function considered in this subsection departs from the standard undergraduate textbook version of the IS-LM model, as it determines the output gap instead of the level of output as a function of the real interest rate. It is, on the other hand, a distant relative of the consumption Euler Equation 4.7. There are two differences: (i) the expectation of the future output gap is ignored (since the model of this subsection abstracts from all the expectational variables); (ii) the real interest rate is defined as the difference between the nominal interest rate and current inflation instead of being described by the stochastic process Equation 4.9. This definition makes room for monetary policy and for inflation in the aggregate demand component of the model.

[18] The original Phillips curve associates inflation to the distance of the unemployment rate from the natural rate of unemployment. This distance is negatively related to growth through Okun's law. Hence the formulation in the text.

[19] There are many ways of deriving the AS curve. For example, with perfect competition and nominal wage rigidity, from Equation 4.1 one gets $P = \frac{\bar{W}}{\alpha} q^{\frac{1-\alpha}{\alpha}}$. Taking logs and differentiating one gets $\pi = kx$ where $k = \frac{1-\alpha}{\alpha}$, where we assume that the percent change of output is measured from the natural level of output.

Substituting the LM into the IS equation and setting $m = 1$ to simplify notation (and without loss of generality), one gets the Aggregate Demand (AD) schedule

$$x_t = d_0\mu - d_1\pi_t \qquad (4.14)$$

where $d_0 := \frac{\phi}{\sigma+\phi}$ and $d_1 := \frac{\phi-1}{\sigma+\phi}$. Since $\phi > 1$, then $d_1 > 0$.

The IS-LM-PC framework boils down to the the AD-AS system consisting of Equation 4.14 and the Phillips curve. Solving this system for x, π we get

$$x^K = \frac{d_0}{1 + kd_1}\mu$$

$$\pi^K = \frac{kd_0}{1 + kd_1}\mu$$

Changes in the growth rate of money supply affect both nominal and real variables.[20] This is due to nominal rigidity.

When wages are perfectly flexible, the aggregate scale of activity is always at the full employment level, so that

$$x^F = 0$$

$$\pi^F = \frac{d_0}{d_1}\mu = \frac{\phi}{\phi - 1}\mu$$

In this case, of course, changes in monetary policy affect only nominal variables.

4.5.2 Expectations Enter the Scene

Friedman's critique of the Phillips curve led to the *Expectations Augmented Phillips curve* (EAPC), i.e.,

$$\pi_t = kx_t + \pi^e_{t+1} \qquad (4.15)$$

---

[20] To complete the argument, notice that the IS-LM-PC model in structural form is a system of three equations in three unknowns, namely the equilibrium levels of the output gap, inflation, and the nominal interest rate. The reduced form of the model therefore consists of x^K, π^K and $i^K = \phi\left[(1+k)\frac{d_0}{1+kd_1} - 1\right]\mu$. It is necessary to assume that the expression in brackets is negative, so that an increase of the quantity of money pushes the interest rate down. At this point, however, we must reinterpret i as a component of the nominal interest rate which can be positive or negative. For instance, we can denote the nominal interest rate properly speaking with $i_n = \bar{i} + i$, where $\bar{i}$ is a given benchmark. Hence i turns out to be a component of the nominal interest rate which can be negative. The Zero Lower Bound is hit when i is negative and equal to $\bar{i}$ in absolute value.

where π_{t+1}^e is the expectation of inflation in $t + 1$, taken in t.[21] The IS-LM-EAPC framework boils down to the system consisting of the AD and EAPC equations, Equations 4.14 and 4.15. Solving this system for x_t, π_t we get

$$x_t = \frac{a}{k}\mu - bd_1\pi_{t+1}^e \tag{4.16}$$

$$\pi_t = a\mu + b\pi_{t+1}^e \tag{4.17}$$

where $a := \frac{kd_0}{1+kd_1}$, $b := \frac{1}{1+kd_1}$. The reduced form of the AD-EAPC system consists of the *output gap equation* Equation 4.16 and the *inflation equation* Equation 4.17. Notice that the latter is a linear relationship between current and expected inflation, given the growth rate of money supply. To close the model, we need *a theory of expectation formation* to be applied to the expectation of inflation.

4.5.3 Adaptive Expectations

As anticipated in the previous section, Friedman proposed an *adaptive heuristic* to model expectations formation. In the Adaptive Expectations (AE) setting, expectations are updated according to the following rule:

$$\pi_{t+1}^e = \pi_t^e + \rho(\pi_t - \pi_t^e) \tag{4.18}$$

where $0 < \rho \leq 1$. The expression in parentheses is the forecast error $e_t := \pi_t - \pi_t^e$. The product ρe_t[22] is the "error-correction" mechanism.[23]

Equation 4.18 can be rewritten as

$$\pi_{t+1}^e = (1 - \rho)\pi_t^e + \rho\pi_t \tag{4.19}$$

that is, the expectation of inflation in $t+1$ is a weighted average of the expected and actual levels of inflation in t.[24]

---

[21] This can be conceived also as the equation of the expectations augmented AS curve (EAS).

[22] Denoting with $\Delta_{t,t+1}^e := \pi_{t+1}^e - \pi_t^e$ the change in expectations, the adaptive nature of the updating rule emerges nicely if we rewrite Equation 4.18 as follows: $\Delta_{t,t+1}^e = \rho e_t$. From this expression it is clear that in an adaptive setting (i) expectations of inflation are revised upward (downward) if inflation has been underestimated (overestimated) and (ii) the magnitude of this revision is proportional to the error made.

[23] When maximum weight is given to the forecast error, i.e., $\rho = 1$, we get *static* or *naive* expectations. In this special case $\pi_{t+1}^e = \pi_t$.

[24] Iterating Equation 4.19, it is easy to infer that the expectation of inflation in $t + 1$ is a weighted average of past values of inflation with exponentially declining weights:

$$\pi_{t+1}^e = \rho\pi_t + (1 - \rho)\rho\pi_{t-1} + \ldots = \rho \sum_{s=0}^{\infty}(1 - \rho)^s \pi_{t-s} \tag{4.20}$$

Notice that only the past values of the variable to be forecast play a role in the AE mechanism. Additional information which may be relevant to forecast inflation is ignored.

The AD-EAPC system with adaptive expectations boils down to the output gap Equation 4.16, the inflation Equation 4.17 and the AE updating rule Equation 4.19.

The system is recursive. We focus first on the subsystem represented by the inflation equation and the updating rule. From Equation 4.17 we get: $\pi^e_{t+s} = (\pi_{t+s-1} - a\mu)/b$, $s = 0, 1$. Substituting these expressions into Equation 4.19 and rearranging, we get a linear first order difference equation:

$$\pi_t = \frac{a\rho}{1 - b\rho}\mu + \frac{1 - \rho}{1 - b\rho}\pi_{t-1} \tag{4.21}$$

The steady state of Equation 4.21 is $\pi^{AE} = \frac{a}{1-b}\mu$. Thanks to the fact that $b < 1$, steady state inflation is positive and the steady state is stable.[25] Steady state inflation is a multiple of the growth rate of money supply. Recalling the definition of parameters, we get $\frac{a}{1-b} = \frac{d_0}{d_1} = \frac{\phi}{\phi-1}$. Hence we can rewrite steady state inflation as follows:

$$\pi^{AE} = \frac{\phi}{\phi - 1}\mu \tag{4.22}$$

It is easy to see that in the steady state (the long-run equilibrium), expected inflation in every period is constant and equal to actual inflation:

$$\pi^e = \pi^{AE} \tag{4.23}$$

meaning expectations are fulfilled and the forecast error is zero.[26]

Substituting Equation 4.23 for π^e_{t+1} into Equation 4.16, we get the steady state level of the output gap:

$$x^{AE} = 0 \tag{4.24}$$

Equations 4.23 and 4.24 are the long-run solution of the AD-EAPC model with adaptive expectations.[27]

Stationarity implies fulfilled expectations but forecast errors are always present out of the long run equilibrium – i.e., during the transitional dynamics. To see this graphically, we proceed as follows. Updating Equation 4.21 we get

$$\pi_{t+1} = \frac{a\rho}{1 - b\rho}\mu + \frac{1 - \rho}{1 - b\rho}\pi_t \tag{4.25}$$

---

[25] In fact, $b < 1$ implies $1 - \rho < 1 - b\rho$.
[26] From (4.20) assuming that the economy is in the steady state one gets
$\pi^e = \rho\pi^{AE}\sum_{s=0}^{\infty}(1 - \rho)^s$ where $\sum_{s=0}^{\infty}(1 - \rho)^s = 1/\rho$.
[27] Notice that the long run equilibrium with AE is exactly the same solution of the AD-AS system with flexible wages, see subsection 4.5.1 above. Why? Because wages in the AD-EAS system adjust to expected inflation. When expectations are correct, then this adjustment is perfect. In other words, wages are perfectly indexed to inflation and the real wage is at the full employment level.

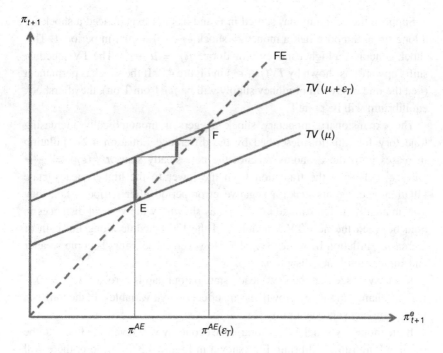

Figure 4.2 AE: Effects of a permanent monetary shock.

Substituting Equation 4.17 into Equation 4.25 and rearranging we get:

$$\pi_{t+1} = \frac{a}{1-b\rho}\mu + \frac{b(1-\rho)}{1-b\rho}\pi_{t+1}^e \qquad (4.26)$$

Equation 4.26 represents the *True Value (TV) schedule* on the $\left(\pi_{t+1}, \pi_{t+1}^e\right)$ plane (see Figure 4.2).

Expectations are correct when

$$\pi_{t+1}^e = \pi_{t+1} \qquad (4.27)$$

Equation 4.9 represents the *Fulfilled Expectations (FE) schedule*, which coincides with the 45-degree line by definition.

We determine the *Fulfilled (or correct) Expectations Equilibrium (FEE)* by solving the system consisting of Equations 4.26 and 4.9. The solution provides the coordinates of the intersection E between the TV and FE schedules in Figure 4.2. It is easy to verify that the FE of π coincides with its actual value π^{AE}.

The error $e_{t+1} := \pi_{t+1} - \pi_{t+1}^e$ is the vertical distance between the TV and FE schedules. In the steady state the error is zero: stationarity implies fulfilled expectations.

Suppose the economy has settled in E and has not experienced a shock for a long time. Suppose that a monetary shock $\epsilon_T > 0$ occurs in period T. This shock generates a higher money growth rate $\mu_T = \mu + \epsilon_T$. The TV schedule shifts upwards as shown by $TV(\mu + \epsilon_T)$ in Figure 4.2. If the shock is permanent (i.e., the rate of growth of money supply will be μ_T from T on), the aftershock equilibrium will be point F.

The expansionary monetary shock triggers a monotonically increasing trajectory for inflation described by the difference Equation 4.21. Inflation increases until the economy reaches the new steady state $\pi^{AE}(\epsilon_T) = \frac{\phi}{\phi - 1}$ $(\mu + \epsilon_T)$. During the transition from the lower to the higher steady state inflation rate, agents make a negative error period after period – i.e., they systematically underestimate inflation – as shown by the vertical distances in bold between the new TV schedule and the FE schedule along the path of increasing inflation betweeen E and F. However, these errors become smaller and smaller until they disappear in F.

It is easy to see that the new steady state output gap is zero: $x^{AE}(\epsilon_T) = 0$ – i.e., the change in money growth has no effect on real variables. In the long run there is money super-neutrality.[28]

If the monetary shock is temporary, the economy will revert gradually to the original long run equilibrium E as shown in Figure 4.3. Therefore, there will be a fluctuation which will be characterized by persistence: both inflation and the output gap will jump up due to the shock and go down gradually to the original steady state over time.

4.5.4 Rational Expectations

The adaptive heuristic proposed by Friedman to model expectation formation was heavily criticized by Lucas, Sargent and the other intellectual leaders of the *New Classical Macroeconomics (NCM)*, essentially because people do not make systematic errors in the real world.[29] The RE school has aimed at modeling a nonmyopic process of expectation formation. In order to present the RE approach in our simple setting, we must rewrite the inflation Equation 4.17.

---

[28] Notice that we get the steady state value of inflation and therefore fulfilled expectations also imposing the condition $\pi_t = \pi^e_{t+1}$ in (4.17). This is somehow obvious because in the steady state also the condition above occurs. In other words, in the steady state current and future inflation are the same and equal to expected inflation.

[29] In the light of plenty of experimental evidence, there are good reasons to object to this objection. In learning-to-forecast experiments, in fact, real human subjects do make systematic errors. See Hommes and Lux (2013).

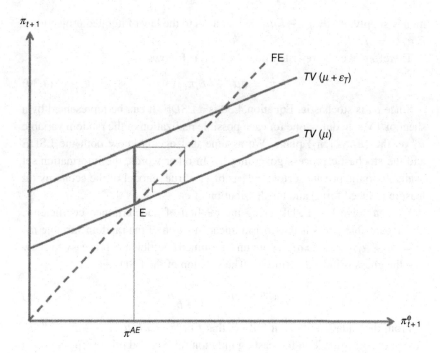

Figure 4.3 AE: Effects of a temporary monetary shock.

First of all, with RE, the expectation of inflation is defined as

$$\pi^e_{t+1} = E_t\pi_{t+1} \tag{4.28}$$

where E_t is the expected value taken in t (and on the basis of the information set available in t) of π in $t + 1$.

Second, we have to introduce a source of randomness. The obvious candidate is the growth rate of money supply. Let us explore first the simplest case:

$$\mu_t = \mu + \epsilon_t \tag{4.29}$$

where ϵ_t is a *monetary shock* (or monetary innovation), a white noise stochastic disturbance (zero mean and constant variance). In words, the (uncertain) rate of growth of money supply in a given period $t + s$ is a random variable with constant expected value $E_{t+s}\mu_{t+s} = \mu$ for any $s = 0,1,2...$ and constant variance, equal to the variance of the monetary shock.[30] The monetary shock can be conceived as the error the agents make in forecasting the growth rate of

---

[30] In this simple setting, there is within-period uncertainty. The agent does not know in t the growth rate of money supply in the same period.

money supply: $e_t^\mu := \mu_t - E_t\mu_t = \epsilon_t$, thanks to the law of iterated projections: $E_t\mu_{t+1} = \mu$.

Therefore, we can rewrite Equation 4.17 as follows:

$$\pi_t = a\mu_t + bE_t\pi_{t+1} \tag{4.30}$$

Since μ_t is stochastic, Equation 4.30 is a LSDE. It can be represented by a sheaf of TV schedules, one for each possible realization of the random variable μ_t on the $(E_t\pi_{t+1}, \pi_t)$ plane. We assume that agents know both the LSDE and the stochastic process governing μ_t. In other words, the information set available to the private sector consists of the "true" model of the economy (at least in reduced form) and the distribution of ϵ_t.

We can solve this LSDE using the method of undetermined coefficients. One reasonable guess is that π_t is a linear function of the random variable μ_t: $\pi_t = \alpha_0 + \alpha_1\mu_t$, where α_0, α_1 are undetermined coefficients. It is easy to show that the guess is indeed verified.[31] The solution of the LSDE is

$$\pi_t^{RE} = a\mu_t + \frac{ab}{1-b}\mu \tag{4.31}$$

From the equation above it follows that $E_t\pi_t^{RE} = aE_t\mu_t + \frac{ab}{1-b}\mu = \frac{a}{1-b}\mu$, so that the error made in forecasting inflation (also called price surprise) is

$$e_t^\pi := \pi_t^{RE} - E_t\pi_t^{RE} = a(\mu_t - \mu) = ae_t^\mu = a\epsilon_t \tag{4.32}$$

In words: the error made in forecasting inflation (price surprise) is proportional to the error made in forecasting money growth (monetary innovation).

In the absence of monetary shocks (and therefore of price surprises), Equation 4.30 can be written as $\pi_t = a\mu + bE_t\pi_{t+1}$. This is represented by the straight line labelled $TV(\mu)$ in Figure 4.4. Substituting $\mu_t = \mu$ into (4.31) and rearranging, we get $\pi^* = \frac{a}{1-b}\mu$. Since $\frac{a}{1-b} = \frac{\phi}{\phi-1}$, we can write:

$$\pi^* = \frac{\phi}{\phi-1}\mu \tag{4.33}$$

π^* is the RE solution of Equation 4.30 in the absence of shocks. Notice that, in the absence of shock, $\pi_t = \pi_{t+1} = E_t\pi_{t+1} = \pi^*$.

The RE solution in the absence of shocks provides the coordinates of the intersection E between the $TV(\mu)$ and FE schedules (see Figure 4.4). In other words, it is the fulfilled (or correct) expectations equilibrium (FEE) in this setting.

---

[31] From the guess follows that $E_t\pi_{t+1} = \alpha_0 + \alpha_1 E_t\mu_{t+1}$. But $E_t\mu_{t+1} = \mu$. Substituting this expression in the LSDE we can infer that the guess is verified with $\alpha_0 = \frac{ab}{1-b}\mu$ and $\alpha_1 = a$. Hence $E_t\pi_{t+1} = \frac{a}{1-b}\mu$.

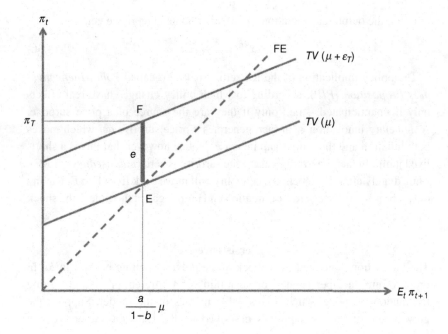

Figure 4.4 RE: Effects of a monetary shock.

The RE solution is exactly the same as the AE solution. The AE solution however is a long-run equilibrium, i.e., the steady state of a dynamic process. The RE solution instead is characterized by the absence of shocks.

Let's consider now what happens when a shock occurs. Suppose the economy has settled in E and has not experienced a shock for a long time. Suppose that a monetary shock ϵ_T occurs in period T. This shock generates a departure of the money growth rate from μ:$\mu_T = \mu + \epsilon_T$. As a consequence, the TV schedule shifts up as shown by $TV(\mu + \epsilon_T)$ in Figure 4.4. If the shock is not anticipated (so that $E_t\pi_{T+1} = \pi^*$), there will be a departure of inflation from π^*. In fact, $\pi_T = a\mu_T + \frac{ab}{1-b}\mu$ as shown by (4.31). Graphically the aftershock equilibrium is point F in Figure 4.4.

Notice that the error is $e_T^{\pi} = \pi_T - \frac{a}{1-b}\mu = a(\mu_T - \mu)$ – i.e., the vertical distance between the TV schedules (before and after the shock) measured at the level of expected inflation. Hence,

$$\pi_T^{RE} = \pi^* + (\pi_T - E_T\pi_T) = \pi^* + a(\mu_T - \mu) = \pi^* + a\epsilon_T \qquad (4.34)$$

This solution can be generalized to any time period:

$$\pi_t^{RE} = \pi^* + a(\mu_t - \mu) = \pi^* + a\epsilon_t \qquad (4.35)$$

Using the output gap equation (4.16), after some algebra we get:

$$x_t^{RE} = \frac{a}{k}\epsilon_t \qquad (4.36)$$

The policy implication of the RE setting is the so-called *Policy Ineffectiveness Proposition (PIP)*, according to which policy changes have real effects only if unanticipated – i.e., only if they are the source of a price surprise. A monetary innovation ϵ_t in fact, generates a price surprise $a\epsilon_t$ which makes both inflation and the output gap increase. Notice however that this is a short-lived jump. In fact, on average, the price surprise is zero (*unbiasedness* of RE). Immediately after the shock, the economy will move back from F to E, leaving only a blip in the time series of inflation and output gap at the time T the shock occurred.

Persistence

The fluctuation generated by a shock in the previous setting is short lived. In order to introduce persistence, one can think of a different process governing the random variable which drives the dynamics of the model. Suppose the growth rate of money supply is described by the following autoregressive process of order one:

$$\mu_t = (1 - \rho)\mu + \rho\mu_{t-1} + \epsilon_t \qquad (4.37)$$

where $0 < \rho < 1$ and ϵ_t white noise.

The expected value is $E_{t+s}\mu_{t+s+1} = (1 - \rho)\mu + \rho\mu_{t+s-1}$ for any $s = 0,1,2\ldots$ Notice that, in the absence of shocks, the steady state of this process is $\mu_t = \mu_{t-1} = \mu$. The monetary innovation is $e_t^\mu := \mu_t - E_{t-1}\mu_t = \epsilon_t$.

We use this definition of money growth to solve Equation 4.30 using the method of undetermined coefficients.[32] The RE solution of Equation 4.30 when μ_t is governed by (4.37) is

$$\pi_t^{RE} = \frac{a}{1 - b\rho}\mu_t + \frac{ab(1 - \rho)}{(1 - b)(1 - b\rho)}\mu \qquad (4.38)$$

In the absence of shocks (and therefore of price surprises), Equation 4.30 can be written as $\pi_t = a\mu + bE_t\pi_{t+1}$. This is represented by $TV(\mu)$ in Figure 4.5.

---

[32] One reasonable guess is $\pi_t = \alpha_0 + \alpha_1\mu_t$, where α_0, α_1 are undetermined coefficients. From the guess follows that $E_t\pi_{t+1} = \alpha_0 + \alpha_1 E_t\mu_{t+1}$. But from Equation 4.37 follows that $E_t\mu_{t+1} = (1 - \rho)\mu + \rho\mu_t$. Substituting this expression in Equation 4.30 we can infer that the guess is verified with $\alpha_0 = \frac{(1-\rho)ab}{(1-b\rho)(1-b)}\mu$ and $\alpha_1 = \frac{a}{1-b\rho}$.

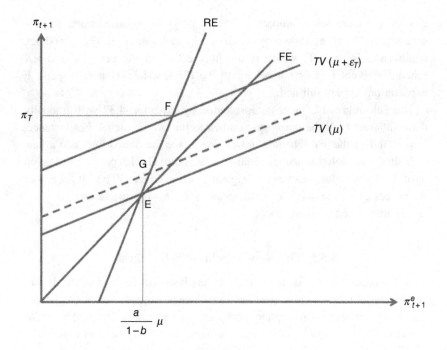

Figure 4.5 Persistence.

Substituting $\mu_t = \mu$ into (4.38) and rearranging we get

$$\pi^* = \frac{\phi}{\phi - 1}\mu \qquad (4.39)$$

π^* is the RE solution of (4.30) in the absence of shocks. Notice that this solution is exactly the same as above.

Notice now that, in the present setting, expected inflation in $t + 1$ is increasing with current inflation in t.[33]

$$E_t\pi_{t+1} = \pi^* + \rho\pi_t \qquad (4.40)$$

This is the EXpectation schedule in Figure 4.5.

The RE solution in the absence of shocks provides the coordinates of the intersection E between the $TV(\mu)$ and EX schedules. By construction it is also the intersection between the TV and FE schedules. In other words, it is the fulfilled (or correct) expectations equilibrium (FEE) in this setting.

Let us now explore the consequences of a shock. Suppose the economy has settled in E for a long time. A monetary shock ϵ_T occurs in T. The money

---

[33] In fact, from the guess it follows $E_t\pi_{t+1} = \alpha_0 + \alpha_1 E_t\mu_{t+1} = \alpha_0 + \alpha_1[(1 - \rho)\mu + \rho\mu_t]$.
Adding and subtracting $\rho\alpha_0$ and recalling that $\pi_t = \alpha_0 + \alpha_1\mu_t$ we obtain (4.40).

growth rate increases on impact: $\mu_T = \mu + \epsilon_T$. As a consequence, the TV schedule shifts up as shown by $TV(\mu + \epsilon_T)$ in Figure 4.5. The aftershock equilibrium is point F, which is the intersection of the new TV and EX schedules. Point F does not belong to the FE schedule. Hence, in point F expectations are not fulfilled.

The auto-regressive process represented by Equation 4.37 will gradually drive inflation (and the output gap) down to the original level. For instance, in period T+1 the TV schedule moves down (see the dotted line) and a new (transitory) RE solution will materialize – i.e., point G. This process will go on until the TV schedule reaches the original position – i.e., $TV(\mu)$. At the end of the process, the economy will settle again in E. This process takes time – i.e., it is characterized by persistence.

4.5.5 The New Neoclassical Synthesis

New Classical Macroeconomics (NCM) has been all the rage in the 1980s. By the early 1990s, a new approach had gained ground, which challenged the perfect competition/complete markets setting generally accepted by NCM theorists. This approach goes under the name of *New Keynesian Economics (NKE)*. By the end of the 1990s, a syncretic approach, the *New Neoclassical Synthesis*, merged insights from both the NCM and NKE schools. The workhorse of the New Neoclassical Synthesis is the *New Keynesian dynamic stochastic general equilibrium (NK-DSGE)* model which, in our simplified setting, boils down to the following equations:

$$x_t = -\frac{1}{\sigma}(i_t - \pi_t)$$
$$i_t = (1 + \gamma)\pi_t$$
$$\pi_t = kx_t + \beta E_t \pi_{t+1} + u_t$$

The first equation is the IS relatiosnship between the output gap and the real interest rate. [34] The second equation is a monetary policy rule, namely a Taylor rule (TR), which defines the policy rate as an increasing function of inflation ($\gamma > 0$).[35]

---

[34] To be precise, the first equation of the standard NK-DSGE model is the so-called "optimizing IS curve," which is essentially the consumption Euler Equation 4.7 where the real interest rate is endogenized as follows $\mathcal{R}_t = i_t - E_t\pi_{t+1}$. Usually, a demand shock is added to the equation. For simplicity and continuity of exposition, we adopt here a simplified variant of the consumption Euler equation, identical to the one used in the previous section. Notice moreover that we ignore demand shocks.

[35] The Taylor rule is an instrument rule, i.e., it is not derived from an optimization problem (it is a rule of thumb, not an optimal rule). The Taylor rule captures a change in the way in which

The third equation is the NK-Phillips curve (NKPC), which associates inflation positively to the output gap and expected inflation.[36] The NKPC plays the role of the AS curve in the NK setting.

Finally we introduce a source of randomness, namely a *supply shock* which is appended to the NKPC. The supply shock follows the auto-regressive process

$$u_t = \rho u_{t-1} + \epsilon_t \qquad (4.41)$$

where ϵ_t is white noise. Notice that $E_t u_{t+1} = \rho u_t$. The NK-DSGE workhorse in our simplified setting therefore is the system of IS-TR-NKPC equations where the supply shock is described by Equation 4.41.

Substituting TR into the IS equation one gets

$$x_t = -\frac{\gamma}{\sigma}\pi_t \qquad (4.42)$$

Equation 4.42 is the equation of the AD curve in the NK context. The NK model boils down to the AD–AS system where the AS is represented by the NKPC curve. Substituting Equation 4.42 into the NKPC, we end up with:

$$\pi_t = au_t + bE_t\pi_{t+1} \qquad (4.43)$$

where $a := \frac{\sigma}{k\gamma+\sigma}, b := \frac{\beta\sigma}{k\gamma+\sigma}$. Notice that both a and b are positive and smaller than one.

Equation 4.43 is the *inflation equation* in the NK setting. It can be represented by a sheaf of TV schedules, one for each possible realization of the random variable u_t on the $(E_t\pi_{t+1}, \pi_t$ plane).

As usual we will solve this LSDE using the method of undetermined coefficients.[37] The solution of the LSDE is

$$\pi_t^{RE} = \frac{a}{1-b\rho}u_t \qquad (4.44)$$

In the absence of shocks (and therefore of price surprises), Equation 4.43 is represented by $TV(0)$ in Figure 4.6.

monetary policy has been carried out, from monetary targeting (whereby the central bank sets the money growth and the interest rate is endogenous) to inflation targeting (whereby the central bank sets the interest rate as a response to inflation and the quantity of money is endogenous). The specific formulation we follow characterizes a regime of *strict inflation targeting* whereby the interest rate responds only to inflation. When the central bank reacts also to changes in the output gap, the Taylor rule characterizes a regime of flexible inflation targeting (which we do not consider for simplicity).

[36]
In the NKPC, expected inflation is weighted by the discount factor β which is smaller than one. This is due to nominal rigidity.

[37]
The guess is $\pi_t = \alpha u_t$ where α is undetermined. From the guess follows that $E_t\pi_{t+1} = \alpha E_t u_{t+1}$. But $E_t u_{t+1} = \rho u_t$. Hence $E_t\pi_{t+1} = \rho\pi_t$. Substituting this expression in the LSDE, we can infer that the guess is verified with $\alpha = \frac{a}{1-b\rho}$.

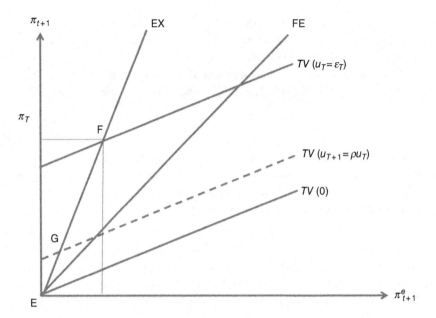

Figure 4.6 Effects of a supply shock in the NK-DSGE model.

$\pi^* = 0$ is the RE solution of (4.43) in the absence of shocks. Notice that, in the absence of shock, $\pi_t = \pi_{t+1} = E_t\pi_{t+1} = \pi^*$.

In the present setting:

$$E_t\pi_{t+1} = \rho\pi_t \tag{4.45}$$

This is the equation of the Expectation schedule in Figure 4.6.

The RE solution in the absence of shocks provides the coordinates of the intersection E between the $TV(0)$ and EX schedules. By construction, it is also the intersection between the TV and FE schedules. In other words, it is the fulfilled (or correct) expectations equilibrium (FEE) in this setting.

Suppose the economy has settled in E and has not experienced a shock for a long time. Suppose that a supply shock ϵ_T occurs in period T. As a consequence, the TV schedule shifts up as shown by $TV(\epsilon_T)$ in Figure 4.6. If the shock is not anticipated, graphically the aftershock equilibrium is point F, which is the intersection of the new TV and the EX schedules. Point F does not belong to the FE schedule.

The auto-regressive process represented by Equation 4.37 will gradually drive inflation (and the output gap) down to the original level. For instance, in period T + 1, the TV schedule moves down (see dotted line) and a new (transitory) RE solution will materialize, i.e., point G. This process will go on until the TV schedule reaches the original position, i.e., $TV(0)$. At the end of the process, the economy will settle again in E. This process is characterized by persistence.

4.6 The Limits of Rational Expectations

There are at least three main reasons to criticize the rational expectations hypothesis.

First of all, the burden of "rationality" imposed on agents in RE models – in terms of content of the information set and computing capability – appears to be out of the reach of real human beings, who are characterized instead by bounded rationality as mentioned above (we will elaborate further on this issue in the next chapter).

Second, the assumption that agents will sooner or later discover the "true model" of the economy simply begs another question: Which model? In a RE framework the true model must be the researcher's model, whose solution is by construction consistent with expectations.[38] Therefore, the model all the agents "have in mind" is exactly the model built by the researcher.

Third, RE usually relies on the over-simplifying assumption of a representative agent. In an heterogeneous agents setting, in order to have a RE equilibrium *all* the agents must converge to the same rational prediction.[39] In principle, however, different agents have different expectations and convergence to RE (through rational learning) is not assured. The persistence of heterogeneity in economic beliefs is in fact a well-known fact of life.

These limits have provided the starting point for a complex web of lines of research. As to the first and second points, for instance, a large literature has developed on statistical or adaptive learning pioneered by Evans and Honkapohja in the early years of the new century, in which agents learn the numerical values of the parameters of the model by running regressions. In simple cases, statistical learning yields convergence to a rational expectations solution (rational learning): agents indeed learn the parameters of the true model of the economy and therefore converge to (uniform) rational expectations. In more complex environments, however, learning may not yield the RE equilibrium.

As to the third line, let us recall the vast literature on heterogeneous expectations and heuristic switching pioneered by Brock and Hommes (1997).

---

[38] This resembles the ontological argument put forward by Saint Anselm of Aosta, according to which God must exist (in reality) simply because the idea of God as the perfect being (in the mind of men) cannot lack the attribute of existence.

[39] See chapter 1 for a succinct discussion of neoclassical models with heterogeneous agents.

In their setting, expectations agents switch from one rule of thumb to another (e.g., from adaptive to fundamental expectations), depending on the relative "fitness" of the rules. As a consequence, heterogeneous expectations can survive and coexist: the aggregate or average expectation is a weighted sum of the individual expectations.

We will elaborate on these issues in depth in Chapter 5. In the following section, we will provide a very simple introduction to the effects of heterogeneous expectations in a macroeconomic setting similar to the one discussed earlier. This discussion will pave the way to a brief introduction to modelling expectations in macroeconomic ABMs.

4.7 Heterogeneous Expectations: A Very Simple Introduction

4.7.1 Heterogeneous-Biased Expectations

Suppose there is a continuum of agents of unit mass. Let's use π^e_{it+1} to denote the expectation (the "belief" hereafter) taken in t of inflation in $t+1$ by agent i, $i \in (0, 1)$. We can model the individual expectation in very general terms as follows

$$\pi^e_{it+1} = f(\pi_t, \alpha_i) \qquad (4.46)$$

where π_t is the current value of inflation and α_i is the individual *bias*. For simplicity, we assume that the function $f(.,.)$ is the same for all the agents, so that expectations are heterogeneous only because of the bias. We assume the individual bias is distributed on the support $(-\alpha_L, \alpha_H)$ with mean α and variance σ^2_α. In the following we will refer to α as the *collective* bias. By construction, the *average expectation* $\langle \pi^e_{it+1} \rangle$ – which we will denote with π^e_{t+1} hereafter – is:[40]

$$\pi^e_{t+1} \approx f(\pi_t, \alpha) + \frac{1}{2} \frac{\partial^2 f(\pi_t, \alpha)}{\partial \alpha^2} \sigma^2_\alpha \qquad (4.48)$$

The average expectation is a function of π_t, and of the mean and higher moments of the distribution of α_i.

---

[40] We can linearize Equation 4.46 around the average bias by means of a Taylor expansion:

$$\pi^e_{it+1} \approx f(\pi_t, \alpha) + \frac{\partial f(\pi_t, \alpha)}{\partial \alpha}(\alpha_i - \alpha) + \frac{1}{2} \frac{\partial^2 f(\pi_t, \alpha)}{\partial \alpha^2}(\alpha_i - \alpha)^2 \qquad (4.47)$$

Taking the expected value of the expression above and recalling that $E(\alpha_i - \alpha) = 0$ and $E(\alpha_i - \alpha)^2 = \sigma^2_\alpha$, we obtain Equation 4.48.

Equation 4.48 is the average EXpectation (EX) schedule on the $\left(\pi_t, \pi^e_{t+1}\right)$ plane. The mean and the variance of the distribution of the bias are shift parameters of the function.

For simplicity, suppose that the function $f(.,.)$ is linear in π_t and takes the following simple form:

$$\pi^e_{it+1} = \pi_t + f(\alpha_i) \tag{4.49}$$

We assume that if the bias is positive (negative), the agent expects inflation in $t+1$ to be higher (lower) than inflation in t.[41]

The average expectation in this case is

$$\pi^e_{t+1} = \pi_t + f(\alpha) + \frac{f''(\alpha)}{2}\sigma^2_\alpha \tag{4.50}$$

Equation 4.50 is the equation of the EX schedule in Figure 4.7. The intercept of this schedule on the x-axis is affected by the mean and the variance of the distribution of the bias.

As usual, the True Value (TV) schedule is represented by the inflation Equation 4.17 which we report here for the reader's convenience:

$$\pi_t = a\mu + b\pi^e_{t+1} \tag{4.51}$$

We now have a system consisting of Equations 4.50 and 4.9. The solution of this system yields equilibrium – i.e., consistency – between (i) the way in which actual inflation is determined by average expected inflation according to Equation 4.8 and (ii) the way in which average expectations are determined according to (4.50). However, individual expectations will not be model-consistent as we will show below.

In equilibrium, actual inflation in the presence of heterogeneous expectations is

$$\pi^H = \pi^* + \psi\left(f(\alpha) + \frac{f''(\alpha)}{2}\sigma^2_\alpha\right) \tag{4.52}$$

where $\pi^* = \frac{\phi}{\phi-1}\mu$ and $\psi = \frac{\sigma+\phi}{k(\phi-1)}$. Therefore, expected inflation in equilibrium is

$$\pi^{eH} = \pi^* + (1+\psi)\left(f(\alpha) + \frac{f''(\alpha)}{2}\sigma^2_\alpha\right) \tag{4.53}$$

Actual and expected inflation do not coincide because of the bias. They are the coordinates of the intersection H between the *TV* and *EX* schedules (see Figure 4.7). Since H does not lie on the FE schedule (the 45-degree line),

---

[41] In symbols: $f'(\alpha_i) > 0, f(\alpha_i) > 0$ if $\alpha_i > 0, f(\alpha_i) < 0$ if $\alpha_i < 0, f(0) = 0$.

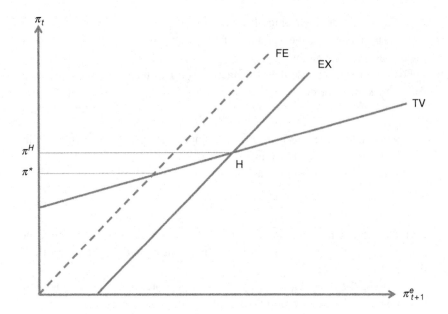

Figure 4.7 Heterogeneous expectations.

expectations are not fulfilled. More precisely, given our assumptions, they are systematically greater than actual inflation.

Of course, this is only the starting point of the analysis, which may become more interesting if one departs from the assumption that the bias is given. The bias can be endogenized, for instance, by considering the complex relationships between the bias and current inflation. This analysis, however, is out of the scope of our introduction.

4.7.2 A Convenient Special Case: Two Types

In order to dig a little deeper into this issue, consider an extremely simplified setting in which the population consists only of two types of agents: high and low. The high type holds a belief characterized by a positive bias $+\Delta$. Symmetrically, the low type has negative bias $-\Delta$. Hence $\pi^e_{Ht+1} = \pi_t + \Delta$ and $\pi^e_{Lt+1} = \pi_t - \Delta$.[42]

Let's denote with ω the fraction of positively biased agents in the population. The *collective* bias – i.e., the weighted average of the optimistic and the

---

[42] In this simplified setting, we assume that the expectation is linear in the bias. Therefore, only the collective bias will play a role in determining the average expectation. Due to linearity, higher moments of the distribution of the bias will not play any role.

pessimistic bias – is $\omega\Delta + (1 - \omega)(-\Delta) = \psi\Delta$ where $\psi := (2\omega - 1)$. By construction, the average expectation is

$$\pi^e_{t+1} = \pi_t + \psi\Delta \tag{4.54}$$

Equation 4.54 is the equation of the *EX* schedule in this simple example. It can be represented as in Figure 4.7 reinterpreting the intercept on the *x*-axis as $\psi\Delta$ and assuming that $\omega > 0.5$ (so that the intercept is positive).

Superimposing the usual TV schedule, one can compute the coordinates of point H in this simplified setting. The solutions are:

$$\pi^H = \pi^* + \psi\Delta \tag{4.55}$$

$$\pi^{eH} = \pi^* + (1 + \psi)\Delta \tag{4.56}$$

Expectations are always individually biased and the individual error is constant and systematically negative (positive) for the positively (negatively) biased individuals. If the fraction of positively biased agents were also constant, then ψ would be constant and the aggregate bias would also be constant. The economy would settle in H with actual inflation systematically lower than expected inflation.

If we assume that agents can switch from a positive to a negative bias and vice versa, however, the population of heterogeneous agents can change over time. Suppose for instance that the fraction of positively biased agents exceeds 0.5 (and becomes therefore the majority); if their bias has been confirmed, i.e., if actual inflation is greater than past inflation, then:

$$\omega = \frac{\lambda(\pi_t - \pi_{t-1}) + 1}{2} \tag{4.57}$$

In this case, it is easy to see that $\psi = \lambda(\pi_t - \pi_{t-1})$. Hence the average expectation equation becomes:

$$\pi^e_{t+1} = (1 + \lambda\Delta)\pi_t - \lambda\Delta\pi_{t-1} \tag{4.58}$$

Plugging the average expectation Equation 4.58 into the inflation Equation 4.17 we get the equilibrium inflation, which follows a first-order law of motion:

$$\pi_t = \frac{a}{1 - b - b\lambda\Delta}\mu - \frac{b\lambda\Delta}{1 - b - b\lambda\Delta}\pi_{t-1} \tag{4.59}$$

It is easy to see that the steady state of Equation 4.59 is $\pi^H = \pi^*$. Imposing the restriction, $\lambda\Delta < \frac{1-b}{b} < 2\lambda\Delta$, the steady state will be stable.

When the economy is in the steady state, expectations are fulfilled *when averaged across agents*. The individual bias, however, is still present. How is this possible? The reason is very simple: the composition of the population in the steady state is such that the aggregate bias of the positively biased individuals is offset by the aggregate bias of the negatively biased ones. In fact, in the steady state $\omega^* = 0.5$. Expectations are heterogeneous and biased at the individual level but they are collectively unbiased.

Graphically, when $\omega = 0.5$ the EX schedule coincides with the FE schedule. Apparently people hold correct expectations, but this is true only on average: half of the population is of a high type and half of the low type.

4.7.3 Heterogeneous Adaptive Expectations

Let's now introduce heterogeneous adaptive expectations. As in Subsection 4.7.1, we consider a continuum of agents of unit mass. The i-th agent updates her expectation according to the following adaptive rule:

$$\pi_{it+1}^e = \rho_i \pi_t + (1 - \rho_i)\pi_{it}^e \tag{4.60}$$

ρ_i is the individual error correction coefficient. We assume the individual coefficient is distributed on the support $(0, 1]$ with mean ρ. Averaging across agents, we get $\pi_{t+1}^e = \rho \pi_t + \pi_t^e - \langle \rho_i \pi_{it}^e \rangle$ where the last term is the expected value of the product of the individual coefficient and the individual expectation in period t.

Notice now that $\langle \rho_i \pi_{it}^e \rangle = cov\left(\rho_i, \pi_{it}^e\right) + \rho \pi_t^e$ where $cov\left(\rho_i, \pi_{it}^e\right)$ is the covariance between ρ_i and π_{it}^e. Hence, the average expectation equation can be rewritten as

$$\pi_{t+1}^e = \rho \pi_t + (1 - \rho)\pi_t^e - cov\left(\rho_i, \pi_{it}^e\right) \tag{4.61}$$

Heterogeneity is captured by the covariance between the individual ρ_i and the individual π_{it}^e, but the latter is in turn defined as in Equation 4.60 (lagged one period). Hence the covariance of ρ_i and the individual π_{it}^e can be recast in terms of variance and higher moments of the distribution of ρ_i and of past values of inflation. Dynamics can indeed be very rich.

4.8 Heterogeneous Expectations in ABMs

In a complex economy and in the presence of cognitive and informational constraints on individual rationality, it is straightforward to assume that agents hold heterogeneous expectations, i.e., they form expectations following different heuristics. This is the most obvious point of departure in building expectation formation in ABMs.

In principle, there is no limit to the creativity of the researcher: since the principle of full rationality is not disciplining economic theorizing, any forecasting heuristic is in principle admissible. This is, of course, a drawback of the AB methodology which goes under the name of wilderness of bounded rationality.

In our opinion, the consequences of this problem may be mitigated by assuming that only few forecasting rules are actually adopted, as experimental evidence suggests. The obvious candidates are expectations adaptive (discussed in the previous section) and its variants. For example, one can incorporate the inertia of the variable to be forecast into the expectation formation mechanism by augmenting static expectation with the second difference of the variable:

$$\pi^e_{it+1} = \pi_t + \lambda_i(\pi_t - \pi_{t-1}) \tag{4.62}$$

Depending on the magnitude of the tuning parameter in Equation 4.62, we get:

- a weak trend-following rule if $0 < \lambda_i < 1$, and
- a strong trend-following rule if $\lambda_i > 1$.

Along similar lines, following a well-known behavioral insight, one can model expectations based on the anchoring and adjustment heuristic:

$$\pi^e_{it+1} = \lambda_i \pi^{av}_t + \beta_i \pi_t + (\pi_t - \pi_{t-1}) \tag{4.63}$$

where π^{av}_t is a moving average of past values of π. Besides AE, other formulations based on linear filters such as extrapolative/regressive expectations have been used in the literature.

As an example, let us consider an agent-based macro-model in which, in order to buy consumption goods, each household visits only a (small) subset of firms – i.e., households do not explore the entire space of purchasing opportunities – so that each firm has some *market power* on its own local market. In other words, there are as many local markets as there are firms.

The firm has to set individual price and quantity under uncertainty.[43] The firm knows from experience that if it charges higher prices, it will get smaller demand but it does not know the actual demand schedule (i.e., how much the consumers visiting the firm would buy at any given individual price). The firm, in fact, observes only the current willingness to pay of the visiting consumers, who change from time to time. Hence the firm is unable to maximize profits setting the marginal cost (which is known) equal to the marginal revenue (unknown). The best the firm can do consists in setting the price as close as possible to the average price level – a proxy of the price set collectively by

---

[43] In the following, we borrow heavily form Assenza et al. (2015).

its competitors[44] – and production as close as possible to expected demand
in order to minimize involuntary inventories (in case of excess supply) or the
queue of unsatisfied customers (in case of excess demand).

In t, the i-th firm must choose the individual price and desired output for $t+1$
$\left(P_{it+1}, Y^*_{it+1}\right)$, where desired output is anchored to expected demand $Y^*_{it+1} = Y^e_{it+1}$. The firm's information set in t consists of (i) the average price level P_t
and (ii) excess demand

$$\Delta_{it} := Y^d_{it} - Y_{it} \tag{4.64}$$

where Y^d_{it} is actual demand and Y_{it} is actual output in t. Δ_{it} shows up as a
queue of unsatisfied customers if positive, and as an inventory of unsold goods
if negative.

Notice that Δ_{it} is a proxy of the forecasting error $\epsilon_{it} := Y^d_{it} - Y^e_{it}$ where Y^e_{it} is
expected demand formed in $t-1$ for t.[45] If there is a positive forecasting error
(i.e., under-estimation of demand), then there will be *a fortiori* excess demand
(a queue of unsatisfied customers). If there is a negative forecasting error (i.e.,
over-estimation of demand), then there will be excess supply (involuntary
inventories) only if the negative error is greater in absolute value than the
discrepancy between expected demand and actual production. This will be the
case, of course, if the discrepancy is sufficiently small.[46]

Given this information set, a firm can decide either to update the current
price or to vary the quantity to be produced – but not both.[47]

The decision process is based on two rules of thumb which govern price
changes and quantity changes respectively. These rules are represented by
simple adaptive algorithms. The price adjustment rule is:

$$P_{it+1} = \begin{cases} P_{it}(1 + \eta_{it}) & \text{if } \Delta_{it} > 0; P_{it} < P_t \\ P_{it}(1 - \eta_{it}) & \text{if } \Delta_{it} \leq 0; P_{it} > P_t \end{cases} \tag{4.65}$$

---

[44] As usual in a monopolistic competition setting, the single firm assumes its price is weighted
almost zero in the average price level.

[45] Δ_{it} coincides with ϵ_{it} iff production plans are fulfilled, i.e., $Y^*_{it} = Y_{it}$. Production plans,
however, may not be fulfilled: actual production Y_{it} can differ from desired quantity Y^*_{it} if
constraints on the availability of capital, labor and funding inhibit the attainment of the desired
scale of activity. In symbols: $Y_{it} \leq Y^*_{it}$. Therefore $\Delta_{it} = \epsilon_{it} + (Y^e_{it} - Y_{it})$, where the expression
in parentheses is a non-negative discrepancy between expected demand and actual production.

[46] Notice that goods are not storable: involuntary inventories cannot be carried over from one
period to the next. Therefore they cannot be employed strategically to satisfy future demand.
They play, however, the very useful role of an element of the information set available to the
firm when setting the price and the quantity for the future.

[47] This is a simplifying assumption, which makes coding less cumbersome.

where η_i is a random positive parameter drawn from a distribution with support $(0, \bar{\eta})$.[48]

The sign of Δ_{it} and of the difference $P_{it} - P_t$ dictate the direction of price adjustment, but the *magnitude* of the adjustment is stochastic and bounded by the width of the support of the distribution. This is one of the main sources of randomness in the CATS model. We also assume that the firm will never set a price lower than the average cost (which includes not only the cost of labour and capital goods but also interest payments).[49]

The firm sets the desired quantity Y_{it+1}^* at the level of expected demand Y_{it+1}^e. Hence the *quantity adjustment* rule can be conceived also as an algorithm for changing demand expectations:

$$Y_{it+1}^* = Y_{it+1}^e = \begin{cases} Y_{it} + \rho \mathbf{1}_{[P_{it} > P_t]} \Delta_{it} & \text{if } \Delta_{it} > 0 \\ Y_{it} + \rho \mathbf{1}_{[P_{it} < P_t]} \Delta_{it} & \text{if } \Delta_{it} \leq 0 \end{cases} \tag{4.66}$$

where ρ is a positive parameter, smaller than one.

$\mathbf{1}_{[P_{it} > P_t]}$ is an *indicator function* equal to 1 if $P_{it} > P_t$, 0 otherwise. Analogously, $\mathbf{1}_{[P_{it} < P_t]}$ is an *indicator function* equal to 1 if $P_{it} < P_t$, 0 otherwise.

The sign of Δ_{it} and of the difference $P_{it} - P_t$ dictate the direction of quantity adjustment. Notice, however, that the *magnitude* of the adjustment is not stochastic, but determined by excess demand. If we assume that the discrepancy between expected demand and desired production is negligible, so that excess demand coincides with the forecasting error, we can interpret Equation 4.66 as a standard *adaptive mechanism* to update demand expectations. By iteration, as it is well known, desired production in t+1 will be determined by the weighted average of past quantities with exponentially decaying weights.

4.9 Conclusions

In this chapter we have focused on (i) the role of uncertainty in shaping microeconomic behavior and (ii) the role of expectation formation in determining macroeconomic outcomes. As to (i), in a risky context – i.e., when the environment is uncertain in a measurable way – agents replace the unknown true value of variables (which are necessary to decision-making) with their probability

---

[48] The distribution from which the idiosyncratic parameter is drawn is the same for all the firms and is time-invariant.

[49] While the attainment of the desired scale of activity is constrained by lack of capital, labor or finance, there are no obstacles to setting the desired price provided the price emerging from Equation 4.65 is greater than the average cost.

distribution and carry on the usual optimization routines. In a straightforward extension of this framework to a multi-period setting, agents form rational expectations of future variables. The cognitive and informational requirements of RE, however, may be out of the reach of agents characterized by bounded rationality. In this case, an adaptive mechanism may be a satisficing heuristic to form expectation.

As to (ii), in the history of macroeconomic thought, AE – proposed by Friedman in the debate over the Phillips curve – have been rapidly wiped out by the RE revolution. This methodological principle has been and still is almost always respected, even if the debate has raged with alternating successes between New Classical and New Keynesian economists. Of recent, skepticism on the appropriateness of RE in macroeconomic models is gaining ground both inside and outside the mainstream.

In a complexity setting, it is straightforward to assume that agents adopt satisficing heuristics also when they must form epectations. AE are formed on the basis of simple rules processing signals that come from the environment and the behavior of other agents. No effort in improving knowledge or changing behavior is carried out. In building ABMs, researchers generally adopt one sort or another of adaptive schemes. A natural extension would be to imagine models whose agents explore their environment and modify their behavioral rules, according to some learning process. This will be explored in the next chapter.

5

Agents' Behavior and Learning

Alberto Russo, Domenico Delli Gatti, Saul Desiderio,
and Ivo Vlaev

5.1 Introduction

The fundamental building blocks of every agent-based model are *agents*. From
a general point of view, in order to build an agent-based model, four main
issues need to be addressed: (i) the *nature* of the agents; (ii) the list of variables
describing their *state*; (iii) the list of the *actions* the agents can perform;
(iv) the structure of their *interaction* with other agents. In what follows, we
will discuss the first three points, while the last will be deeply analyzed in
Chapter 6.

A peculiar feature differentiating agents in agent-based models from those
of mainstream models is their *autonomy* of action. Indeed, agents in a rational-
expectations-cum-equilibrium model behave according to rules that are not
independent of what the others are doing: in any situation, their actions depend
on some variable that is determined by the behavior of the entire system. In a
typical market model, for instance, a firm must know the actual market price
(i.e., market-clearing price) in order to decide its production level, and this
price is determined by the interplay of all the agents populating the economy.
Hence, agents' actions are mutually dependent through the equilibrium state
or, differently stated, the actual implementation of actions depends on the
outcome of actions (outcome $\Rightarrow$ actions). As this simple but representative
example clarifies, mainstream models are dynamically incomplete since no
mechanism for out-of-equilibrium dynamics is provided. Thus, the central
problem characterizing a decentralized market economy – i.e., the coordination
problem – is left aside. On the contrary, the character of autonomy in an agent-
based model consists in the existence of a set of behavioral rules allowing
agents to take decisions in any situation, independently from what the others
are doing and without a central Auctioneer, intervenes as a *deus ex machina*
in determining some sort of equilibrium state. The implementation of actions

81

is not dependent of the outcome of actions. Of course, the final outcome generally will depend on the whole system of interactions among the agents, implying the possibility of individual rationing in case of coordination failures, but this is not an obstacle to the implementation of autonomous decision-making. In fact, what makes this possible is that agents' actions directly influence only other agents' variables, and not also their own variables. To clarify the point, let us imagine a consumer wanting to buy a good from a shop. If the good has already been delivered, the consumer will buy, otherwise it won't. The *outcome* (purchase or not) of the consumer's action clearly depends upon the action taken by the shop (deliver or not), but the consumer's very *action* (try to buy) does not: actions and outcomes are separate, and this is exactly an instance of what out-of-equilibrium means (actions $\Rightarrow$ outcome). The attribute of agents' autonomy, therefore, makes agent-based models the natural candidate to simulate the dynamic evolution of a decentralized, and not necessarily coordinating, market economy.

The dynamic evolution of the economic system depends on the behavioral rules followed by agents. Where do behavioral rules come from? Agents in real economies are intentional subjects, i.e., they have mental representations of the environment, have well defined objectives and act in the attempt of achieving them on the basis of their information set and of their capabilities. Behavioral rules in the real world, therefore, must be related to the cognitive processes that guide actions. Accordingly, in this chapter we focus on agents' rationality, behavioral rules and learning processes.

5.2 Full and Bounded Rationality

Since its first appearance in the works by Adam Smith, modern political economy has basically configured as a theory aimed at understanding the outcome of the interaction among self-interested agents operating under competitive conditions. It is important to stress that the notion of rationality embodied in this theory is simply related to a vague idea of "pursuance of self-interest," that is to a mere tendency toward the matching between preferences and opportunities. Thus, no aspect of optimality was supposed to characterize individual decision-making. Consequently, in giving explanations of economic behaviors, large emphasis was found by psychological inquiries about human "moral sentiments."

This early concern about psychological foundations of economic theory started fading after the advent of Marginalism at the fall of the nineteenth century. Fascinated by the success of classical mechanics, the marginalist school borrowed its analytical tools in the attempt of edifying a theory of a perfectly predictable human behavior. Economics was then pushed in the direction of ever increasing degrees of mathematical formalism, which eventually became the centerpiece of economic disciplines, while any psychological content was limited to only few axioms whose plausibility was all but undisputable. The loose notion of rationality characterizing classical political economy mutated into the so-called full rationality paradigm, which constrained the fickle and inconsistent human being's behavior in the straightjacket of the concept of *homo oeconomicus*, a Laplacean demon provided with omniscience and infallibility. Moreover, the same concept was applied with great ease not only to human beings, but also to any other economic agent – being a bank, a manufacturing firm or a government.

The standard model of economic decision-making, therefore, rests on a set of hypotheses that may be epitomized in the following three propositions:

1. agents are fully informed about the environment;
2. agents are consistent, in the sense that between two alternatives they choose the best one (according to some criterion);
3. deciding agents encounter no limit of time and computational power.

In any model of rational choice, goals are given as a prior and are embodied into a well-defined objective function (utility for consumers, profits for firms), which allows the economic agent to always carry out consistent choices. In addition, economic agents are supposed to choose, from all the possible alternatives, the one entailing the achievement of the maximum of their objective function – in a word, agents *optimize*. Moreover, the full rationality assumption is maintained even in the context of risky choice that is investigated by the Subjective Expected Utility theory. To summarize, the full rationality perspective adopted by neoclassical economics reduces to the following postulates:

1. preferences are well-defined;
2. information about events or probability of events is perfect;
3. agents optimize.

The well-known product of these assumptions is the picture of a suspiciously smart individual. It is therefore natural to ask whether the above claims are a good representation of human behavior when immersed in real worlds – which by their very nature are complex systems because of multiple interactions of many heterogeneous agents.

Since the second half of the twentieth century, Herbert Simon challenged the neoclassical view of human decision-making by pioneering a line of research on the psychological foundations of actual economic behavior, suggesting that human minds are characterized by *bounded rationality* because they suffer of some sort of cognitive limitation, both in the amount of available information and in the ability of processing it in the correct way. In the wake of Simon's work, two strictly interdependent strands of investigation developed: *experimental economics*, whose research is aimed at empirically testing neoclassical theoretical predictions by means of laboratory experiments (from theory to data), and *behavioral economics*, whose objective is to employ the available empirical evidence about human behavior in order to work out new and more realistic representations of economic decision-making (from data to theory). More recent is the advent of *neuroeconomics*, which exploits the modern techniques of brain scanning to derive new insights about human economic behavior relating actions to brain activation areas.

We have now to characterize the concept of bounded rationality in deeper details, starting by a clarification of what it is *not*. In first place, bounded rationality is not an "optimization under constraints," and is not even an inferior form of rationality; it is not a mistake or a deviation from theoretical norms. Bounded rationality, in practice, must not be confused with the intelligence that may characterize irrational decision-makers. On the opposite, it is the kind of rationality that necessarily characterizes real agents when called to face problems in a real environment. In fact, advocates of bounded rationality focus their analysis on the *procedural* rationality, that is on the very process of how agents materially make choices given their preferences and the perceived opportunities offered by the structure of the environment, while neoclassical theory ignores the actual implementation of the choice and concentrates only on the prediction of the best outcome, which fully rational agents are supposed to attain (*substantial* rationality). In other terms, to be procedurally rational means to adopt a method to possibly find a *satisficing* solution for a given problem (Simon, 1987), while to be substantially rational means to know the best solution of the problem. But optimizing rationality guarantees the correspondence of substantial and procedural rationality if, and only if, all the consequences of alternative actions can be consistently conceived in advance, at least in a probabilistic sense. In such an ideal situation, optimizing behavior is sufficient to give a good representation of mental processes, regardless of the actual implementation of decisions. But for complex systems like real economies, this possibility is generally ruled out because the dynamics produced by an interactive population gives rise to uncertainty that can not be reduced to risk. As a consequence, in similar situations real economic actors do not possess well-defined models of the environment surrounding them, and the degree of rationality we can realistically ask our agents should decline.

In large complex economies, deductive means of reasoning are inapplicable or ill-defined; instead, individuals build internal mental models to represent the world, learn from the outcomes of previous choices and extrapolate from the particular to the general. Simply stated, agents employ some form of *induction*. Thus, in large interactive systems, individual decision processes become unavoidably *adaptive* – that is, adjusted in the light of realized results – and the search for actions aimed at increasing individual performance stops as soon as a *satisficing* solution has been found. Adaptation is a backward-looking, sequential, path-dependent phenomenon and is based on quick, resource-saving *heuristics*. Bounded rationality, consequently, is the evocative term used to label decisional processes of ecologically rational adaptation – that is processes of selective adaptation providing outcomes that are not necessarily optimal, but which give the opportunity to survive most of the times in a given environment.[1]

All in all, while the *rational agent model* is about how to make good decisions, *bounded rationality* is about trying to predict what people actually do. Since there is only one way to be "fully rational," while the ways of not being fully rational are infinite, a complete theory of bounded rationality does not exist and, consequently, many models of bounded rationality can be generated. For instance, instead of assuming a given set of alternatives, which the deciding agent picks from, one can postulate a process generating the alternatives. Instead of assuming a given and known probability distribution of choice outcomes, one can introduce some mechanism allowing the estimation of the probabilities or the deployment of some strategy to face the uncertainty without assuming the knowledge of the probabilities. Finally, as an alternative to the assumption that agents can maximize their utility function, one may postulate a decision strategy giving only satisfactory outcomes. Models of bounded rationality cannot be, therefore, universal strategies to be used as general-purpose tools, but rather they are unavoidably context-dependent, fast and frugal heuristics. Nevertheless, some regularity exists as the literature on experimental and behavioral economics show.

5.2.1 Empirical Microfoundations of Individual Behavior

While discussing the concept of bounded rationality, we have already pointed out how major contributions in detecting failings of neoclassical theory

---

[1] Mainstream economics also recognized real agents' cognitive limitations, but rejected bounded rationality as irrelevant and still retained the full rationality hypothesis on the basis of Friedman's notorious *as-if* argument, stating that the survival-of-the-fittest mechanism would let only optimizing firms to survive at equilibrium. A simple counter-argument to Friedman's claims is based on the observation that in any environment individual full rationality is not a necessary condition to survive; at most, it is only sufficient to be slightly smarter than the others.

came especially from cognitive psychology, behavioral and experimental economics and recently from neuroeconomics. Agent-based modelers can benefit from the results of these disciplines that contribute to the development of alternative schemes for the representation of bounded rational individual decision-making.

Cognitive psychology is principally concerned about the activities of judgment and choice, assuming that at the basis of human decision-making two different cognitive processes coexist: intuition and reasoning. While reasoning is a voluntary, slow, controlled, serial and effortful cognitive process, on the opposite intuition is a fast, associative and effortless mechanism producing automatically spontaneous judgments (or thoughts) just as if they were perceptions. The neoclassical picture describing economic decision-making is uniquely based on reasoning, while in reality most of decisions (and the economic ones are not an exception) are typically based on intuitive judgments, with reasoning simply relegated to the task of monitoring the quality of judgments produced by intuition. Thus, cognitive psychology offers a strong empirical support to the bounded rationality arguments, offering at the same time useful bases for constructing alternative behavioral models.

One of the central assumptions for economic theory is that of well-defined preferences, which can be considered a valid hypothesis whenever preferences are independent of the context. But several experiments by cognitive psychologists demonstrated that often the opposite is true because of the so-called framing effect. As we will see, framing effects are pervasive and cause preferences to be in many cases ill-defined, or dependent on the context in which they are originated.

Intuitive judgments depend on *accessibility*, that is the easiness with which particular mental contents come to mind (Higgins, 1996). Accessibility, on its turn, is a feature of human mind influenced by the framing of the object being observed. Changes in the framing may induce the accessibility of different intuitive judgments, which consequently trigger a different evaluation of the problem. Thus, framing effects (Tversky and Kahneman, 1981) make preferences context-dependent, and constitute a violation of the preference invariance property (Arrow, 1982; Tversky and Kahneman, 1986), which basically states that preferences are not affected by variations of irrelevant features of options and outcomes. How the context may imply different preference structures by affecting accessibility will be illustrated through a series of examples. Each example at one time shows both a failure of neoclassical assumptions and a possibility for alternative bounded rational behavioral models.

Framing effect. Many experiments have demonstrated that people actually evaluate risky decision outcomes framing the problem in terms of gains and losses, showing that the carriers of utility are changes in wealth and not levels of wealth as assumed by subjective expected utility theory. When a problem of risky choice is stated (framed) in terms of changes, people show clear risk aversion, but when the same problem is represented in terms of levels, a weak attitude to risk-taking emerges. On the basis of the evidence that changes are relatively more accessible than absolute values, Kahneman and Tversky (1979) proposed a model of risky choice called prospect theory. It states that individual preferences are described by a value function, which is increasing and concave with respect to gains, decreasing and convex with respect to losses and zero at the origin, where it also displays a kink. Alternative theories of risky choice aimed at relaxing or removing the original axioms of expected utility theory are the *weighted utility theory* (Chew and MacCrimmon, 1979), the *expected utility without the independence axiom* (Machina, 1982), the *regret theory* (Loomes and Sugden, 1982) and *rank-dependent expected utility* (Quiggin, 1982, 1993).[2]

Reference points. Another powerful example of framing effect is given by the case of reference-dependent evaluations in risky contexts. Human perception is biologically designed to favor the accessibility of changes and differences instead of levels (Palmer, 1999). Hence, *reference-dependence* means that perception is usually based on an anchoring reference value that is used as a vantage point: the perceived attributes of a focal stimulus reflect the contrast between that stimulus and a context of prior and concurrent stimulus. A simple example is the following one. Consider three buckets of water characterized by different temperatures: the left one contains cold water, the middle one contains tepid water, and the right one contains hot water. Consider that the left hand of a person is immersed in the hot bucket and the right hand in the cold one. After initial intense sensations of cold and heat, these sensation wanes; when both the hands are immersed in the middle bucket, the experience is heat in the left hand and cold in the right hand.

The violation of the rationality axiom of irrelevance of irrelevant alternatives constitutes further evidence of the importance of reference points in decision-making. There are in fact cases in which decision-making is a problematic task because the options at stake differ by features that are not easily comparable – that is, the decision cannot be taken because of a lack of reference points. In the first step of a classic experiment conducted by Tversky, undergraduate students are called to decide between renting room A, cheap but far away from the university, and renting room B, expensive but close to the university. The choice is not so obvious because the characteristics of the rooms (cost and

---

[2] See also: Chew et al. (1987) and Yaari (1987).

proximity to the university) are difficult to compare with each other, and in fact the sample of students splits equally between A and B, signaling an objective difficulty in deciding. In the second step, A and B are flanked by a third option, room C. The characteristic of room C is to be patently worse than A, because it is more expensive and more distant from the university. According to neoclassical precepts, the addition of C should be irrelevant, but Tversky discovered that most of the students now prefer room A, whose attributes are more easily comparable with those of C. Since most of respondents find it hard to opt between A and B, adding option C induces students to implicitly restate the problem into a choice between A and C only.

Hyperbolic discounting. Another example we show, witnessing how reference points may have a role in shaping individual preferences, is the phenomenon of *time-inconsistency* detected in the intertemporal choice problem. In mainstream models where agents are called to trade off costs and benefits that occur at different periods, usually it is assumed that future events are discounted by the exponential factor $1/(1+r)^t$, where r is a *constant* rate. Such a formulation assures preferences are always consistent along time, since the same time windows exhibit same discounting factors regardless of their absolute position in time. However, since the first experiments by Thaler (1981), also confirmed by later studies (e.g., Benzion et al., 1989; Holcomb and Nelson, 1992; Pender, 1996), a hyperbolic time-discounting function, at a rate $1/(1+kt)$, has proved to fit experimental data better than the exponential model. The main property of hyperbolic discounting is to have a discount factor r, which is decreasing in time. In fact, same time windows show different discounting according to their absolute position in the time horizon; for example, discounting between period t and $t+1$ is larger than discounting between $k+t$ and $k+t+1$ with $k>0$. This characteristic entails, therefore, time-inconsistency in people's preferences since, when future become near future (i.e., the time window approaches the moment of decision-taking), its discounting becomes more and more dramatic, producing an "immediacy effect," according to which present time is disproportionately preferred. Thus, people with hyperbolic discounting have the systematic tendency to change their mind as the time goes by.

Mental accounting. The next example of framing effect (Tversky and Kahneman, 1981) constitutes a violation of the neoclassical prediction according to which wealth is fungible, a property that is irrelevant due to the source of the wealth. In the experiment, a group of consumers had to suppose of having purchased in advance the tickets for a theater show at the price of $10, later discovering, at the time of the show, to have lost the tickets. A second group of consumers, instead, had to imagine of losing a $10 bill while going to the theater to buy the tickets. Then, the components of both groups were asked to declare whether they would have attended the show anyway. According to the full-rationality theory, the two groups should have given the same answer, since losing $10 worth of tickets is equivalent to losing a $10 bill, because the effect on the budget constraint is equivalent. Nonetheless, almost all the people from the group supposing the loss of the ticket replied that they would have not gone to the show, while the 88% from the other group announced that they would have attended the show in spite of the loss of the $10 bill. The authors explained such results introducing the concept of "mental accounting," according to which people are inclined to organize their expenditures in mental categories such as food entertainment or general expenses. For the two groups, the economic value of the loss ($10) is the same, but its framing is different. In fact, it is likely that those people losing the tickets behave as if they debited the loss into the mental count for entertainment, while the others to the count of general expenses. Hence, for the first group, the loss of the ticket makes the cost of the show to rise from $10 to $20, a cost which many respondents find excessive, while for the others it remains to $10.

Risk attitude. A famous instance of framing effects is given by the Asian disease problem, which offers a striking example of violation of the preference invariance property assumed by neoclassical economics. The problem is stated as follows (Tversky and Kahneman, 1981):

Imagine that the United States is preparing for the outbreak of an unusual Asian disease, which is expected to kill 600 people. Two alternative programs to combat the disease have been proposed. Assume that the exact scientific estimates of the consequences of the programs are as follows:

If Program A is adopted, 200 people will be saved;

If Program B is adopted, there is a one-third probability that 600 people will be saved and a two-thirds probability that no people will be saved.

Which of the two programs would you favor?

If the problem is presented in this version, most of respondents are in favor of program A, indicating risk aversion. The same dilemma is then submitted to another sample of respondents in an alternative but logically equivalent form:

If Program A' is adopted, 400 people will die;

If Program B' is adopted, there is a one-third probability that nobody will die and a two-thirds probability that 600 people will die.

A neat majority of respondents now prefers program B', showing risk-proclivity. Although the two versions of the problem bear exactly the same informative content (A = A$'$ and B = B$'$), they evoke different ideas and emotions and induce opposite choices. The reason resides in the difference of framing that causes the problem to allow for a dissimilar accessibility of judgments in respondents' mind. In fact, since certain options are generally over-weighted because their outcome is easier to evaluate, program A will be disproportionately attractive and preferred to program B because it makes easily accessible the positive image of saving 200 people for sure. Besides, for the same reason of over-weighting of certain outcomes, program B$'$ is preferred because program A$'$ calls to mind the negative image of a condemnation to sure death for 400 people; as a consequence, respondents accept the gamble embodied in program B$'$ in the hope of avoiding a grim fate to 400 people. According to the full-rationality paradigm, if A is preferred to B, then A$'$ must be also preferred to B$'$. But, as experimentally proved, this is not the case. Therefore, even though far from being a proof of irrationality of people, this example shows how preferences may even be reversed by the particular accessibility of sentiments and intuitions triggered by the framing of the context.

5.2.2 Agents' Behavior and Heuristics

Even when preferences are well-defined, people do not always show the kind of rationality that is supposed by neoclassical economics to characterize human behavior. This is true in at least two meanings. As already stated, in complex environments, adaptive behaviors based on rules of thumb, or *heuristics*, become the standard. As is logical, this is true in the judgment process too. Kahneman and Tversky (1974) in fact argue that people rely on a limited number of *heuristic methods* to overcome the operational complexity of tasks such as assessing probabilities and deducing environmental features. But there is also another difficulty that weakens the descriptive ability of the full-rationality paradigm: people display the tendency to erroneously interpret the facts that are relevant to a problem of choice, and often their errors are systematic. Generally, heuristics are efficient because they represent quick and parsimonious decisional rules that help to survive in everyday life and, in this sense, they are *ecologically* rational. But when used in more complex problems or when the available decisional time is minimal, they are often misleading and incorrect. Kahneman and Tversky (1974) identify some practical rules used in judgment:

- The first one is availability. In general people estimate the frequency of an event based on the ease with which analogous events are remembered. Experiments show that people are inclined to deem the cases of killings more frequent than the cases of suicide not because killings actually are, but because they strike people's mind much more. Consequently, killings are more available to memory.

- The second heuristic is representativeness, which works when people are called to estimate conditional probabilities. The task of estimating $P(sample\ A \in class\ B)$ is carried out simply on how well the sample represents the class, without considering how large the class is. Suppose you want to evaluate whether a shy man is a salesman or a librarian. Since librarians are shy more often than salesmen, one is more inclined to say that the shy man is a librarian. But this evaluation is likely to be incorrect because it does not consider that in the population there are many more salesmen than librarians. The heuristic of representativeness is then at the root of the so-called base rate fallacy.[3]

- The third heuristic is anchoring, a widespread strategy used in evaluating a given situation which consists of choosing an initial reference point and then in adjusting the evaluation as new information becomes available. The principal drawbacks of anchoring are that the reference point may be totally independent from the object of evaluation, or that the final judgment tends to be too much closely related to it.[4]

Furthermore, some contributions (Damasio, 1994; Loewenstein et al., 2001; Slovic et al., 2002) highlight the role of *emotions* in shaping agents' behavior and thus economic choices. For instance, Slovic et al. (2002) introduce affect heuristics to describe how the decisional process is affected by the emotions associated with objects or the mental images of those objects. The influence of particular feelings/affective reactions or moods are typically experienced at the unconscious level and may shape agents' behavior without them being aware of it. Through repeated interactions, agents may learn how to automatically react to stimuli and can develop a set of automated (and implicit) actions, thus resulting in fast decisions (as opposed to more elaborate and slow decisions based on logical reasoning).

In order to develop a consistent set of behavioral rules followed by a bounded rational agent, who tries to make inferences from the real world under constraints of limited time, limited knowledge and limited computational capabilities, it is useful to discuss the notion and the content of a specific vision of bounded rationality proposed by Gigerenzer et al. (1999): the *adaptive*

---

[3] This mistake simply amounts to confound conditional with marginal probabilities.
[4] The most common biases produced by these heuristic of judgments are non-regressive prediction, neglect of base-rate information, overconfidence and overestimates of the frequency of events that are easy to recall.

toolbox, which collects a set of heuristics based on three premises (Gigerenzer and Selten, 2001b):

- *Psychological plausibility.* The aim is to develop a model of the actual behavior of humans (or animals) based on their cognitive, emotional and behavioral characteristics.
- *Domain specific.* The toolbox provides a collection of heuristics that are specialized rather than general (as in the case of Expected Utility Theory).
- *Ecological rationality.* The success of heuristics is based on adaptation to the structure of the environment (both physical and social).

Heuristics are composed of building blocks with three main functions: search a direction, stop search and make a decision. In more detail, we have the following rules whose combinations give rise to heuristics:

- *Search rules.* Searching information or alternatives is modeled as an adaptive procedure that is repeated until it is stopped.
- *Stopping rules.* They terminate searching procedures whenever a satisfactory condition is reached, preventing search rules from wasting limited resources.
- *Decision rules.* Once search is stopped and a certain amount of information has been gathered, a simple decision rule is applied. It may include the adoption of social norms, cultural habits or well-established conventions.

For example, think about a population of firms and workers that interact in a spatial labor market:

- Consider that the worker j has a reservation wage w_j and visits firms from the nearest to more distant firms; this is a *search rule*.
- The agent visits a certain number of firms in her neighborhood until the distance is not larger than 100 Km; this is a *stopping rule*.
- Based on previous rules, the worker j has a list of firms, each offering a given wage; now, two cases can be considered in the *decision rule*:
    1. There is at least one firm for which the offered wage is higher than the reservation wage plus transport costs (*tc*); then, the worker j decides to accept the wage w_i paid by the firm i for which the difference $w_i - (w_j + tc)$ is the highest in the list of observed firms; but
    2. in the other case, the worker j prefers to be unemployed, given that the offered wage by firms does not cover the reservation wage augmented by the transport costs.

The combination of the three rules – search, stopping and decision – gives rise to a heuristics that guides the behavior of an agent who wants to be employed by a firm in her neighborhood, gaining a wage that is above the reservation wage and also enough to cover the transport costs.

5.3 Learning

In general, learning is the object of study by different disciplines such as psychology and pedagogy but, in recent years, it is more and more capturing the attention of economists. For our scope, it is necessary to understand when learning gains a prominent role for economic theory, what the objects of learning are and how it can be embodied in economic models.

As already stated, once the hypothesis of perfect information is removed, some sort of bounded rationality becomes the normal status and, consequently, artificial agents have to be modeled with some sort of limitation in their cognitive and decisional capabilities. Moreover, agents may be allowed to change their attitude and their knowledge through some learning mechanism.

As a consequence of limited information, the typical situations where learning may occur are those in which:

- agents have a limited or even a wrong comprehension of their environment;
- they master only a subset of all the actions that can be conceived in order to face a given situation;
- they have an imprecise understanding of their own goals and preferences.

From this categorization, it immediately follows that theoretical models may tackle the issue of learning formalization. Their scope of investigation involves the exploration of world state-spaces modeling the learning process at different levels of abstraction. We can classify the objects of learning in the following order:

1. *Models of the world*: Learning is modeled as a search for more satisfactory representations of the functional structure of the environment in which the agent is operating.
2. *Parameters within a given model*: In this narrower case, it is assumed that the model of the world is given in its functional structure, and that learning amounts to an inferential process on the true value of some unknown parameter, as in Bayesian or statistical learning.
3. *Actions*: Learning assumes a constant or even irrelevant representation of the world, and amounts to choose from a list of different possible actions that convey more satisfaction, as in simple stimulus-response models of learning.

4. *Realized outcomes*: The process of learning is modeled in a reduced form being just represented as a dynamic process in the space of realized outcomes (as in models of economic growth with technological progress).

The order of classification reflects different degrees of abstraction in the way of modeling the learning process. Instance (1) is the deepest representation of learning since it deals with the very agent's cognitive process. Of course, it may also imply the other three cases because learning in the space of world representations involves also the possibility of parameter estimates or the choice of actions. Finally, instance (4) is the most abstract representation of learning since it is assumed that the problem of modeling the actual cognitive processes is already solved from the start, and learning is simply represented in a reduced form.

Given the underlying object of learning, we can trace another distinction of learning processes according to the restrictions imposed on the domain in which learning dynamics can occur. A closed learning process takes place whenever the assumption of a small world is retained, that is when agents are supposed to hold in mind from the start a finite and complete list of all the things that are possible objects of learning. This is the case of adaptive learning, which typically finds its representations in evolutionary games. Conversely, more realistic open-ended learning dynamics become the norm in *truly* evolutionary environments, where not only adaptation, but also discovery and persistent emergence of novelties are involved.

So far we have shown when learning becomes a relevant issue for economic theory and what its manifestations are. Hence, it is now necessary to understand how learning could be actually implemented in economic models. In the literature on agent-based models, several kinds of representation of human learning process have been employed. Most of these learning criteria have been developed as optimization tools in uncertain environments, where the maximization of very rugged objective functions could not be attained through ordinary differential calculus. However, it must be emphasized that the relationship between learning theory and agent-based modeling is twofold:

- From one side, an agent-based model can be used as a computational laboratory in order to test the effectiveness and the implications of learning rules.
- On the other side, learning mechanisms can be implemented in agent-based models as agents' behavioral rules in order to increase their degree of realism.

The way in which agents learn depends on the amount of information and on their ability to process it. Therefore, the choice for the most suitable representation of their *forma mentis* has to be based on environmental and agents' characteristics. If the model contemplates a situation of perfect information, then agents can be conveniently supposed to be optimizers; on the contrary, if the environment is a poor supplier of information and agents are unsophisticated, the best way to represent their learning behavior will be necessarily simple and adaptive. As recommended by behavioral and experimental economics, in order to make a good choice it is fundamental to take into account the results emerging from *laboratory experiments* with human beings and minding, in particular, the discrepancies between them and the predictions of mainstream economic theory.

Since agents can learn individually only on the basis of their own past history or they might be involved in some social learning process occurring when interaction is at work, two kinds of individual learning will be reviewed, both applicable in agent-based models: *statistical learning*, recently developed in the bosom of mainstream economics, and *fitness learning*, whose first appearance can be traced back to 1920s Skinnerian psychology. Afterward, a section is devoted to a brief sketch of *social learning*. Finally, a comparison between individual and social learning is provided.

5.3.1 Individual Learning 1: Statistical Learning

The statistical learning literature suggests incorporating a learning behavior expectation formation in order to limit the hyper-rational intelligence of agents (Evans and Honkapohja, 2001). The starting point is to assume bounded rationally agents are allowed to learn the parameters of the model by acting as econometricians who run regressions to improve their knowledge when called to forecast unknown variables. In this way, the forecasting rule must be explicitly expressed as a dynamical econometric model representing the perceived law of motion (PLM) of the forecast variables. Recalling the above categorization of learning, this is precisely an example belonging to the second type. The second step is to allow adaptation of expectations as soon as new data become available to agents. In formal terms, the prediction p_t^e is supposed to be a function of a data set X_t:

$$p_t^e = \Phi(X_t, \theta_{t-1})$$

where function $\Phi(\cdot)$ is the PLM and θ_{t-1} is a vector of previously estimated unknown parameters. Finally, the specification of an updating rule for the estimates θ_{t-1} – like, for instance, *recursive least squares* – completes the adaptive forecasting apparatus. At least in simple cases of closed learning dynamics, statistical learning leads models to converge to some Rational Expectations solution, thus providing a sort of asymptotical justification to rational expectations. Besides, it can help solve the problem of multiplicity of equilibria. For example, in the cobweb context, if agents estimate prices by computing the sample mean from past values, it is possible to show that learning expectations will converge over time to their RE counterparts.

Obviously, the statistical learning approach raises several questions. Even if we affirm that agents are bounded rational in origin, we must admit that they can learn from their own mistakes, possibly behaving as a rational agent at the end of a learning process. But we must also note that an easy criticism to these learning procedures is that they usually require that the agents own the high skills of an econometrician. Another question is the following: Are we sure that learning procedures always promote convergence to the same equilibrium of the perfect foresight assumption? Departing from the case of simple linear systems, the answer is often negative as, for example, showed Bullard (1994). He considers a quite simple and standard two periods OLG model and shows how even the assumption that the agents are able to use a least square regression to estimate an unknown value of a parameter; such an assumption is not enough to always ensure convergence to the perfect foresight equilibrium. He calls this kind of learning dynamic, which is different from the convergence to the rational steady state, *Learning Equilibria* because they are exclusively generated by the adopted learning mechanism. In other words, what Bullard shows is the possibility of *self-fulfilling* mistakes.

Learning equilibria can also emerge as consequences of further relaxing the degree of rationality. For example, once it is assumed that agents behave as econometricians, they may well face the same kinds of problems in choosing the most appropriate specification of their statistical representation of the real world, with the consequence that this model may be wrong. This is an instance of learning of the first type, where agents need to learn the model of the world. One major problem in choosing the model is the proper consideration of all the variables that are actually relevant to the process being forecast: agents start by using a particular conditional mean for the predicted variables, and can change it if it is rejected by data – but nothing makes it sure the correctness of the variable choice. This depends on the initial conditions of the forecasting procedure: when agents start predicting a process with an over-parameterized model that includes more variables than necessary, they can learn over time to get rid of the irrelevant ones. But if, on the contrary, they are estimating the conditional mean of the process by employing a model which disregards some of its relevant variables, agents are in general not able to detect the misspecification of the model because the regression residuals are orthogonal to the variables included in their informative set, and they might induce the model to converge toward what is called *restricted perception equilibrium*

(RPE). In econometric jargon, this is a problem of endogeneity, which can be also determined by other forms of model misspecification. A particular type of RPE is one that characterizes a situation in which a nonlinear process underlies the dynamics of the economy and is predicted by means of a linear model. When the mean and the correlations in the data generated by the true nonlinear process coincide with those predicted by the linear model, the equilibrium is reached.

5.3.2 Individual Learning 2: Fitness Learning

Within the fitness learning approach, two broad classes of learning proce-dures can be identified (Duffy, 2006): *reinforcement models* and *evolutionary algorithms*.

Reinforcement Models

Rooted in Skinnerian behaviorist psychology and first appearing in mathemat-ical psychology studies, reinforcement, or stimulus-response, learning finds its rationale in the so-called Thorndike's "law of effect," which basically states that actions that in the past have proven to be relatively more (less) successful have higher (lower) probabilities to be played again in subsequent periods. An agent that employs reinforcement learning is therefore called to experiment on how much utility he can gain from the use of different possible actions, attaching to each of them a probability of reutilization that increases with the acquired payoff. As a by-product, actions that are not sufficiently experimented from the beginning are then less likely to be played over time. An important feature of reinforcement learning is that it requires very low levels of rationality from agents, since no information about other agents' behavior or environmental characteristics is demanded – only knowledge of a set of actions and of individual past history is necessary. From an optimization viewpoint, reinforcement learning is therefore able to attain local optima if the environment is stable, since iterated experimentation correctly reveals actions' payoffs.

One of the first applications of reinforcement learning procedures to the modeling of economic behavior is Arthur (1991). In this model, agents are supposed to be endowed with a fixed set of possible actions. To each action i at time t a "strength" s_t^i, or *fitness* or propensity is assigned; this strength is the cumulated of all past payoffs earned by action i and determines the probability p_t^i of playing action i according to the formula $p_t^i = s_t^i/C_t$, where C_t is a normalization factor tuning the speed of learning. Whenever action i

brings a relatively higher payoff, its probability of reuse increases through the strength s_t^i; therefore, this payoff-based increase of probabilities is interpreted as if the agent can *understand* the goodness of action i.

Numerous variants of reinforcement learning procedures have been proposed and applied in order to match different experimental data. For instance, Roth and Ever (1995) borrow from Arthur the general apparatus with the exception of the probability-updating rule, which is given by the linear relation

$$p_i = \frac{s_i}{\sum_j s_j}$$

where j denotes all the actions different from i. Other versions instead employ the exponential choice rule

$$p_i = \frac{\exp s_i}{\sum_j \exp s_j}$$

More sophisticated approaches include the possibility for agents to learn actions' payoffs by observing other agents' behavior as well, or to use more advanced inductive techniques, such as Q-learning,[5] which is closely related to dynamic programming.

The work by Brock and Hommes (1997) represents a cross-point for bounded rationality, expectations and reinforcement learning, since it is one of the first examples of modeling heterogeneous expectations as the endogenous outcome of a decision problem in which agents, in a cobweb context, have to choose a predictor – i.e., a function of past history – from a set of alternatives on the basis of costs and benefits.

Reinforcement Learning in the Brain

Models from computer science have been useful modeling how biological decision-making systems learn to assign values to actions. Reinforcement learning theory has also been informed by recent mechanistic approaches in cognitive neuroscience, which searches for a formal model of how organisms acquire complex behaviors by learning to obtain rewards and to avoid punishments (Sutton and Barto, 1998; Dickinson and Balleine, 2002; Rangel et al., 2008; Glimcher et al., 2009). In behavioral and cognitive neuroscience, reinforcement learning has been employed as a theory of motivated action – i.e., actions resulting from computation of value – and also a model how the brain decides what actions to take. In contrast to economic theories assuming the existence of a unitary system for estimating the value of alternative actions, models of reinforcement learning posit the existence of three competing

---

[5] See Section 5.3.2.

systems for action control. Modern versions of reinforcement learning specify how different action control systems, which are embodied in contrasting neural networks and functions, can be independently or jointly activated to control action (see Vlaev and Dolan, 2015).

Researchers have identified three control systems for action: a *goal-directed* (or model-based) controller, a *habitual* (or model-free) controller and an *innate* (or Pavlovian) controller. The key insights is that in contrast to a unitary-utility approach, the utility of competing actions need not be integrated across systems to form a unitary estimate prior to the initiation of action; rather each system can itself initiate action.

Goal-directed actions require the most complex information processing, because they are based on an explicit model of the structure of the environment, which requires a representation of the contingency between the action and the outcome(s) and a representation of the value of each outcome. Goal-directed actions require three core computational processes:

- valuation (costs and benefits) of outcomes (*outcome value*),
- probabilistic estimation of the contingency between the action and the outcome (*action-outcome contingency learning*),
- planning which incorporates those calculations and engages in modeling and searching through decision trees containing sequences of state-action-outcomes in order to calculate the optimal sequence of actions (i.e., involves representing explicit models of the world or the organism).

Therefore, goal-directed action control learns the transition structure of the environment separately from the outcome values (the latter makes goal-directed actions sensitive to the current motivational state of the organism). There are different of ways a model-based system could operate. For example, Daw et al. (2005) offer a possible implementation. In such models, learning is modeled as a Markov decision process, in which experience is structured as a set of trials with a set of end or terminal states where a decision episode can end. This process is also represented as a decision-tree system. Usually, outcomes (rewards) are delivered only in terminal states. Choice in such tree systems depends on scalar values that represent predictions of the future utility of executing a particular action at a given state. Thus, for example, if the outcome is devalued, the tree system can use that information to guide action at distal states, because action values are derived by considering what future states would result. Note that the agent may start without knowing the exact marking process, and this process can also change over time – which is why those models are known as reinforcement learning, i.e., the agent has to learn the process and find the optimal course of action. Therefore, the key difference between this computational approach and the standard Expected Utility is that the former acknowledges that fully optimal choice in unknown Markov decision process is computationally intractable, and therefore may rely on approximations.

In computational terms, according to Daw et al. (2005), a Markov decision process comprises sets S of states and A of actions, a transition function $T(s, a, s') \equiv P(s(t + 1) = s' | s(t) = s, a(t) = a)$ specifying the probability that state s' will follow state s given action a, and a reward function $R(s) \equiv P(r(t) = x \text{ units} | s(t) = s)$ specifying the probability that a reward is received in terminal state s. The state-action value function $Q(s, a)$ is the expected probability that a reward will be received, given that the agent takes action a in state s and chooses optimally thereafter. This process is formally represented with a recursive function:

$$Q(s, a) \equiv \begin{cases} R(s) & s \text{ is terminal}(a = \oslash) \\ \sum_{s'} T(s, a, s') \cdot max_{a'}[Q(s', a')] & otherwise \end{cases}$$

Habitual actions are stimulus-response associations learned through repeated practice and rewards in a stable environment. *Habits* are instrumental responses based on adaptive state-action contingencies or associations (also known as operant conditioning), thus avoiding the need to compute the expected outcomes. Habitual model-free learning is most often described with temporal difference equations. Basically, the habitual system needs to solve two problems (see Rangel et al., 2008). First, given a policy π (it specifies the action that the animal takes in every state), it needs to compute the value of taking every action a in every state s. This is given by a model known as Q-learning:

$$Q^\pi = E[rt + \gamma r_{t+1} + \gamma^2 r_{t+2} + \gamma^3 r_{t+3} \ldots | s_t = s, a_t = a, a_{t+1} = \pi(s_{t+1}, \ldots)]$$

where r_{t+k} denotes the reward that is received at time $t + k$ and $\gamma > 0$ is the discount rate (this equation can also be written in a recursive form, of course). In order to learn $Q^\pi(s, a)$, the habitual system uses $\hat{Q}(s, a)$ as an estimator of $Q^\pi(s, a)$. To make sure that $\hat{Q}(s, a)$ becomes a good estimate of the value function, the models define a prediction error:

$$\delta_t = r_t + \gamma \cdot max_{a'}[\hat{Q}(s_t + 1, a')] - [\hat{Q}(s_t, a_t)]$$

that measures how close the estimate is to satisfying the equation for $Q^\pi(s, a)$ above. If $\delta_t > 0$, the value of the action is overestimated; if $\delta_t < 0$, the value is underestimated. One can then use the prediction error to update the estimates of the action values as follows:

$$\hat{Q}(s_t, a_t) \leftarrow \hat{Q}(s_t, a_t) + \eta \delta_t$$

where η is a number between 0 and 1 that determines the learning rate/speed. This model guarantees that, under specific technical conditions, the estimated action values converge to the values produced by the optimal action policy (i.e., the agent can learn the optimal choice policy by following the algorithm and selecting the actions with the largest values).

It is important to note that similarly to the tree system, habitual control depends on scalar values (predictions of the future utility of a particular choice/action at a particular state); but contrary to the tree system, if an outcome is devalued, the habit system's values are insensitive to such changes because the values are stored scalars. In this sense, habitual learning is model-free, because the agents do not need to know the transition function or the reward function. Habit learning explains various behavioral conditioning phenomena (see Dolan and Dayan, 2013), such as blocking, overshadowing, inhibitory conditioning, and also disorders of compulsivity (Voon et al., 2015). The beauty of those models is their computational simplicity, given that the agent does not need to keep track of long sequences of rewards to learn the value of actions.

Innate actions are evolutionarily appropriate responses to specific predetermined stimuli, although associative learning allows organisms to deploy them in response to other stimuli – such behaviors are also known as unconditioned and conditioned Pavlovian responses respectively (Mackintosh, 1983). Thus, Pavlovian learning of state-outcome contingencies allows organisms to learn the predictive value of a state/cue, which reflects the sum of rewards and punishments expected to occur from it (see Seymour and Dolan, 2008). Such value expectancies can instigate two fundamental types of evolved reactions:

- Approach: Designed to decrease the distance between the organism and a feature of the environment using responses such as locomotion, grabbing, consumption, fighting, mental approach/focusing.
- Avoidance: Responses aim to increase the distance by moving away, flight, freeze, mental avoidance.

Note that even though some of those specific actions can be employed in goal-directed behaviors (e.g., animal defending a held resources may employ cost-benefit planning), the signature of innate actions is their automaticity regardless of whether or not they lead to immediate reward in the given situation. Such innate actions can underpin a surprisingly wide range of human behaviors that have important consequences, such as overeating, addiction, obsessive-compulsive behaviors, and opting for immediate smaller rewards at the expense of delayed larger rewards (see Dayan et al., 2006).

Formally, the value of Pavlovian action (approach or avoidance) is the value of the state $v(t)$ – i.e., it requires learning of the Pavlovian contingency – the predictive value of the state – i.e., the mean reward – learned as $v(0) = 0$, and

$$v(t + 1) = v(t) + \eta(r(t) - v(t))$$

where $r(t)$ is the reward delivered on trial t, and η is a learning rate. This is an instance of the Rescorla and Wagner (1972) rule, which is also found in temporal difference learning (Sutton, 1988). Note that Pavlovian also does not really refer to a way of doing computations as much as the flexibility permitted in learned relationships between stimulus, action and outcome (see Dayan and Berridge, 2014, for a model/tree-based version of Pavlovian values).

There is also emerging evidence about the neural interactions between habits and goal-directed control (Dayan et al., 2006). Habits require extensive experience including schedules of reinforcement involving single actions and single outcomes, which implies that behavior must be initially goal-directed and gradually becomes habitual over the course of experience. This view is supported by explicit evidence for the transfer from dorsomedial to dorsolateral over the course of training (see Dolan and Dayan, 2013, for review). This is further supported by evidence that instrumental learning tasks always involve model-based and model-free processes (Collins and Frank, 2012).

In contrast to a unitary-utility approach, the utility of competing actions need not be integrated across systems to form a unitary estimate prior to the initiation of action: rather, each system can itself initiate action. A good demonstration of this is that innate and instrumental systems can come into conflict, and in animals there is a limitation to the extent that evolutionarily incongruent actions can be reinforced. For example, it is not possible to fully condition pigeons instrumentally to withhold a key peck in order to gain access to a visible food reward: they continue to peck the key, being unable to withhold the innate pecking response despite the fact that it is never reinforced (Williams and Williams, 1969). By contrast, although the three systems are theoretically capable of producing action independently and according to their own criteria, they are not mutually exclusive; for example, where Pavlovian and instrumental conditioning are congruent there is evidence that appetitive conditioned stimuli strengthen instrumental behavior, an effect known as Pavlovian Instrumental Transfer (Dickinson and Balleine, 2002; Talmi et al., 2008).

The interaction between the three systems adds considerable explanatory power over and above a unitary decision process, accounting for a greater array of real-world choice phenomena (Dolan and Dayan, 2013; Story et al., 2014; Vlaev and Dolan, 2015). The three-system approach is therefore capable of uniting the interpretation of a variety of additional effects with relevance to economic choice.

Less common than reinforcement learning are the belief-based learning algorithms. The major difference is that in the latter case, agents recognize they are engaging in a game with other players. Actions are then a best response to their beliefs, which must be updated according to past histories. The need to consider other players' data makes belief-based models more demanding as far as agents' memory is concerned, and this may explain why they are less frequently used in agent-based models, where huge collections of data are usually generated.

In general, both reinforcement and belief-based learning models have proven to be better predictors of human behavior than is the concept of static Nash equilibrium.

Evolutionary Algorithms

A shift of perspective, from the individual to the collective, is the characteristic of the second class of learning procedures. Inspired by biological principles, they are aimed at discovering the process of diffusion of a set of strategies inside a population of agents. Therefore, evolutionary algorithms are best suited to model the collective behavior of a population of agents than individual behaviors and, in fact, the most conspicuous shortcoming is their difficult interpretation.

Widely used in game-theoretic literature, the simplest class of evolutionary algorithms is that of *replicator dynamics*. The focus is not on how an individual makes practice with a fixed set of strategies, but on how their use spreads across the population. The idea informing replicator dynamics is basically the same behind reinforcement learning: strategies whose fitness is above average see their proportion in the population increase according to some recursive updating rule. As an example, consider the following differential equation:

$$\dot{x}_i = x_i[f_i(x) - \phi(x)], \quad \phi(x) = \sum_{j=1}^{n} x_j f_j(x)$$

where x_i is the fraction of type i in the population (the elements of the vector x sum to unity), $x = (x_1, \ldots, x_n)$ is the vector containing the distribution of the different types that composes the population, $f_i(x)$ provides the fitness of type i, and $\phi(x)$ is the average fitness of the population (given by the weighted average of the n types' fitness).

Originally developed by Holland (1975) as optimization stochastic tools, *genetic algorithms* have become more and more popular in modeling human behavior in multi-agent systems after their implementation by Sargent (1993). In spite of a great variety of algorithms, a typical structure can be identified:

- the objective function, whose optima have to be searched by the genetic algorithm, must be specified, together with the parameters and their admissible values;
- the possible parameter vectors are defined as strings of length L: thus, each element of the string represents a particular value for a parameter. Since in principle the number of possible strings could be infinite, generally researchers work with a finite N-sized population of strings;
- the performance of each of the N strings of length L is evaluated using the objective function;
- finally, mimicking biological processes, N new strings are generated from the old ones until some criterion is satisfied.

The final process of generation is the characterizing element of genetic algorithms and needs some clarification.

- First, imitating the Darwinian survival-of-the-fittest, a sample of N strings is randomly drawn from the initial population, with the only condition that its average performance is above the average performance of the population.
- Second, pairs of strings are randomly picked from the sample, which then undergo two operations, typical of *DNA*:

  – *crossover*: cuts and recombines two strings in order to get two new strings,
  – *mutation*: randomly changes the value of some element of the strings in order to add new information.

- Finally, the recombined and mutated new N strings are then evaluated using the objective function.

Genetic algorithms, as well as their close relative *genetic programming* (Koza, 1992), are affected by a general ambiguity of interpretation. For example, the N individual strings may be thought of as representing the actions of N interacting individual agents. Alternatively, one can imagine a single agent experimenting different possible decisions that are represented by the strings.

Another typology of evolutionary algorithms is given by the *classifier systems* (Holland, 1986). At half way between reinforcement learning mechanisms and genetic algorithms, classifier systems are best interpreted as models of individual learning. Their basic structure consists of four parts (Duffy, 2006):

1. a set of if-then decision rules (the classifiers);
2. an accounting system devoted to assessing the strength of classifiers;
3. an auction-based system determines which classifiers are to be used;
4. a genetic algorithm which is used to introduce new classifiers.

(For some examples on genetic algorithms and classifier systems see Booker et al., 1989.)

5.3.3 Social Learning

By introducing genetic algorithms, we have already noticed their ambiguous interpretation, as they can be also thought of as a whole population trying to collectively learn some optimal behavior, rather than as an individual's learning process.

In this section we deal with collective, or social, learning from the standpoint of the individual agent: we mean that social learning is intended as the process through which single agents elicit information from the others, determining the spreading of private information to the whole population. Within this context, social learning requires a particular form of interaction among agents (see Chapter 6): *observation*. The immediate consequence of observing others' behavior is a process of information transmission among individuals (*observational learning*). This kind of interaction usually takes place in a network structure, where agents directly interact with each other; in other cases it is an average behavior or information to be observed (mean-field type interaction).

Observational learning can take many forms:

- The strongest, but also the least realistic, especially in a competitive market environment, is that of *directly observing others' private information*. As an example, a firm may come to knowledge of the profitability of a new technology from its competitors, if they know.
- More plausible than this is the *observation of the signals received by others*. In the same example, a firm may observe realized profits of those competitors that have adopted the new technology.
- Finally, the simplest and most likely form of observation is the mere *watching of the actions undertaken by others*. If competitors are adopting the new technology, the firm may deduce that it is convenient to do so.

Observation of actions can logically lead to *imitation*, or to its opposite: *contrarianism*. When agents face "strong" or Knightian uncertainty, in the sense that risks related to different scenarios cannot be calculated, they tend to conform to the opinion of the rest of the world, according to the presumption that it is better informed; in this way, the behavior of a society of individuals, each of which trying to imitate others, leads to a sort of conventional view (Keynes, 1937).[6] Though imitative behavior shapes individuals' decisions in many situations, this does not exclude that agents can follow a contrarian (or anti-coordination) behavior resulting in more profitable actions. Indeed, we should consider that contrariety is pervasive in human experience and that, as stressed long ago by Niels Bohr, *contraria sunt complementa* – i.e., contraries are complement (Kelso and Engstrom, 2006). Therefore, while some forces may act to coordinate actions, anti-coordination behavior may also arise and influence collective dynamics. Moreover, while imitation leads to homogeneity, the presence of both imitation and contrarianism preserves the heterogeneity of agents' behavior.

Far from being an irrational individual attitude, imitation naturally emerges under *strong uncertainty*. In the context of limited information and bounded rationality, imitation can be interpreted as an ecologically rational rule-of-thumb for saving time and costs in decision-making. In spite of this, imitation can give rise to *herding*, an inefficient collective behavior where the rate of social learning is generally low. The most extreme case of herding is given by the so-called *informational cascade*, a pathological process of blind imitation where no one is learning anymore. Herding and informational cascade have often been proposed as explanations for the emergence of irrational speculative bubbles in financial markets (Banerjee, 1992; Bikhchandani et al., 1992; Welch, 2000).

In contexts where uncertainty can be reduced to risk, as in a game theoretic framework, the rational learning of an unknown state of nature is generally based upon a Bayesian updating of beliefs. In contexts of true uncertainty, as in agent-based models, observation itself becomes an individual choice: agents must be endowed with rules for deciding who to observe and how to exploit the observed information. As an example, the agents may observe a subset of the population and then imitate the behavior of the one attaining the best relative performance (*imitate-the-best*). Imitation can be, therefore, not only a consequence of observational social learning, but also a very deliberate activity of the agents within their behavioral strategy.

---

[6] Recent advances in neuroscience have highlighted the neural basis of imitation through the discovery of "mirror neurons" in monkeys (Rizzolatti et al., 1988) and in humans (Rizzolatti et al., 1996).

5.3.4 Individual vs. Social Learning

Consider the following example of a standard Cournot oligopoly game (Vriend, 2000). There are n firms producing the same homogeneous goods and competing in the same market. The only decision variable for each firm i is the quantity q_i to be produced. Production takes place simultaneously for all the firms and, once firms sell the output in the market, in the aggregate $Q_1 = \sum_i q_i$, the price P is determined based on the (inverse) demand $P(Q) = a + bQ^c$, where a, b and c are positive parameters. Assume that the production costs are such that there are negative fixed costs K, whereas the marginal costs are k. We can imagine that firms happen to have found a well where water emerges at no cost, but each bottle costs k, and each firm gets a lump-sum subsidy from the local town council if it operates a well. Given these assumptions, each firm might be willing to produce any quantity at a price greater than or equal to k. A firm wants to produce a level of output that maximizes its profit. If the firm does not know the level of optimal output, it can try to learn a level of output which is good. As suggested by Vriend (2000), we can employ a genetic algorithm in two ways:

- *Social or population learning*: The genetic algorithm is a rule that characterizes the population of firms which look around, tend to imitate, and recombine ideas of other firms that appeared to be successful; the more successful these rules were, the more likely they are selected for the process of imitation and recombination, where the measure of success is given by the profits associated to each rule.
- *Individual learning*: Instead of being characterized by a single output rule, each firm now has a set of rules in mind, where each rule is again modeled as a string, with a fitness measure of its strengths or success (the profits generated by that rule when it was activated) attached. Each period uses only one of these rules is used to determine the output level actually supplied to the market; the rules that are more successful in the recent previous periods are more likely to be chosen. This is also known as a classifier system (as already seen). Therefore, instead of looking how well competitors with different rules were doing, a firm now checks how well it had been doing in the past by using these rules itself.

As for the results of the computational exercise proposed by Vriend (2000), social learning quickly converges to a higher and less volatile level of output, while individual learning leads to lower and more volatile output. Due to a spite effect, the population of firms tends to converge to the Walrasian output (that emerging for a very large n). Under social learning, in fact, given that if the output is *below* the Walrasian level it happens that the rules of firms producing at the *higher* output levels are selected to be reproduced, while the rules of firms producing at the *lower* output levels are selected when output is *above* the Walrasian level. Instead, in the case of individual learning, the different production rules that compete with each other do not interact, given that each firm actually applies only *one* of the production rules, and the spite effect does not affect social learning at the level of the population.

However, individual and social learning represent two extreme forms of learning, while various intermediate levels of learning are possible: for instance, a population can be characterized by different types of agents that interact with each other but that learn only from agents of the same type.

5.4 Conclusions

In this chapter we discussed some basic issues regarding the nature of agents, the variables that shape their state and the actions they can perform. The relatively recent wave of studies in cognitive psychology, behavioral economics, experimental economics and neuroeconomics highlights the falseness of mainstream economics in assuming full rationality as a guide to individual behavior. Bounded rationality can be considered an alternative behavioral paradigm for economic agents, as opposed to the neoclassical hypothesis of constrained maximization. Indeed, in a complex environment in which information is limited and incomplete, the behavior of agents tends to be based on heuristics, that is relatively simple rules of decision that agents use to try to reach a satisfying choice. Moreover, agents may learn from their behavior and from the interaction with other agents and the environment. When we consider the economy as a whole, we must consider that agents can directly interact with other agents when taking decisions or learning about the working of the economy. The interaction of heterogeneous agents can lead to complex dynamics at the level of the whole system. For this reason, the macro level can be different from the simple sum of micro entities. This is the topic which we will discuss in the next chapter.

6

Interaction

Alberto Russo, Gabriele Tedeschi, and Giorgio Fagiolo

6.1 Introduction

It is a fact of life that the preferences, information, and choices – hence the behavior – of an agent affect and are affected by the behavior of the agents she interacts with. In fact, there is a two-way feedback between individual and aggregate behavior: agents' interaction affects the evolution of the system as a whole; at the same time, the collective dynamics that shape the social structure of the economy affect individual behavior.

For example, consider the case of the adoption of a new technology by initially uninformed consumers. Each agent, based on her preferences, may have some ex-ante evaluation about the quality of new products introduced in the market. However, by interacting with their peers, agents may gather fresh information about the new product and, eventually, they may decide whether to buy it or not. This influences the adoption rate of the product, which can be in turn exploited by other consumers as a parameter to be employed when subsequently considering whether to buy the product or not. Therefore, individual decisions may be affected by agent interactions, then impact on the aggregate state of the system, which can in turn feed back to individual behaviors.

Traditionally, economic theory has largely overlooked the importance of interactions among economic agents. In standard economic theory, interactions are treated as externalities or spillovers. In general equilibrium theory (GET), the presence of externalities is often treated as a pathology of the model, leading to possible nonexistence of equilibria. Therefore, in the model it is often assumed that externalities do not simply exist – i.e., that agents only interact indirectly through a nonagent – that is prices, whose role is to aggregate individual information. Hence, in GET, agents are totally disconnected, dots living in a vacuum without any connections (links) between them.

109

To appreciate the importance of externalities in mainstream economics, one has to resort to game theoretic models. In this setup, agents interact directly with all the other agents in the game. Interactions are captured via strategic complementarities: the payoff of any single agent depends directly on the choices made in the game by all the $N - 1$ other agents. This configures a scenario completely at odds with the one portrayed in GET, namely one where agents live in a fully connected world, where they are linked with anyone else.

In reality, however, interaction structures may be very distinct from the ones employed in these two extremes. Agents may indeed interact with subsets of all the other agents, and these sets of "relevant others" may be strongly constrained by geography (i.e., interacting with your neighbors) or social norms. Interactions may also change across time, both exogenously (e.g., because agents change their geographical or social location) or endogenously (i.e., agents may decide not to interact with others anymore). Understanding how this dynamic is intertwined with that describing the state of the system becomes therefore critical in order to gain a better knowledge of economies.

In this chapter, we will examine the relationships between agents established by their *interactions* – a distinctive feature of ABMs which we have emphasized in Chapters 2 and 3. We will go in depth in dissecting the various ways and means of interaction among agents in Section 6.2. In Sections 6.3 and 6.4 we will present and discuss some modeling building blocks using network theory, which is a powerful set of formalisms that are particularly well suited to model interaction structures in ABMs.

6.2 Modeling Interactions

Different approaches may be adopted to describe the connections among agents: interaction may be local or global, static or dynamic, direct or indirect, deterministic or stochastic, exogenous or endogenous.

Local interaction characterizes models in which agents interact with a *neighborhood* consisting of a subset of the agents' population. This may be due to *transaction costs, geographical distance* – as in the locational model by Gabszewicz and Thisse (1986) – or *closeness in characteristics*, as in Gilles and Ruys (1989, also see Kirman, 1994). When these costs become negligible, interaction becomes global: individual behavior depends on the behavior of the entire population. In such a case, before taking a decision, agents may collect information about each and every distinct decision made by the other agents in the population, or, more often, respond to some average behavior of all the other agents.

When interaction is local, there are at least two ways to model interaction structures. On the one hand, if agents can be assumed to be able to potentially reach any other agent in the population but only interact with a few of them in any period, one may use the metaphor of a random graph. In a random graph, as in Kirman (1983) and Ioannides (1994), the partner(s) of an agent are picked at random. This may describe a case where agents do not have preferred partners with whom to interact, and simply make random encounters or phone calls to other agents in order to gather the information they need.

On the other hand, local interaction may be constrained by geography or social norms. In that case, a stochastically or deterministically determined subset of the population will form the neighborhood of the agent.[1]

The rule defining the set of interacting agents (the structure of interactions) can be *exogenous* – when agents cannot change the interaction over time – or *endogenous*, e.g., when an agent is able to choose to interact with a specific neighbor or not. When interaction rules are exogenous, the modeler can choose to describe them in a *deterministic* or *stochastic* way.

In deterministic case, the more convenient way to model local interactions is via a lattice structure. Agents can be placed on the nodes of a lattice, i.e., a homogeneous and regular graph where each node has a fixed number of links. Lattices are characterized by their dimension. One-dimensional lattices are simply lines, where nodes are connected only with their left and right neighbors.

In order to avoid the fact that agents at the boundaries of the line would only have one neighbor, one may connect the left and right boundary of the lattice obtaining a circle, where all nodes have exactly two neighbors (see Figure 6.1, left). In a one-dimensional lattice, interaction structures can only differ by their size. Indeed, one can assume that instead of interacting with left and right neighbors only, each agent has a certain radius of interaction even larger than one. In this way, one can suppose that each node can interact with, say, the k agents to the left and to the right in the circle, thus allowing for a larger overlap of agent interaction sets. Of course, when k becomes larger or equal than $N/2$ (N being the number of nodes) one recovers a situation where each agent interacts with all the others.

Two-dimensional lattices are instead checkerboard-like structures, where each node is connected to its four nearest neighbors – north, south, east, and west (see Figure 6.1, right). This, of course, does not apply to nodes on the

---

[1] In Chapter 2, we have shown the effects of local interaction in a Schelling segregation model. In a complex environment, where information and cognitive capabilities are scarce (i.e., in a bounded rationality setting), local interaction is a more realistic modeling device than global interaction.

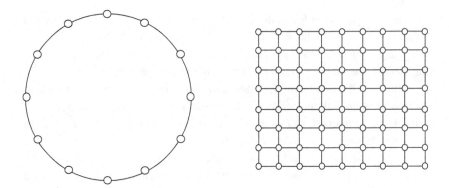

Figure 6.1 Left: A one-dimensional lattice with no boundaries. Right: A two-dimensional lattice with boundaries.

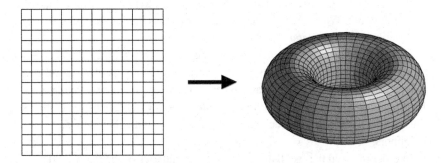

Figure 6.2 From a two-dimensional lattice with boundaries to a two-dimensional lattice with no boundaries (torus).

edges and on the corners, who have respectively three and two neighbors. In order to solve this problem, one can think to fold the east and west side of the lattice together, thus obtaining a cylinder-like object, and then join the two circle-shaped edges of the cylinder to obtain a torus (see Figure 6.2).

The case where agents interact with their north, south, east, and west neighbor is called a Von Neumann neighborhood. This is equivalent to the introduction of a Manhattan norm on the lattice – where the distance between any two nodes is given by minimum number of edges that must be traveled in order to go from one node to another one – assuming that agents only interact with partners that lie one step away. More generally, one can define Von Neumann neighborhoods by assigning a certain interaction radius $r \geq 1$ and assume that agents interact with partners lying not farther than r (see Figure 6.3).

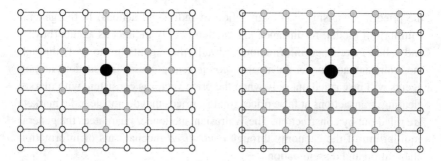

Figure 6.3 Von Neumann (left) vs. Moore (right) neighborhoods in a two-dimensional lattice.

An alternative way to model neighborhoods in a two-dimensional lattice is to assume Moore neighbors. This starts from the definition of a norm where the distance between any two nodes is equal to the minimum difference between their x (horizontal) and y (vertical) coordinates. A Moore neighborhood is then defined assuming that agents only interact with other agents distant less than a certain radius r. In case $r = 1$, one has that each agent will interact not only with its north, south, east, and west partners as in the Von Neumann case, but also with agents located north-east, north-west, south-east, and south-west, thus leading to an 8-person neighborhood (see Figure 6.3). Note that Moore neighborhoods have larger overlaps, whilst Von Neumann sets are largely much more non-overlapping.

When local interactions are modeled stochastically, on the contrary, one can assume that agents, in each time period, may choose a certain set of others with whom to interact, but they do so with a certain probability. For example, agents may draw in each time period a number $k = 1, 2, \ldots, N - 1$ of other agents completely at random, or based on some exogenous information about the structure of the economy and their state (i.e., with probabilities inversely depending on the geographical distance between agents, or on some variable that measures the similarity or dissimilarity between agents according to some socioeconomic characteristics).

Another important distinction is between direct and indirect interactions. *Direct* interaction occurs when the choice of each agent is affected by the behaviors of other agents – for instance, because payoffs change as a consequence of the choices made by other agents, or via expectations thereof, or alternatively through a search and matching mechanism in a fully decentralized market setting. Agent interactions are indirect when they are mediated by a variable or a mechanism which transmits the effects of agents' behavior – e.g., the price mechanism – via aggregation of individual actions. In the general equilibrium model, for instance, interaction is only indirect as agents (buyers and sellers) exchange information with all other agents (at no cost) through the Walrasian auctioneer during the *tatonnement* process. Transactions among agents will be carried out only when the price vector is consistent with market clearing; transactions at false prices (that is, prices that do not clear the market) are ruled out by construction. The Walrasian auctioneer guarantees the general equilibrium of the economy through *centralized* mechanisms of information elaboration and dissemination.

Finally, the structure of interactions is *static* when the set of neighbors is determined once and for all, or *dynamic*, when it evolves over time depending on model assumptions, as in the case of *endogenous evolving networks*. It must be noted that in the dynamic interaction case, the structure of interactions can change exogenously (because the modeler introduces some exogenous shocks or rule that changes from time to time the relationships among the agents), or endogenously (when within the model it is assumed that agents hold some behavioral rules that allow them to decide whom to interact with on the basis of the status of the system).

The "best" approach to model agents' interaction simply does not exist: "the choice of a model should depend on circumstances to be modeled in a broad sense, and on the purpose of the model" (Vriend, 2006). In the following, we will overview the most popular interaction structures.

6.2.1 Local Exogenous Interaction

We start describing the mechanisms of interaction when the structure of inter-linkages is local and exogenous, i.e., agents interact with a subset of all the others, and interactions are determined *ex-ante* and not modifiable by the agents. We begin with cellular automata, a useful metaphor that illustrates how complex behavior can arise from simple rules and basic interaction structures. We then introduce local games on lattices. Finally, we discuss applications of local interactions in economics.

Cellular Automata

A cellular automata (CA) is perhaps the simplest dynamic model of interaction between agents that can be conceived (Wolfram, 2002). In its basic implementation, it describes a population of N agents or cells, distributed on the nodes of a 1-dimensional lattice without boundaries (i.e., a circle). Time is discrete and agents can be in one out of two possible states, say on or off. Each cell only interact with two neighbors, the one at its left and the one at its right. At time $t = 0$, each cell is initialized in one of the two possible states. From then on, at each time $t > 0$, every cell has the option to update its status, independently on all the others, using a deterministic behavioral rule. A rule is simply a map that transforms current local configurations – i.e., the state at time $t - 1$ of the agent that is called to update its choice and the states at time $t - 1$ of its two neighbors – into the next state of the agent itself. Rules are therefore lookup tables that associate a response to each possible local configuration. In the setup just described, a rule is therefore a map that to each of the possible $2^3 = 8$ local configurations, associates either on or off. Thus, the space of all possible rules in this case is $2^8 = 256$. It is easy to see that the cardinality of this space explodes if we allow cells to be in $S > 2$ states and to interact with $S > 2$ nearest neighbors. Simulation of this simple model easily generates complex behavioral patterns. Indeed, there exists a large region of the space of rules where the long-run behavior of the system – i.e., the configuration of cell states in the lattice, evolves in a way that is neither chaotic nor simple, and produces unpredictable patterns that lie at the edge of chaos. Hence, the take-home message of this class of models is that complex aggregate behavior can be generated by a very simple model where agents behave myopically and directly interact with their neighbors.

Local Games on Lattices

The cellular-automata model introduced in the last section is an extremely streamlined description of a dynamic system populated by agents that take decisions and interact. Indeed, behavioral rules are simply mechanistic maps that convert local configurations in a response. No strategic considerations are made by the agents when making their decisions. To allow for more strategy in a context where agents interact dynamically with their nearest neighbors, one may simply assume that agents are still placed over a lattice but they play noncooperative bilateral games with each neighbor (Fagiolo, 1998). More precisely, suppose that a 2-by-2 symmetric stage-game payoff matrix is given, for example, that of a coordination game where agents must choose between two actions, say A and B, knowing that their payoff will be larger if they play the same action of their opponents. One may therefore assume that agents are initially endowed with either A or B, and from then on they are matched with their neighbors to play the bilateral game just described. Agents may then decide which action to actually perform in the current period by best replying to the current local configuration, i.e., they may choose A or B depending on which one delivers the total maximum payoff against the actions played at time $t-1$ by each of the neighbors. Suppose that in each time period only one agent may possibly revise its choice. It will change only if by doing so it better coordinates its action with those of its neighbors, otherwise it will stay put. It is therefore instructive to study which one will be the long-run state of the system. Will the system converge to a coordinated equilibrium where everyone will play A or B, or are mixed equilibria likely to emerge? The answer to this question depends on both the stage game payoffs, assigning the reward that agents get if they play A (resp. B) if their opponent plays B (resp. A), and the way payoff ties are resolved – i.e., which action is chosen if the total payoff to A from interacting with the neighbors is exactly equal to that of B. Indeed, if ties are resolved by tossing a coin – i.e., choosing at random between A or B – it can be seen that the system will surely converge to a state where everyone play either A or B. However, which action will be selected in the long run depends on its risk efficiency – i.e., on the average payoff it delivers against itself and the opposite action. The action that does best on average will be selected.

Economic Applications

In economics, earlier contributions on how to model interactions among a large number of heterogeneous agents are based on a *stochastic* approach, which has originally been proposed to assess the role of direct interaction in a General Equilibrium framework. As noted by Hommes (2006), stochastic interaction may lead to complex collective dynamics.

Exogenous *local* interactions have been introduced in a pioneering contribution by Föllmer (1974), who studies the dynamics of an exchange economy in which agents have stochastic preferences as proposed by Hildenbrand (1971). The novelty of Follmer's approach with respect to Hildebrand is that the probability law that governs individual preferences depends on the behavior of agents in a neighborhood which is defined *ex ante* and is not changing over time. In such a framework, local interactions may propagate through the economy and give rise to aggregate uncertainty causing large price movements and even a breakdown of equilibria. Agents in the Föllmer model are placed on lattices and interact with their nearest neighbors in a homogeneous (i.e., all agents have the same number of neighbors and they are spread uniformly across the space) and symmetric way (i.e., if agent i affects agent j, also j affects i).

In a stylized model of a supply chain, Bak et al. (1993) show that small shocks can cause large fluctuations when producers hold inventories of goods and they locally interact with each other. In this case, agents are located on trees or chains, describing different layers of the economy (i.e., from producers of basic goods to consumers) and interactions are asymmetric. Agents in bottom layers are affected by the choices of upstream agents (i.e., their suppliers) but they do not affect them, as they only influence the choice of downstream agents (i.e., to whom they sell). However, even though interactions naturally go from upstream to downstream sectors of the economy, small shocks that are originated downstream (e.g., at the level of final demand) may well crawl up and be diffused throughout the whole economy via the amplifying effect of local interactions. Indeed, if interactions structures are deep enough, small shocks that can initially affect a smaller number of agents and then die away may resonate through the system and trigger mechanisms that lead more and more agents to eventually revise their state, thus generating avalanches that can potentially affect the whole system. Interestingly enough, the size of such avalanches is unpredictable in the model and can range from very small to very large magnitudes. In particular, very large avalanches are not exponentially rare, but their probability decays with a power-law shape, a pattern that we have encountered (and will encounter) many times in this book.

Stiglitz and Greenwald (2003) show that local interaction among producers may lead to a financial collapse. In their simple model, firms are located on a circle and each firm sells an input to her neighbor: hence firm i is at the same time a downstream firm with respect to firm $i-1$ and an upstream firm for firm $i+1$. A bank provides credit to all the firms in order to finance production. If an upstream firm cannot repay the loan, also the downstream firm may go bankrupt and so on, in a vicious circle of defaults.

Delli Gatti et al. (2006) build on this framework in a model (see Figure 6.4) where downstream firms (producers of consumption goods) are connected to upstream firms (producers of intermediate goods) through "trade credit" (whereby the latter finance the provision of intermediate goods to the former), all firms are connected to banks through "bank credit" (to finance labor costs), and banks are connected through the "interbank market" (to manage liquidity). Credit interlinkages spread financial distress and may facilitate bankruptcy avalanches.

In the case of *global* interaction, each agent can interact, or is likely to interact, with all other agents. For instance, Feldman (1973) describes an economy in which agents may make Pareto-improving transactions through pairwise interactions generated by *random matching*, without a central price signal. A static equilibrium can be computed for this class of models. In the model of Diamond (1989), a multitude of buyers and sellers interact through pairwise transactions and the law of one price no longer holds; on the contrary, a distribution of prices emerges. The absence of a Walrasian auctioneer generally prevents the attainment of a Pareto optimum.

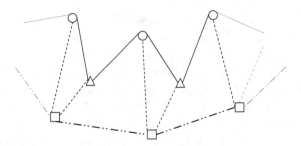

Figure 6.4 The network structure of the economy in Delli Gatti et al. (2006): downstream firms (circles), upstream firms (triangles), and banks (squares).

In the presence of externalities, the interaction among different agents may affect aggregate results leading to complex collective dynamics. This is the case of *herding*. For example, in the game-theoretic model proposed by Banerjee (1992), agents are located on a segment and make decisions sequentially. Each agent makes her choice on the basis of a private signal and a public signal, which consists of the previous choices made by other agents. The Nash equilibrium of this game can be socially inefficient if the population is large enough: for example, all clients end up at the worst restaurant. Bikhchandani et al. (1992) notice that, after a while, cumulated actions contain so much information that the single agent has an incentive to ignore his own information and an "informational cascade" starts. Kirman (1993) observes a similar dynamic pattern in the evolution of two strands of opinion in a population. Other examples of global interaction over an exogenous network structure can be found in models describing the adoption of new technologies when the profitability of a technology depends on the number of firms that already adopted it (David, 1985; Arthur, 1990).

Some typical structures emerge out of exogenous interaction, as the star, the circle, or a small world, which will be explored in Section 6.3. Let us now discuss endogenous interaction.

6.2.2 Endogenous Interaction

There are different ways of describing endogenous interactions in ABMs (Vriend, 2006). In a multi-agent setting, markets may be characterized by *procurement processes* (Tesfatsion and Judd, 2006) which generally take the form of *decentralized search and matching*. Procurement processes are market-specific and can take the form of auctions, negotiated markets or pairwise bargaining markets, characterized by different buyer-seller relationships (see

Kirman, 2010). Due to the absence of any exogenously imposed market-clearing mechanism, the economy may self-organize toward a spontaneous order, which is generally characterized by emerging properties such as self-sustaining growth and fluctuations, endogenous crises, persistent involuntary unemployment, unsold production, or credit rationing. In what follows, we survey a few examples of endogenous interaction patterns in ABMs. These range from the Schelling segregation model to self-organization of trade in actual markets, all the way to artificial societies like the Sugarscape, ABMs of the labor and credit market, and of the macroeconomy.

Residential patterns in Schelling's model. Schelling (1971) proposes a pioneering ABM – succinctly presented in Chapter 2 – in which residential patterns (with neighborhood segregation) emerge from agents' interaction. There is a finite number of agents located on a bounded lattice (a grid). Each cell can be occupied by only one agent at a time and each agent can interact only with the agents located in the eight cells around it (Moore neighborhood). The agent's preferences are defined by the number of similar or dissimilar neighbors where similarity is defined according to a predetermined criterion, e.g., race or ethnicity. For instance, we can assume that the agent is satisfied with her position if at most 50% of her neighbors are dissimilar. Starting from an initial spatial allocation of agents, all unsatisfied agents (in a random order) move to the nearest empty location looking for a satisfactory position. After a time step, a new list of unsatisfied agents is compiled and the whole process of searching preferred locations is iterated again. Iteration goes on until no agents want to move anymore. The final outcome is a steady state spatial allocation which exhibits a segregated residential pattern: segregation emerges from agents' interaction which, in turn, is influenced by the dynamic evolution of agents' locational choices.

Interaction-driven macroscopic patterns in Sugarscape. Imagine a very simple artificial economy in which sugar is the only commodity and agents need sugar to survive. The spatial dimension of Sugarscape (Epstein and Axtell, 1996) is a torus, i.e., a lattice without bounds. Each cell can be occupied by only one agent at a time, and each agent can interact only with the agents located in the four cells around it (Von Neumann neighborhood). At each site, sugar grows at a given rate (up to a maximum). An agent which occupies a site increases its wealth by accumulating the sugar available at that site. She has a given information set, i.e., she can observe how much sugar is present in different sites, up to a limit. Moreover, agents are characterized by heterogeneous metabolic rates which determine how much sugar each agent needs per time step – that is, consumption. As a consequence, if an agent has enough sugar to consume it survives, otherwise it dies (because of negative wealth). For each time step, agents are randomly ordered and they decide to move around looking for sugar according to this stochastic list. As in the case of the residential pattern in Schelling's model, the overall configuration of agents' locations evolves over time as agents decide to move around in Sugarscape.

In a slightly more complex environment in which spice is added to sugar, trade enters the scene. In this case, agents directly interact with neighbors through trade (according to the marginal rates of substitution implied by agents' utility functions). Epstein and Axtell (1996) show that decentralized (bilateral) bargaining among different agents may lead to "market clearing," that is price dispersion decreases over time (without the intervention of an auctioneer). Many other characteristics may be added to this simple computational framework such as credit, mating, spreading of diseases, combat, cultural transmission, and so on, building up a complex artificial society.

The self-organization of markets. Kirman and Vriend (2001) provide a model of the evolving structure of an actual market inspired by an empirical analysis of the Marseille wholesale fish market. They focus on two features: price dispersion and buyer-seller loyalty. Before the market opens, sellers purchase the fish they want to sell during the day, though demand is uncertain. When the market opens, buyers choose a seller, forming various queues in the market hall. Then, sellers sequentially make a take-it-or-leave-it offer to buyers at given posted prices. When all queues have been handled, the (morning) market is over. In the afternoon session, unsatisfied buyers may choose other sellers, forming new queues, and the process is repeated. Since fish is perishable and therefore non-storable, when the market closes sellers get rid of the unsold stock of fish.

In such a framework, sellers follow alternative rules of behaviors based on their relative fitness (that is, the actual payoff realized when using a certain rule): better rules are more likely to be used again. The interaction structure is endogenous because the seller-buyer networks evolve based on agents' choices. These choices, in turn, are influenced by the evolution of the interaction structure. For instance, loyalty can emerge endogenously from interaction if the fitness of the involved buyer and seller is higher when they form a partnership.

Vriend (1994) adopts a computational approach to the analysis of buyer-seller networks based on communication, the information agents have on possible trading partners. Sellers (firms) produce commodities without knowing the demand for their products. Then, they (randomly) send (costly) messages to potential partners. Buyers (consumers) have three options: shop around randomly, stay loyal to the current supplier, or follow one of the information signals they receive.

Interaction is endogenous because firms choose to reach a target network of potential partners by advertising. Moreover, consumers may or may not follow the information signals they receive (depending on the success of past decisions), so influencing firms' profit which, in turn, is a signal firms use to revise their production and advertising strategies. Finally, agents learn from experience and modify their behavior accordingly, shaping the evolution of the buyer-seller network. Depending on the distribution of information, a certain pattern of agents' interaction prevails and markets emerge as self-organized structures.

Howitt and Clower (2000) provide another example of market self organization. Traders follow simple behavioral rules and transactions are coordinated by specialist trading firms that bear the costs of market disequilibrium. Starting from an initially autarkic situation (in which there are no institutions that support exchange), simulations show that a fully developed market economy will emerge spontaneously. Moreover, in virtually every case where a market economy develops, one of the commodities traded will emerge as a universal medium of exchange (commodity money) being traded by every firm and changing hands at every transaction.

Economic growth in open-ended economies. To study the determinants of economic growth in a simple production economy, Fagiolo and Dosi (2003a) develop the so-called island model. In this model, the economy is populated by a set of stylized entrepreneurs (firms) that produce a homogeneous good under increasing returns to scale in the number of exploiters of a given technology. Technologies are randomly distributed in an infinite lattice and can be thought as islands with mines on them from which entrepreneurs can dig the homogenous product. Each firm can exploit one island in each time period, but each mine can be exploited by many entrepreneurs simultaneously who therefore produce using increasing returns to scale. Interactions in this models occur at different scales. First, firms using the same technology interactions via returns to scale. Second, firms can decide to leave the island they are exploiting and start exploring the sea (i.e., nodes of the lattice without islands) in search of other, new technologies. During this journey, firms can receive signals sent by firms working on other islands. If they do so, they can decide to follow the signal, move toward the island from which the signal was sent, and start producing there. Finally, when explorers find a new island, its new productivity (i.e., the amount of product per firm that can be produced) will increase the more productive the worker was in the past, which depended also on how many other firms were producing there, i.e., a sort of interaction from the past. The model is able to produce simulated time series for the aggregate output that are statistically similar to those observed in the realworld. Furthermore, the long-run performance of the economy (i.e., in terms of long-run average growth rate) depends on the rate of interactions between agents, as well as on other parameters. In general, there needs to be a balance between the extent to which agents exploit existing resources in the model and that at which they explore in search of new technologies in order to attain a high long-run performance. If agents exploit or explore too much, the economy slows down into a stagnating pattern.

ABMs of the labor market. In ABMs of the labor market – see for instance Russo et al. (2007) – firms set their demand for labor (and post vacancies accordingly) on the basis of their desired level of production. Unemployed workers send out job applications to firms posting vacancies. Firms may select applications focusing on some characteristics of the applicants, such as skill, specialization, productivity, or emphasizing loyalty. Once an applicant is selected, the worker and the firm bargain over the wage and when they reach an agreement a match occurs. If job applications are not enough to fill all the vacancies, the firm hires all the applicants but employment and production will be set below the desired scale. If, on the other hand, vacancies are not enough to satisfy all the applications, the firm can reach the desired scale of activity, but some applicants will stay unemployed (Fagiolo et al., 2004a; Richiardi, 2006; Russo et al., 2007; Neugart, 2008).

ABMs of the credit market. In ABMs of the credit market, the key issues are the determination of the interest rate on loans and the total size and allocation to borrowers of credit extended by lenders. In some models of a fully decentralized credit market (see, e.g., Gaffeo et al., 2008; Grilli et al., 2012), borrowers contact a given number of randomly chosen lenders to get a loan, starting from the one which charges the lowest interest rate. Each lender sorts the borrowers' applications for loans in descending order according to the financial soundness of borrowers, and satisfy them until all credit supply has been exhausted. The contractual interest rate is determined using an optimization strategy (Delli Gatti et al., 2005) or a rule of thumb (see Delli Gatti et al., 2008). Along these lines, Delli Gatti et al. (2010) propose a model to analyze a credit network composed of downstream (D) firms, upstream (U) firms, and banks. The production of D firms and of their suppliers (U firms) is constrained by the availability of internal finance – proxied by net worth – to D firms. The structure of credit interlinkages changes over time due to an endogenous process of partner selection, which leads to the polarization of the network. As a consequence, when a shock hits a significant group of agents in the credit network and agents' leverage is critically high, a bankruptcy avalanche can follow. This mechanism can be regarded as a network-based financial accelerator.

ABMs of the stock market. In ABMs of the stock market, agents can place market orders or limit orders for arbitrary quantities (see Chiarella et al., 2009; Tedeschi et al., 2009). Limit orders are stored in the book and executed when they find a matching order on the opposite side of the market. A market order is filled completely if it finds enough capacity on the book, partially otherwise. The order-driven market mechanism avoids the limitations of the market-maker approach in which there is no explicit trading mechanism. In fact, the market maker, who is typically risk neutral and endowed with unlimited liquidity, absorbs excess demand and makes trading always viable, regardless of its size. For relevant contributions in this field (see Lux and Marchesi, 2002; Hommes, 2006; LeBaron, 2006).

ABMs of the macroeconomy. Delli Gatti et al. (2011) and Riccetti et al. (2014) propose a macroeconomic ABM characterized by decentralized search and matching, i.e., a macroeconomic framework in which a relatively large population of heterogeneous agents (households, firms, banks, the government, and the central bank) interact in four markets (credit, labor, goods, and deposits) according to a decentralized search and matching mechanism. Agents follow (relatively) simple rules of behavior in an incomplete and asymmetric information context. Households shop for goods visiting firms and start buying from the supplier posting the lowest price. Firms set the price and the quantity to produce on the basis of expected demand. If desired employment is higher than the actual workforce, they post vacancies. Unemployed household members search for a job visiting firms that post vacancies. If they need external funds, firms ask for a loan at a bank starting from the bank that offers the lowest interest rate.

For instance, in Riccetti et al. (2014), in each of the four markets two classes of agents interact on the demand and the supply sides respectively. They obey the following matching protocol: (i) A list of agents is picked at random from the population of agents on the demand side – firms in the credit and in the labor market, households in the goods market, and banks in the deposit market. (ii) The first agent in the list observes a random subset of potential partners and chooses the one posting the lowest price. (iii) The second agent on the list performs the same activity on a new random subset of the updated potential partners list. (iv) The process is repeated till the end of the list of agents on the demand side. (v) A new list of agents is picked at random from the population of agents on the demand side and the steps (i) to (iv) are repeated.[2] The matching mechanism goes on until either one side of the market is empty or no further matchings are feasible. The patterns of agents' interaction change as agents made their choices and collective dynamics feed back to individual decisions, including the choice of the best partner(s). Accordingly, the pattern of interactions is fully endogenous.

Dosi et al. (2010) explore a different scheme of endogenous interaction in a context in which innovation is embodied in capital goods. Capital-goods producers send "brochures" with information on new vintages of machine tools to a subset of potential customers, i.e., producers of consumption goods who use capital as an input. The latter choose whether to buy new capital goods or use the existing machine tools of a previous vintage. The two-way feedback between the adoption of new technologies and the volume and composition of demand generation suggest the presence of two distinct regimes of growth (or absence thereof) characterized by different short-run output and employment fluctuations.

Finally, a spatial structure of interaction can be incorporated in a macroeconomic ABM. For example, in Dawid et al. (2012), consumption goods are sold at local market platforms (malls), where firms store and offer their products and consumers come to buy goods at posted prices. In this model, while market demand for consumption goods is determined locally in the sense that all consumers buy at the local mall located in their region, supply is global because every firm might sell its products in all regional markets of the economy. Labor markets are characterized by spatial frictions determined by commuting costs that arise if workers accept jobs outside their own region. Finally, households and firms have access to all banks in the economy and therefore credit markets operate globally. Accordingly, different assumptions on the local or global dimension of agent interaction can be explored in order to understand the interplay between local/regional/global market dynamics.

---

[2] For example, in the labor market, firms (on the demand side) enter the matching process and have the possibility to employ one worker (on the supply side). In the first step of the procedure, the first firm on the list of firms, say F_1, observes the reservation wage of a subset of the list of workers and chooses the worker asking for the lowest wage, say worker H_1. The list of potential workers is updated eliminating worker H_1, and the process is iterated.

6.3 Networks: Basic Concepts and Properties

It is always possible to represent, at least theoretically, agents' interactions by means of a *network* or graph.[3] Therefore, network theory is a useful tool in order to have an analytical description of the interaction structure in a multi-agent framework.

There is an obvious link between the conceptual framework of ABMs and *network theory*. Consider for instance a financial or credit network in which agents are linked by borrowing/lending relationships. In this type of network, it is important to understand how the interaction structure affects the way in which defaults spread through connections (financial contagion). Network theory is key in understanding this phenomenon as it provides the basic mathematical concepts needed to describe the set of interactions among agents, as well as the tools needed to analyze the collective, *emerging properties* of this set. Interaction patterns, in turn, affect the state and control variables of the agents.

In fact, one may claim that each ABM maps onto one or more networks (since the structure of interactions could be either fixed or changing over time), and the mathematical properties of these networks can be used to analyze and eventually forecast, at least for some variables, the behavior of the agents in the ABM. For these reasons, the quest for a deeper integration with network theory has become an important topic in the research agenda of the ABM literature, with a growing amount of research effort especially devoted to problems of interaction over fixed networks (Wilhite, 2006) and of endogenous network formation (Vriend, 2006). So far, however, the ABM and the network literatures have grown along different trajectories. In his well-known book on networks – especially tailored for the economics profession – Jackson (2008) makes only a marginal reference to ABMs, while Vega-Redondo (2007) is entirely silent on the subject in his monograph more oriented toward the physics community. Among the few systematic efforts to better integrate the two approaches, it is worth mentioning the ambitious theoretical framework proposed by Potts (2000), which is explicitly geared toward multi-agent simulation modeling and relies heavily on network theory. According to Potts (2000), there is an evolutionary common ground shared by the different heterodox economic schools, in which evolution is to be understood in its broadest meaning as a process of self-transformation of

---

[3] In this book we use the words "graph" and "network" as synonyms. Graph is the term mainly used in the mathematical literature (see, for instance, Bollobas, 1998, or Chung, 1997). Among physicists, network is more popular (Caldarelli, 2007; Newman, 2010).

agents. In this ever changing process, what matters most are connections, since the latter determine the dynamical behavior of the system as a whole.

When the modeler wants to observe what happens to model dynamics given an exogenous structure of interaction, a *static network* may be sufficient to characterize the local or global interaction among agents. In this case, one can investigate the impact of the given *network topology* (or of alternative topologies) on model results. On the other hand, when the modeler wants to capture the partners' choice, an *evolving network* must be explored. In this case agents decide with whom they want to interact. Their choices affects aggregate dynamics and, at the same time, macro properties influence the social structure of the economy giving rise to a coevolution of the network and macro variables.

Two remarks are in order: First, it must be noted that some of the interaction structures already introduced in this chapter easily fall in a network framework. For example, one- or two-dimensional lattices are particular types of networks, namely regular networks invariant to roto-translations. They are regular as all nodes hold the same number of links. They are invariant to roto-translations as the way in which we move the graph in a higher dimensional space does not change its properties. Second, a distinction must be made between models of network evolution and the use of network theory within ABMs. A large literature, mostly grounded in physics, has developed simple stochastic models attempting to describe and explain how networks evolve and reach stable equilibrium states as time goes by (Newman, 2010). Similarly, game-theoretic models have been developed in order to understand which type of network is going to have efficient properties where agents on it must bargain or split a certain amount cooperatively (Jackson, 2008), or whether some equilibria may be reached when agents play noncooperatively and are placed on endogenous or exogenous networks (Vega-Redondo, 2007). On the contrary, a network formalism can be used in ABMs to micro-found the structure of agent interactions and their evolution. However, agents in economic ABMs are typically more sophisticated than simple players in the game or anonymous nodes in cellular automata. They typically behave in richer ways, interacting in different markets and performing a number of different tasks (deciding how much to produce, form expectations, react to system-level inputs, etc.). Therefore, network theory is an extremely useful tool in ABMs but can never replace agent-based modeling as such.

Let us now start with some preliminary notions. A *network* – denoted by G – is a mathematical object composed by *nodes* (or vertices, denoted by V) connected by *links* (edges, E). In symbols: $G = (V, E)$, where V is typically assumed to be a subset of $\mathbb{N}$, while $E \subset \mathbb{N} \times \mathbb{N}$ can eventually map onto any subset of $\mathbb{R}^N$. For example, let $V = \{1, 2, \ldots, n\}$ represent a finite index set mapping onto individuals connected by acquaintance. Then, we can use

Table 6.1 *Adjacency matrix for the graph of Figure 6.5.*

	1	2	3
1	0	1	0
2	1	0	1
3	0	1	0

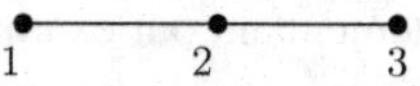

Figure 6.5 Network among 3 nodes.

V to represent individuals in a graph, and consequently we represent two individuals being acquainted by adding to E one element (i, j) with $i, j \in V$ if the corresponding individuals are connected.

In the social sciences, nodes may represent different agents: women, men (distinguished by age, nationality, wealth, etc.), households, banks, firms, countries, etc. Links may represent different social classes, friendship or professional acquaintance, assets, liabilities, etc. Links could have different weights, which represent the strength of the relationship among nodes.[4]

For this more general setting, a functional representation seems straightforward. Let $l_{i,j}$ be a function whose arguments are vertices and having a suitable co-domain. For instance, with $l_{i,j} \to \{0, 1\}$ we represent the relative frequency of interaction (or any *ex-ante* probability measure on a suitably defined interaction space) between i and j. $l_{i,j} = 1$ if the edge between i and j is in E, otherwise $l_{i,j} = 0$. Moreover, we assume that $l_{i,j} \equiv l_{j,i}$. In this case, $V = \{1, 2, 3\}$ with $l_{1,2} = l_{2,3} = 1$ and $l_{1,3} = 0$ yields the graph shown in Figure 6.5.

Within this setting, a convenient representation of a graph is given by the *connectivity or adjacency matrix*, C. Each element $c_{i,j}$ of this matrix stores the image of $l_{i,j}$ associated to each point (i, j) of its (finite) domain. The matrix showed in Table 6.1 reproduces the same network showed in Figure 6.5.

Three remarks are in order: First, the elements of the main diagonal in our example are zero, i.e., no agent links with itself or, in network jargon, the graph has no *self loops*. This is not necessarily the best option in all cases.

---

[4] The most typical networks have a well-established and codified treatment in graph theory. Therefore we will introduce only those concepts and terms that are strictly necessary for our purposes and will not get systematically into the details of graph-theoretic concepts and terminology. A number of rigorous and readable books are now available (Caldarelli, 2007; Goyal, 2007; Vega-Redondo, 2007; Jackson, 2008; Newman, 2010), along with the classical presentation of Bollobas (1998).

Table 6.2 *Adjacency matrix for a digraph.*

	1	2	3
1	0	1	1
2	1	0	1
3	0	1	0

Second, the off-diagonal elements in our example are either zero (the nodes identified by the corresponding row and column are not linked) or one (nodes are linked). Some models require *multiple edges*, which would mean that the elements of the matrix can take on values (represented by integers) larger than 1. In this case we talk of a *multigraph*.

Third, edges in the graph shown in Table 6.1 are *undirected*. The adjacency matrix is therefore *symmetric* since $l_{i,j} \equiv l_{j,i}$ for each $i,j \in V$. An edge, however, may be *directed*. A directed edge can be thought as a one-way road between two points and be represented graphically by an arrow. A graph characterized by directed edges is referred to as a *digraph* and is represented by an asymmetric adjacency matrix.

For instance, by adding to the graph of our example a directed edge between 1 and 3 – i.e., setting $l_{1,3} = 1$ but $l_{3,1} = 0$ – we generate a digraph. The corresponding adjacency matrix is shown in Table 6.2.

The context must dictate which representation is preferred, since there are plenty of examples of both symmetric and asymmetric relationships in the real world. For example, a network representing email messages is unavoidably directed, since each message goes just in one direction. Instead, a network representing parental relationships is undirected since two agents in this network are either related to each other (they are the mother and father of a child) or not.

As mentioned earlier links can be *weighted*. Their weight mirrors the strength of relations among the connected nodes. Returning to Figure 6.5, suppose the three nodes represent banks. In this case, the weight of links can represent the overall value or number of transactions between banks i and j in a given day. We can define, thus, the weighted adjacency matrix W, whose elements $w_{i,j}$ represent daily value of transactions among linked banks. Echoing the matrix setting, we define W of the bank network as

$$W_{i,j} = \begin{cases} w_{i,j} & \text{if } l_{i,j} = 1 \\ 0 & \text{if } l_{i,j} = 0, \end{cases} \tag{6.1}$$

where $l_{i,j}$ is the link between banks and $w_{i,j}$ its weight.

So far, we have discussed situations where only one type of relationship among agents is described. More generally, agents may entertain different types of interactions at the same time. Going back to the case of social interactions, individuals may exchange information using different means, such as personal encounters, phone calls, emails, different direct messaging services, as well as online social networks. Each distinct interaction channel would require a different graph to be formally described in terms of networks. However, all these different linkages may be modeled simultaneously in terms of a multi-layer network (MLN). An MLN is simply a collection of different layer networks where nodes remain the same in each different layer. Layers represent different interaction types and one can think to links in each layer as having a different color. By aggregating all the layers together, an MLN representation envisages a graph where between any two nodes there can exist many (weighted, directed) links, each with a different color, representing the different interaction types coexisting in the social system.

Going back to a simple network, a network is said to be sparse when there are few edges with respect to the number of nodes. Real networks are, almost without exception, sparse, since the capacity of agents to interact doesn't grow proportionally with the dimension of the system. Models of complex networks generally display this feature, assuming that the expected number of vertices connected to a given one remains finite as the size of the network tends to infinity.

In a sparse network, heterogeneous local structures become very important in determining the properties of the network. This feature is captured by the key notion of *neighborhood* (a notion which we have already encountered in the previous sections). The neighborhood $\psi(i)$ of the i-th agent is the set of agents with whom i has a direct link. Neighborhoods find ubiquitous application in network theory, especially within the social and economic domain. In social-economic systems, individuals tend to link with people they are close to. A clear manifestation of this phenomenon is shown in the identification of groups inside the network. These groups can mirror friendship, loyalty, cooperation, or segregation.[5]

The cardinality of the neighborhood $\psi(i)$ which we denote with k_i is the *degree* of the i-th agent, the simplest measure of connectivity:

$$k_i = \sum_{j \in \psi(i)} l_{i,j} = |\psi(i)| \qquad (6.2)$$

[5] Pioneering research on this subject has been carried out by Jacob Moreno in the 1920s and 1930s on the friendship patterns within small groups. Anatol Rapoport (1961) was one of the first theorist to stress the importance of the friendship graphs of school children. Milgram's experiments on the "small-world effect" originated the popular notion of "six degrees of separation" (Milgram, 1967).

In digraphs we must distinguish between *in-degree*, i.e., the number of edges pointed to some vertex, and *out-degree*, i.e., the number of edges pointing away from it. In-degree k_i^{in} and out-degree k_i^{out} are defined respectively as

$$k_i^{in} = \sum_{j \in \psi_{in}(i)} l_{i,j}^{in} = |\psi_{in}(i)| \qquad k_i^{out} = \sum_{j \in \psi_{out}(i)} l_{i,j}^{out} = |\psi_{out}(i)| \quad (6.3)$$

All networks may be conceived as the outcome of a generative process, which mathematically takes the form of an algorithm. At this point it is convenient to introduce a fundamental distinction between *deterministic graphs* and *random graphs*. The former are the outcome of a deterministic sequence of steps, while the latter's development involves one or more stochastic processes.

The most important deterministic network structures in economic applications are the following:

- *Complete networks*: Each vertex is connected to all the other vertices.
- *Star networks*: Every link ends in a certain agent (the star node).
- *Wheel networks*: Agents are arranged as $[i_1, \ldots, i_n]$ with $l_{2,1} = l_{3,2} = \cdots = l_{n,n-1} = l_{1,n} = 1$ and there are no other links.

Panels (a) (b) (c) in Figure 6.6 represent these typical network structures when there are 4 agents. Panels (a) and (b) represent undirected graphs so that the in-degree is equal to the out-degree. In panel (a), for each node i, $k_i = 3$; in panel (b) the star node 1 has a degree 3, whereas the other nodes' degree is equal to 1. Panel (c) represents a wheel, i.e., a digraph such that for each node i, $k_i^{in} = k_i^{out} = 1$.

If a network is random, all the observables defined over it, including the degree, are random variables, which take their values in agreement with a specific probability measure. Therefore we can define the *probability degree distribution* $p(k)$ as the probability that a vertex chosen uniformly at random has degree k. In the applied network literature, it is usual to represent networks by means of the *decumulative distribution function (DDF)* or – less frequently – by means of the *cumulative distribution function (CDF)* corresponding to $p(k)$.

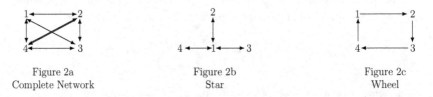

| Figure 2a | Figure 2b | Figure 2c |
| Complete Network | Star | Wheel |

Figure 6.6 Different networks' topologies.

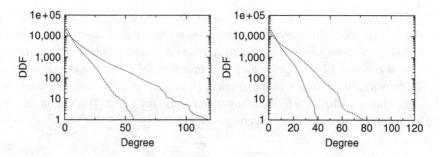

Figure 6.7 DDF of degree for incoming (dotted line) and outgoing (solid line) links in 1999 (left) and 2002 (right).

As we will show, different network topologies have different degree distributions. A well-established stylized fact of real-world networks, however, is that the degree distribution is generally right-skewed, i.e., it is characterized by a long right tail of values that are far above the mean. In other words, there are few nodes with many links (*hubs*) and many links with few nodes. Networks whose degree distribution is approximately shaped as a power law are called *scale free*.

This property is displayed at best by plotting the DDF. Consider, for example, the DDF of the in-degree (lender bank) and out-degree (borrower bank) for the Italian interbank market in 1999 and 2002 (see Iori et al., 2008) shown on a double logarithmic scale in Figure 6.7. The plots show that the degree distribution is right skewed in both periods since the values follow an approximately straight line.

There are many properties closely related to the degree distribution. *Resilience, clustering, community structure* and *assortative mixing* can be counted among the most frequently used in social sciences.

Resilience denotes the robustness of the network's structure to the removal of nodes. When a vertex i is removed from a network, the average distance among nodes increases. As this process goes on, ultimately some nodes will be disconnected. Nodes can be removed in many ways. They may be attacked randomly or according to some of their intrinsic properties (such as their degree). Depending on the rules used to remove nodes, the network shows different levels of resilience.[6]

---

[6] For instance, Albert et al. (2000) show that social networks, usually characterized as scale-free, are remarkably robust to random attacks but extremely vulnerable to attacks targeted at nodes with the highest degree (hubs). To prove this claim, the authors remove nodes in decreasing order of connectivity, showing that as a small number of hubs are removed, the average distance of the scale-free network increases rapidly.

Clustering denotes the organization of the network in neighborhoods, cliques, or motifs. In many social networks, we find that if node i is linked to node j and node j to node h, then there is a fairly high probability that i and h are also linked. This property, therefore, measures the number of triangles in the network. In the jargon of social sciences, for example, clustering answers to the question whether a friend of my friend is also my friend. This notion can be quantified by means of a clustering coefficient c_i:

$$c_i = \frac{2}{k_i(k_i - 1)} \sum_{j,h \in \psi(i)} l_{ij} l_{ih} l_{jh} \qquad (6.4)$$

Then the average clustering coefficient

$$C = \frac{1}{N} \sum_i c_i \qquad (6.5)$$

is an overall statistical measure of the density of interconnected vertex triplets in the network.

The concept of *community* provides a powerful extension of the notion of clustering, by looking at groups of vertices such that there is a higher density of links within groups than between them.[7] The presence of subsets of highly interconnected nodes is a key feature of empirically observed social networks. Usually these communities, which are sparsely interconnected, reflect agents' preferences and choices. As an example, one might imagine a social network representing friendship relationships; in this case, communities describe how agents choose their friends, eventually forming distinct social groups among individuals sharing some common characteristics. Within social networks' theory, this kind of selective linking, based upon similarity, is called *assortative mixing*. A classic example of assortative mixing is given by the study of school integration and friendship segregation in America. Many studies have shown that students are more likely to become friends of other students belonging to their own ethnic group (Catania et al., 1997).

One of the characteristics shared by connected agents can be degree itself. Positive assortativeness (or assortativity), defined as positive degree-degree correlation, has been detected in many social networks (Newman, 2003a,b). In this case *assortative mixing* can be detected by means of the correlation between some node i's degree and the average degree of its neighbors, where the latter is defined as

$$k_{nn,i} = \frac{1}{k_i} \sum_{j \in \psi(i)} k_j \qquad (6.6)$$

---

[7] The field of community-oriented research is quite heterogeneous and rapidly growing. For a recent review the reader can refer to Fortunato (2010).

If $k_{nn}(k) = \{k_{nn,i}|k_i = k\}$ increases (decreases) with k, there is assortative mixing (disassortativity), that is high-degree nodes are more likely to be connected to high-degree (low-degree) nodes.[8]

6.4 Static and Dynamic Networks

In this section, we present and discuss different network formation mechanisms. First, we deal with several stochastic processes generating the link formation mechanism. In this context, we assume that links, after their creation, do not change over time, so $\frac{\delta l_{i,i}}{\delta t} = 0$. In this case, the network is static. Then, we move on to describe dynamic processes of link formation. In this context, the evolution of the link structure is dependent on agents' experience from using their active edges, so $\frac{\delta l_{i,i}}{\delta t} \neq 0$. In this case, there is a continuous feedback mechanism between agents' behavior and network evolution: agents learn and adapt to a changing environment and this in turn leads to an evolution of the network structure which, then, feeds back into the incentives of individuals to form or sever links. In this case, the network is dynamic.

6.4.1 Static Networks

The simplest way to introduce networks within ABMs is to think that the environment acts as a constraint on interaction, and that agents must learn how to behave within this constraint. The issue at stake, then, is how economic outcomes are affected by network structures over which agents make their decisions. By keeping the interaction environment (here represented by the network) fixed, we can analyze, either analytically or with the help of simulations, how state variables[9] evolve within that environment. This view of the environment is common in sociological literature, where a great emphasis is put on the networks in which agents are "embedded"(White, 1981; Granovetter, 1985). The relevance of this approach for economics was outlined by the early study of Baker (1984), who showed that the volatility of option prices depends on the structure of the communication network in the market. Many recent contributions have confirmed this finding, analyzing the many different ways in which network structure affects economic behavior.[10]

---

[8] For a more rigorous treatment in terms of conditional probability, see Caldarelli (2007, par. 1.3).

[9] State variables may represent many economic indicators, such as agents' wealth, knowledge, firms' output, and many more.

[10] There are models of network structure in foreign exchange markets (Kakade et al., 2004), in labor markets (Calvo-Armengol and Jackson, 2004), communication and information (DeMarzo et al., 2003), to name just a few.

Random Interactions: The Poisson Model

Thanks to its simplicity and mathematical tractability, the *binomial or Poisson model* is one of the most popular models of network formation. The network structure generated by the model is defined as a random network.

The model is initialized with a set of N isolated vertices. Each pair of vertices is then connected with a given probability q. It is easy to see that, according to the model, a graph having m links appears with probability $q^m(1-q)^{M-m}$, where $M = \frac{1}{2}n(n-1)$ is the maximum possible number of links for an undirected graph.[11] Since, for each vertex, links are added through $N-1$ independent draws with common parameter q, the degree follows a common binomial distribution:

$$p(k) = \binom{N-1}{k} q^k(1-q)^{N-1-k} \tag{6.7}$$

where $p(k)$ is the probability that a randomly chosen node has degree k. As it is well known, in the limit where $N \to \infty$, the binomial distribution is well approximated by the Poisson distribution with fixed parameter z:

$$p(k) = \frac{z^k e^{-z}}{k!} \tag{6.8}$$

Of course, in both formulations agents on average have the same degree value:

$$z = \frac{qN(N-1)}{N} = q(N-1) \sim qN \tag{6.9}$$

The mathematical simplicity of the model comes with a cost. The Poisson model, in fact, does not feature many properties which are routinely detected in real networks. For example, the clustering coefficient C is low[12] and equal to $q = \frac{z}{N}$. Therefore C tends to zero as the system gets larger and larger. Moreover community structure and assortative mixing are absent in a random graph.

On the other hand, one of most well-known properties of the Poisson model is the occurrence of a phase transition in connectivity when q increases beyond a threshold. In fact, at a critical value for q the system passes from a state in which there are few links and components are small, to a state in which an extensive fraction of all vertices are joined in a single giant component (see Figure 6.8). Crossing the threshold, therefore, has dramatic effects on whichever interaction process is taking place over the network, favoring

---

[11] If the graph is directed, the maximum number of links is $M = n(n-1)$.
[12] This is because in a random graph the probability of a link between two nodes is given. Therefore it will not increase if the nodes in question are already neighbors of another agent

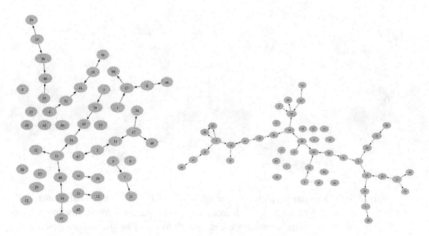

Figure 6.8 Poisson random graph with 50 nodes below the phase transition (left) and at the phase transition (right).

coordinated/homogeneous outcomes over uncoordinated/heterogeneous ones, for example.

The interaction mechanism underlying the Poisson model is inherently symmetric. It may be translated in ABM jargon as follows: in every period, each agent interacts – i.e., she exchanges information, broadly speaking – with a set of other agents chosen at random from the population. This mechanism could be interpreted as a stochastic collection of information. The dynamics generated by this process are not easy to predict.[13]

The Small-World Model

We have seen that Poisson networks are essentially devoid of local structure. This conclusion is easily extended to the broader class of "generalized random graphs" introduced by Newman (2003c), which fall outside the scope of the present book. On the other hand, local structure, for instance under the form of high average clustering coefficient, is a distinctive property of real-world social networks. Milgram (1967) designed an experiment in which people would attempt to relay a letter to a distant stranger by giving the letter to an acquaintance, having the acquaintance give the letter to one of his or her acquaintances, and so on. He found that, for the letters that made it to their target, the median number of intermediate acquaintances was five. This result

---

[13] When agents interact in complex systems, their outcomes are difficult to predict. For example, Ellison and Fudenberg (1995) present a model in which random local interaction generate an inefficient outcome (inefficient conformism).

(a)   **(b)**

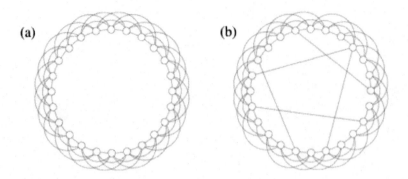

Figure 6.9 (a) Regular graph with $n = 25$ nodes and $z = 3$. (b) Small World graph with $n = 25$ nodes and $z = 3$ created by choosing at random a fraction p of edges in the graph and moving one end of each to a new location, also chosen uniformly at random.

became the source of the popular notion of "six degrees of separation" between any two individuals in the world.

Milgram's result implies that in real social networks, distances between individuals are as low as in a random network, notwithstanding the fact that most of the interactions, contrary to what happens in random graphs, are local and high clustered. The so-called small-world model of Watts and Strogatz (1998) explains this paradox with the help of network theory. In order to describe the model, we must introduce the notion of *average path length* Λ as the average geodesic (i.e., shortest) distance between node pairs in a network:

$$\Lambda = \frac{1}{\frac{1}{2}n(n-1)} \sum_{i>j}^{n} d_{ij} \tag{6.10}$$

where d_{ij} is the geodesic distance from node i to j. In the terminology of network theory, small worlds exist when a network exhibits both high average clustering coefficient and low average path length.

The starting point of the small-world model is an r-dimensional lattice with periodic boundary condition.[14] If $r = 1$, this network can be represented as a ring whose vertices are connected to their z closest neighbors, as shown in Figure 6.9a.

The small-world model is then created by taking a small fraction of the edges in this graph and "rewiring" them. The rewiring procedure involves

---

[14] A lattice (with periodic boundary condition) is a deterministic network where each node has a fixed (and equal) number of neighbors, whose value is determined by a distance threshold $\bar{d}$. If $\bar{d} = 1$, the lattice can be depicted as a grid spanning a r-dimensional space.

going through each edge in turn and, with probability q, reconnecting that edge to a new one chosen uniformly at random from the lattice, except that no double edges or self-edges are included. With probability $1 - q$, thus, the edge is not reconnected. When $q = 0$, the small-world network is obviously coincident with the original lattice. In this case, the clustering coefficient is $C = (3z-3)/(4z-2)$, which tends to $3/4$ for large z, which means that average clustering is nonvanishing in the limit of large network size. The regular lattice, however, does not show the small-world effect, since the average geodesic distance grows linearly with n. In fact, in this case the mean geodesic distances between vertices tend to $n/4z$ for large n. When $q = 1$, every edge is rewired to a new random location and the graph is almost a random graph with typical geodesic distances on the order of $\log n - z \sim \log n$, but very low clustering $C \sim z/n$. Via numerical simulation, the authors have proved that, between the extremes $p = 0$ and $p = 1$, there is a region in which clustering is high and average path length is simultaneously low. In this region, a small-world network configuration finally emerges.

The small-world effect has important implications for the dynamics of processes taking place on networks. In particular, any coordination process will be facilitated, thus increasing the likelihood of a coordinated outcome, since communication across the entire set of agents is made simpler by low-average distances, even if interaction is mostly local. Following this idea, Wilhite (2001) has built a simple bilateral search and trade model, comparing by simulation alternative network configurations with respect to their ability to deliver a single equilibrium market price under the same trading mechanism. In this framework, the small-world network is seen as an intermediate configuration between purely global (i.e., equivalent to a complete network) and purely local interaction. Simulation results show that, although the complete network converges more rapidly to equilibrium than any other configuration, the small-world network is able to reach equilibrium with a significant saving of search efforts. Thus small-world networks emerge as a more realistic configuration for market exchange, since they take into account the fact that economic agents are willing to economize on search efforts, while on the same time retaining the efficiency of global interaction.

6.4.2 Dynamic Networks

In economics the assumption of static network is satisfactory only as an initial approximation, since what is most important is the mechanism underlying link formation, i.e., network evolution. Why do different individuals interact with each other? Which motivation pushes agents to communicate with particular individuals and, perhaps, to follow their indications?

Some agents may prefer to trade with some others according to, for instance, to their geographical position, their loyalty, or their popularity. In general, this means that there is some variable which affects linking probabilities, introducing a deviation from symmetric models like the Poisson network: some agents are preferred as partners because of some quality, which may be network-related or not. In both cases, this quality may be interpreted as a *fitness measure* of the agent over the network in question. To illustrate this idea, in this subsection we are going to present the well-known model of preferential attachment, which employs degree itself as a fitness measure, along with its generalization to arbitrary fitness measures.

Fitness networks

A classical example of network formation is given by the work of Price (1965) on citations among scientific publications. In this study, nodes are represented by articles, and a directed edge indicates that article i cites article j. Let $p(k)$ be the fraction of vertices with in-degree k, i.e., with k citations. According to the model, new nodes are continually added to the network. Each new vertex has a certain out-degree (number of cited papers), which is fixed permanently at the creation of the vertex. The out-degree may vary across nodes but its average value z is constant over time. The model finally dictates that the probability of a new article linking to an existing one is proportional to the in-degree k of latter:

$$p(k) = \frac{k}{D_{in}} \tag{6.11}$$

where D_{in} stands for the sum of in-degrees across agents, which acts as a normalization constant. It is possible to show that, under this assumption, the in-degree follows a power-law distribution $p(k) \propto k^{-a}$ (e.g., Vega-Redondo, 2007, pp. 67–70), which is a good descriptor of the empirical degree distribution found in citation networks, as well as in many other domains. For instance, Simon (1955) found that the power-law distribution of wealth could be explained as a consequence of a "rich get richer" process which is similar to the Price model. Barabasi and Albert (1999) applied an equivalent preferential attachment scheme to an undirected network in order to obtain a growth model for the Web, which has become a widely employed benchmark in the field of complex networks. Other models, like Dorogovtsev and Mendes (2001), have removed some of the constraints of the original Price's model, e.g., by allowing the addition of new out-going edges from incumbent nodes or the deletion/rewiring of existing links.

An important generalization of the preferential attachment scheme is provided by Bianconi and Barabasi (2001). In their model, each newly appearing vertex i is given a fitness value f_i that represents its attractiveness and hence its propensity to accrue new links. It is worth noting the difference between preferential attachment and fitness: when one considers a fitness algorithm, it is true that the larger the fitness the larger the degree; but the converse implication does not hold anymore, since the larger degree becomes only a consequence of an intrinsic quality. It is easy to see that fitness-based linking lends itself more naturally to economic interpretation than preferential attachment. For instance, it seems reasonable to expect that agents entering some market will observe incumbents' performance or reputation, and they will accordingly decide to communicate with and/or conform with the most successful ones.

A simple example of fitness algorithm is implemented by Tedeschi et al. (2012). In this model, directed links are created and deleted by agents seeking advice from a single other agent, who is selected as advisor on the basis of a fitness parameter given by its wealth. Agents start with the same initial wealth W_t, but some agents may become richer than others as time goes by. Agents' fitness at time t is defined as their wealth relative to the wealth $W_t^{\max}$ of the wealthiest agent:

$$f_t^i = \frac{W_t^i}{W_t^{\max}} \tag{6.12}$$

Each agent i starts with one outgoing link with a random agent j, and possibly with some incoming links from other agents. Links are rewired at the beginning of each period in the following way: each agent i cuts its outgoing link with agent k and forms a new link with a randomly chosen agent j, with the following probability

$$p_r^i = \frac{1}{1 + e^{-\beta^i(f_t^j - f_t^k)}} \tag{6.13}$$

Otherwise, he maintains its existing link with probability $1 - p_r^i$. The rewiring algorithm is designed so that successful agents gain a higher number of incoming links. Nonetheless, the algorithm introduces a certain amount of randomness, and links with more successful agents have a positive probability to be deleted in favor of links with less successful agents. This randomness helps to unlock the system from the situation where all agents link to the same individual.

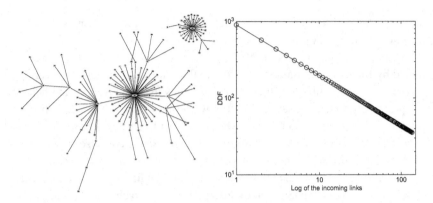

Figure 6.10 Network configuration (left side). The decumulative distribution function (DDF) of the in-degree (right side).

In Figure 6.10 (left side), we plot one snapshot of the configuration of the resulting network. The graph shows that few rich agents coexist and compete for popularity. Moreover the network is very centralized, with a small number of rich agents. The topology of the network is different from that of a Poisson random graph, which would require degrees to follow the binomial (or Poisson) distribution, but closer to the topology of real-world networks, where some agents are found to have a disproportionately large number of incoming links while others have very few. In fact, Figure 6.10 (right side) shows that the decumulative distribution function (DDF) of the in-degree follows a power-law distribution.

It is important to emphasize that in this model links are reupdated every time step via the agents' fitness. In this way, the network topology evolves and changes during the simulation. This mechanism of link formation allows authors to study under which assumptions a successful agent endogenously rises and falls over time, and how imitation affects the network structure and the agents' wealth. The evolutionary dynamics is clearly shown in Figure 6.11, where the authors plot the index of the current winner (black-solid line), the percentage of incoming links to the current winner (red-dotted line), and his fitness (green-dashed line), as function of the time.

In fact, as the successful agent acquires an increasing number of links (red line), one or more of his followers may become richer than the winner himself, as signaled by the fact that the fitness (green line) of the winner becomes, at times, smaller than 1. As other agents become rich, they start to be imitated more and more and eventually one of them becomes the new successful agent.

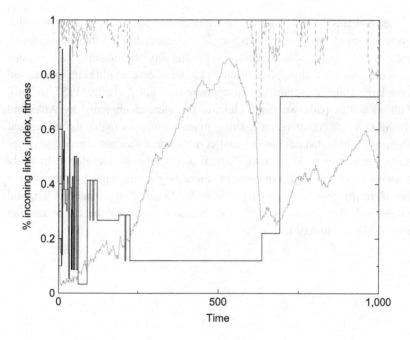

Figure 6.11 The index of current winner (solid line), the percentage of incoming link to current winner (dotted line), and fitness of current winner (dashed line).

6.5 Conclusions

Understanding the influence that socioeconomic systems has on agents and the generation of complex environments by heterogeneous individuals requires an exploration of the phenomena which emerge when different types of agents interact and the influence that the system has on the mechanisms driving agent interaction. In other words, agent interaction becomes a crucial point to understand how a macro coherent behavior may emerge from individual behavior. Since interaction depends on differences in information, motives, knowledge, and capabilities, this implies heterogeneity of agents and externalities. Thus economic organization may be achieved in a way that is parallel and distributed (that is, without a devise acting as a central coordinator). Self-organization, i.e., a process where a structure appears in a system without a central authority or external element imposing it, is a possible description of the *invisible hand* or of *spontaneous order*. The analysis of agents' interaction becomes, thus, the ingredient to understanding the bijective mapping between individuals and environment.

Network theory deals with the structure of interaction within a given multi-agent system. Consequently, it is naturally interested in the statistical equilibrium of these systems, to be defined as the stability of probability distributions of observables, which implies "a state of macroscopic equilibrium maintained by a large number of transition in opposite directions" (Feller, 1957, p. 356). Following this path, we come close to the idea, championed by Aoki and Yoshikawa (2006), of reconstructing macroeconomics under the theoretical framework of statistical physics and combinatorial stochastic processes. Not surprisingly, the same methods (which were originally developed to study systems made of large numbers of interacting micro-units by means of a set of macro state variables) are now of fundamental importance in the field of network theory and, for the same reasons, they are expected to take an increasing role in ABM.

7

The Agent-Based Experiment

Jakob Grazzini, Matteo Richiardi, and Lisa Sella

7.1 Introduction

This chapter deals with the problem of analysing the behaviour of an agent-based (AB) model. The problem is similar to the one faced by any modelling methodology: the researcher sets up the rules of the game, but does not know in advance the implications of those rules. Actually, it is in this *a priori* uncertainty about the model outcomes, and the relationship between the model outputs and the model inputs, that rests the value of developing a model. However, the techniques to gain understanding about the model behaviour differ substantially across modelling methodologies, and they remain quite underexplored in the AB literature. In a simulation model, only inductive knowledge about its behaviour can be gained by repeatedly running the model under different samples from the parameter space.

The analysis of this inductive evidence has to confront with the *a priori* unknown stochastic properties of the model. The easiest case is when, for any values of the parameters, the model is stationary and ergodic: in these circumstances it is generally possible, with a reasonable number of experiments, to characterise both the equilibrium properties of the model and the adjustment dynamics to the equilibria. On the other hand, non-stationarity renders the analytical concepts of equilibrium and adjustment dynamics inapplicable, while non-ergodicity might hinder the same possibility of fully describing the behaviour of the model. A preliminary analysis to discriminate between these cases is therefore necessary, and it can only be done by statistical testing. In this chapter, we will provide examples of the tests that can be used to detect both stationarity and ergodicity.

These properties in turn affect the types of subsequent analyses that can be performed, and the interpretation of the results. The techniques that are used to describe the relationships between the different variables of the model are referred to in general terms as *sensitivity analysis* (SA). Although a complete survey of these techniques is outside the scope of this chapter, we briefly describe them and offer an example of how they can be applied to a specific AB model.

The chapter is structured as follows. Section 7.2 introduces the notion of *statistical equilibria*, and discusses the effects of non-stationarity. Our starting point is the input-output transformation (IOT) function that we derived in Chapter 3:

$$y_t = g_t(\mathbf{Z}_0, \boldsymbol{\theta}) \tag{7.1}$$

which relates the initial conditions $\mathbf{Z}_0 = \{X_0, s\}$ (the initial state of the system X_0 and the random seed s) and the parameters $\boldsymbol{\theta}$ to the outcome of interests y. Section 7.3 surveys the main techniques to gain understanding of this function, that fall into the broad discipline of SA. Finally, Section 7.4 offers our conclusions.

To proceed in this analysis, a first step is to choose the outcome variables y to focus on, and the time period. In order to understand the behaviour of the system, we have to characterise its regularities.

7.2 Long-Run and Transient Equilibria

7.2.1 Definitions

As we have seen at the beginning of this book, in chapter 2, one important difference between analytical models and AB models lies in the definition of equilibrium. In analytical models, equilibrium is defined as a consistency condition in the behavioural equations: agents (whether representative or not) must act consistently with their expectations, and the actions of all the agents must be mutually consistent. This is the methodological prescription of rational expectations, which we examined in Chapter 4, and logically operates at an individual level before action (and interaction) takes place. Like a man standing on one foot who gets pushed away but manages to remain poised on his one leg, the system is always in equilibrium, even during a phase of adjustment after a shock has hit. AB models, on the other hand, are characterized by adaptive expectations, according to which consistency might or might not arise, depending on the evolutionary forces that shape the system. An equilibrium can therefore be defined only at the aggregate level and only in statistical terms, after the macro outcomes have been observed.

Definition For each statistics $y_t(\mathbf{Z}_0, \boldsymbol{\theta})$, a statistical equilibrium is reached in a given time window $(\underline{T}, \bar{T})$, if y_t is stationary.

Stationarity of y_t implies that each observation carries information about some constant properties of the data generating process (DGP). By stationarity, here and in the rest of the chapter, we mean weak stationarity. A stochastic process y_t is (weakly) stationary if $E(y_t) = \mu$, that is, its expected value is independent of t, and if $Cov[y_t, y_{t+h}]$ exists, is finite and depends only on h and not on t. Note the difference between weak and strict stationarity. Strict stationarity requires that y_t has the same distribution for every t, and the joint distribution of $(y_t, y_{t+1}, y_{t+2}, \ldots, y_{t+h})$ depends only on h and not on t. Note that strict stationarity does not necessarily imply weak stationarity, as finite variance is not assumed in the definition of strong stationarity. An example of a stationary process is white noise $y_t \sim WN(0, \sigma^2)$, with

$$Cov[y_t, y_{t+h}] = \begin{cases} \sigma^2 & \text{if } h = 0 \\ 0 & \text{if } h \neq 0 \end{cases}$$

White noise is stationary but may not be strictly stationary.[1] Examples of non-stationary series are the returns in a stock market, where there is clustered volatility (the variance changes over time): trend stationary series that can be transformed to stationary series by subtracting a function of time, and difference stationary series that can be transformed into stationary series by first differentiation.

The statistical equilibrium can then be described by the mean of y_t between $\underline{T}$ and $\bar{T}$, which we denote as μ^*:

$$\mu^* = E[y_t | t \in (\underline{T}, \bar{T})] = g^*(\mathbf{Z}_0, \boldsymbol{\theta}) \tag{7.2}$$

We then distinguish between two types of statistical equilibria: long-run equilibria and transient equilibria.

Definition A simulation model is said to reach a long-run statistical equilibrium if $y_t(\mathbf{Z}_0, \boldsymbol{\theta})$ is stationary in $(\underline{T}, \underline{T} + \tau), \tau \to \infty$. On the other hand, a statistical equilibrium is said to be transient if $y_t(\mathbf{Z}_0, \boldsymbol{\theta})$ is stationary in $(\underline{T}, \bar{T})$ but is no longer stationary in $(\bar{T}, \bar{T} + \tau), \tau > 0$.

Long-run equilibria are stable regularities of the system: once the system is in a long-run equilibrium, it cannot move out. Because the system is deterministic, for any given value of the initial conditions (including the random seed) and the parameters, there can be at most one long-run statistical equilibrium y^*. However, there might be many transient equilibria: for instance, a model can oscillate between two (or more) transient statistical equilibria.

---

[1] A Gaussian white noise, where y_t is identically independent distributed (i.i.d.), Gaussian $y_t \sim N(0, \sigma^2)$ is strictly stationary.

A hypothetical example of a long-run equilibrium is the "natural" unemployment rate in a model of the labour market, while an example of a transient equilibrium could be the (supposedly constant) speed of adjustment to this long-run steady state. Once the model is in the long-run equilibrium, period-to-period deviations from the natural unemployment rate are mainly due to noise and no further adjustment can be detected: the transient equilibrium has vanished. Alternatively to the case of a constant speed of adjustment, long periods of sustained unemployment might take place before the unemployment rate eventually sets to its long-run level. If the unemployment rate were approximately constant during those periods, they would define (possibly many) transient equilibria. Finally, we might have a model where the unemployment rate can be either low or high, with random switches from one (transient) equilibrium to the other. Note that a model can display both transient and long-run equilibria (as in the speed of adjustment example), only transient equilibria (the multiple unemployment regimes), or only a long-run equilibrium (one long-run steady state, but variable speed of adjustment).

7.2.2 Uniqueness and Multiplicity of Equilibria

The condition under which the model, *irrespective of the initial conditions*, will always converge to the same statistical equilibria $\mu^*(\mathbf{Z}_0, \boldsymbol{\theta}) = \mu^*(\boldsymbol{\theta})$ is *ergodicity* of the time series y_t. Intuitively, this means that the model will always exhibit the same type of qualitative behaviour, irrespective of the initial conditions: therefore, if a (long-run or transient) equilibrium is reached, it will be the same in all simulation runs, given the same values of the parameters $\boldsymbol{\theta}$. Starting from a different initial state $\mathbf{X}_0$ or employing a different seed s might change the timing of the equilibrium, that is the period of time over which y_t is stationary, but it would not change the equilibrium level μ^*.

On the other hand, non-ergodic models are sensitive to the initial conditions – including the random seed. This is due to strong persistence in the underlying processes: the random seed representing the legacy from the past. Run the model twice, with the same values of the parameters and the same initial state but different seeds, and the model will display different transient equilibria, and finally set to different long-run equilibria (long-run, steady-state levels).

To continue with our previous example, non-ergodicity implies multiple unemployment regimes, but in a fundamentally different way from the multiple transient equilibria of our ergodic example. In the ergodic case, the model is able to *endogenously* switch between different regimes (hence the equilibria are transient), while in the non-ergodic case each regime defines a parallel universe with no possibility of travelling across different universes. Multiple long-run equilibria are possible only in non-ergodic models. This can be an interesting feature of the model that can open up new possibilities for policies (which might be able to provide appropriate 'reset' events and exogenously move the system away from one 'bad' equilibrium to a 'good' one).

More technically, ergodicity is a property that concerns the memory of a process. An ergodic process is characterised by weak memory, so that as the length of the time series we observe increases, our understanding of the process increases as well. In a non-ergodic process, by converse, persistence is so high that little information is provided by analysing a sub-sample of the process, no matter how long this time series is.

Ergodicity is sometimes defined as

$$\lim_{n \to \infty} \frac{1}{n} \sum_{k=1}^{n} Cov(y_t, y_{t-k}) = 0 \tag{7.3}$$

which means that events far away from each other can be considered as almost independent. This implies that if some event *can* happen, by waiting long enough it *will* happen, regardless of what has happened in the past or what will happen in the future.

If y_t is ergodic, the observation of a unique time series provides information that can be used to infer the model IOT function in Equation 7.1: the process is not persistent and in the long-run different time series (produced by the same IOT function) will have the same properties. If the number of observations of one single time series increases, the information we have about the IOT function increases as well.

Note that stationarity and ergodicity are different concepts, and one does not imply the other. A typical example of a stationary non-ergodic process is a constant series. Consider a process that consists in the draw of a number y_1 from a given probability distribution, and remains constant thereafter: $y_t = y_1$ for every t. The process is strictly stationary (yet degenerated since y_t is extracted from a distribution with mean y_1 and variance 0) and non-ergodic. Any observation of a given realization of the process provides information only on that particular process and not on the IOT function. An example of a non-stationary but ergodic process, discussed in this chapter, is $y_t = y_{t-1} + u_t$, $u_t \sim N(0, 1)$.

An implication of the uniqueness of the long-run equilibrium in ergodic models is that if the expected value and the variance exist and are finite, the simulated mean $m(\theta)$ converges, both over time and over the replications s of the simulation, to the theoretical limiting expected value of the underlying IOT conditional on the parameters used for the simulation, $\mu^*(\boldsymbol{\theta})$:[2]

$$\lim_{t \to \infty} m_t(\boldsymbol{\theta}) = \lim_{s \to \infty} m_s(\boldsymbol{\theta}) = \mu^*(\boldsymbol{\theta}) \tag{7.4}$$

The properties of the time series generated by the model are constant both in time and across replications: therefore, they can be inferred from the sample moments. In other words, the simulated mean of y, computed either over time or over replications, is a consistent estimator of the theoretical limiting expected value. On the contrary, if y_t is stationary but not ergodic, different long-run equilibria are obtained for the same values of the parameters, depending on the initial conditions. This can be regarded as a case of multiple statistical equilibria.

Moreover, the transient equilibria, if any, are also independent on the initial conditions. However, since the transient equilibria are defined over a finite period of time, they *will* inevitably differ when computed for different initial conditions, and convergence over time is simply not defined. Consider again our example of a constant speed of adjustment to the long-run equilibrium. Here y_t is the period-to-period speed of adjustment, defined as $y_t = |\frac{u_t - u_{t-1}}{u_{t-1}}|$, with u being the unemployment rate, while $m(y_t)$ is the average speed of adjustment between $\underline{T}$ and $\bar{T}$.

If we run the simulation for different initial conditions Z_0, we obtain different average speeds of adjustment, irrespective of whether the model is ergodic or not, simply because each of these averages are computed over a limited number of simulated observations (the limited length of the adjustment process $\bar{T} - \underline{T}$). However, if the model is ergodic, the differences between different runs are not statistically significant, so that we can increase our knowledge of the theoretical limiting moment of the underlying DGP conditional on the parameters used for the simulation: $\mu^*(\boldsymbol{\theta})$, by averaging over the moments m_s computed for different seeds (more in general, for different initial conditions):

$$\lim_{s \to \infty} m_s(\boldsymbol{\theta}) = \mu^*(\boldsymbol{\theta}) \tag{7.5}$$

The simulated moments are consistent (over the replications) estimators of the theoretical limiting moment.

Note how flexible and powerful this descriptive apparatus is. For instance, a model can show a long-run statistical equilibrium for, say, GDP. This means that after an initial adjustment period up to $\underline{T}$, the GDP series becomes stationary with constant mean and variance. If the system receives a transitory

---

[2] If y_t is strictly stationary, any simulated moment – not only the mean – converges to its theoretical counterpart, if it exists.

shock, it moves away from the statistical equilibrium. However, once the shock has passed, if the model is ergodic it comes back to the previous steady state, after an adjustment phase. If we re-run the model and shock it 100 times, it would always come down to the same equilibrium: we will say in Chapter 9 that this means that the model is well suited for estimation. Moreover, it might happen that during the adjustment process some other transformation of the state of the system, for instance the speed of adjustment to the equilibrium level of GDP, becomes stationary. This new regularity breaks down when GDP reaches its steady state: it is therefore a transient statistical equilibrium.

It is possible that a model displays no absorbing equilibrium for a given variable of interest. To continue with our example, think of the evolution of GDP, with business cycle fluctuations of different amplitude and duration, and intermittent crises. This is an interesting case for many AB modellers, who essentially see the world as a disequilibrium process. Even in such situations, however, it might be possible to find long-run statistical regularities with respect to some other variable – for instance, the distribution of the length and depth of recessions. Moreover, there might be other regularities which are only transient, and vanish as the simulated time goes by (think for example of the effects of fiscal policies on GDP growth, which are very different depending on whether the economy is close to full employment or not). Again, if they are stable enough across different replications, they might be used to characterise the behaviour of the model (hence for estimation, see chapter 9). If, on the other hand, the model exhibits no regularities whatsoever, no matter how the data are transformed, then one might argue that it is of limited explanatory (not to say predictive) help: 'everything can happen' is hardly a good theory. So, when AB researchers speak of disequilibrium or out-of-equilibrium analysis, what they really have in mind is transient statistical equilibrium analysis of some sort.

To recap, understanding whether a simulated time series produced by the model is stationary and whether it is ergodic is crucial for characterizing the model behaviour. The prescription therefore – following Hendry (1980) – can only be 'test, test, test'.

A number of stationarity tests are available and can be performed on the simulated time series (see, e.g., Grazzini, 2012). Non-parametric tests are in general more suited for AB models, as they do not impose structure on the IOT function of the model, which at this stage of the analysis is still largely unknown. Moreover, the limited power of many non-parametric tests can in principle be overcome by increasing at will the length of the artificial time series, something that cannot obviously be done with real data.[3]

---

[3] Computing time can of course be an issue, in practice.

On the contrary, ergodicity is in general not testable in the real data, as we typically have only one historical time series available. This of course does not mean that the issue must be ignored in empirical applications: if the real world ('Nature') is non-ergodic, using the observed data to make inference about the real-world IOT function, or about the structure of the underlying DGP, is more problematic. Indeed, it is difficult to claim that Nature is in facts ergodic and that present events are not affected by (at least some) event of the past. All the researcher is left with in this case are statements about the true DGP that are *conditional* on the realization of these past events.[4]

In an AB model, the function to be described is the *model* IOT function; fortunately, the "veil of ignorance" about this function is much lighter than with real data, as the model DGP is known, while the real world DGP is unknown. In other words, the researcher is the God of her artificial world, although a non-omniscient God: she sets up the rules of the game, but does not know in advance what the results will be. However, she can replay her artificial worlds at will, thus generating new time series that can provide more information on the behaviour of the system.

This difference has an important implication: the ergodic properties of a simulation model are in principle testable, as we can produce as many time series as we wish, as long as we wish. And they *should* be tested, as we cannot be content with conditional statements on initial conditions in understanding our system behaviour: real initial conditions being in some sense legitimised by history, while the initial conditions chosen by the experimenter being often more arbitrary.[5]

7.2.3 Implications of Stationarity and Ergodicity

To summarise, if the model is ergodic – with respect to an outcome y and for given values of the structural parameters θ – each simulated time series y_t can be used to characterize the IOT function at the given values of the parameters once enough time is passed to wash away the memory of the initial conditions. If, in addition, the model is also stationary in a given time interval, the time series can be used to characterise the (long-run or transient) equilibria of the system.

On the other hand, if the model is non-ergodic, each time series y_t is only informative of one possible outcome given the values of the parameters. Then, multiple runs of the model should be used and variation across runs exploited

---

[4] Whether this is satisfactory or not depends on the objectives of the analysis.
[5] An ergodicity test for AB models is described in Grazzini (2012).

in order to characterise, in distributional terms, the properties of the system at the sampled values of the parameters.

A natural question then arises whether it is more convenient to always treat the model as non-ergodic, and examine the outcomes of multiple runs – i.e., many short time series – rather than only one long time series. The answer is that it is often important to characterise the equilibrium of the system, that is its stationary behaviour, possibly after a prolonged phase of adjustment: analysing long time series allow to test for stationarity and identify the equilibrium.

A second remark concerns the fact that the stationarity/ergodicity analysis is only valid locally, i.e., for specific values of the parameters: the model DGP can be stationary or ergodic for some values of the parameters, and non-stationary or non-ergodic for some other values. Hence, in principle, the analysis should be repeated for every sampled point of the IOT function, assuming by a continuity argument that the results also hold in between different points in the parameter space. When the form of the model DGP induces to expect some discontinuity in the behaviour of the system for specific values of the parameters, these values should be included in the experimental design and duly explored. More generally, the choice of the points in the parameter space are to be sampled, which, together with the overall design of the experiments that are performed in order to gain understanding about the IOT function, is the focus of sensitivity analysis.[6]

7.3 Sensitivity Analyis of Model Output

The statistical techniques to analyse the behaviour of the IOT function are called sensitivity analysis (SA). SA represents not only the final step in analysing the model behaviour, but can also be regarded as an essential step in the model building process itself since it provides the analytical tools which allow to simplify the model structure by identifying its nonrelevant parts.

More, SA can be defined as "the study of how uncertainty in the output of a model can be apportioned to different sources of uncertainty in the model input" (Saltelli et al., 2004). Such definition reflects the modeller's imperfect knowledge of the system, i.e., imperfect knowledge of the IOT function. By means of SA, the relative importance of the parameters in influencing the model output can be assessed. This also allows the modeller to identify possible interactions among the input factors and hence critical regions in the input factor space, with respect to the conditions of most sensitivity of the model output to some specific factors.

---

[6] See for instance Box et al. (1978), and Kleijnen and van Groenendaal (1992).

7.3.1 Settings for SA

There exist three main settings for SA, namely factor screening, local SA and global SA (Saltelli, 2000).

1. *Factor screening* aims to design experiments that identify the most influential factors in models characterised by a large number of inputs. Often, only a few input factors have a significant effect on the model output. Screening experiments can be used to rank the input factors in order of importance. The experiments are generally one-at-time (OAT) designs, which evaluate the main effect of changes in single factors (Daniel, 1973), as well as factorial experiments, which evaluate both the main effects and the impact of factor interactions.[7]

2. *Local SA* focuses on the impact of small variations in the input factors around a chosen nominal value (base point). It generally assumes linear input-output relationships and involves the evaluation of the partial derivatives of the output functions with respect to the input factors. The experiments are generally OAT designs.

3. *Global SA* involves the estimation of the factor probability density functions, investigates the role of their scale and shape and allows for the simultaneous variation of all factors over the whole factor space. The sensitivity is measured over the entire range of each input parameter. Global SA is particularly relevant for AB models as linear OAT sensitivities are ill-suited for nonlinear models characterised by high factor interaction and input uncertainty of various order of magnitude (Cukier et al., 1973).

7.3.2 Strategies for SA

Different SA strategies may be applied, depending on the setting. Moreover, given the manifold purposes of SA, a preliminary characterisation of its objectives is essential. In particular, of fundamental importance is the adoption of the most suitable measure of sensitivity depending on the desired definition of factor importance. In fact, each importance measure generally produces its own factor ranking. Most measures rely on variance decomposition formulas of the model output with respect to the input factors, since the variance is

---

[7] In particular, full factorial designs and fractional factorial designs are commonly adopted. A full factorial design is applied when the factors assume discrete values and considers all possible combinations of values across all factors, allowing the modeller to assess both the main effects and the impact of factor interactions. A fractional factorial design consists of a carefully chosen subset of the experimental runs of the corresponding full factorial design.

generally regarded as a proxy for uncertainty.[8] In choosing the appropriate sensitivity measure, a model-free approach should be followed, i.e., choosing a sensitivity measure which is independent of the model characteristics, such as linearity, monotonicity or additivity.

Saltelli et al. (2008) describe four basic strategies, together with some associated sensitivity measures, namely factor prioritisation, factor fixing, factor mapping, and metamodelling.

1. *Factor prioritisation* identifies the factor X_i as the most influential, causing on average, keeping its distribution fixed, the greatest reduction in the variance of the output Y. The associated sensitivity measure is the first-order sensitivity index S_i of X_i on Y, i.e., the average partial variance of Y conditional on the distribution of X_i. In formulas,

$$S_i = \left(V_{X_i}\left(E_{X_{-i}}\left(Y|X_i\right)\right)\right)/V(Y) \qquad (7.6)$$

   where X_{-i} indicates all factors but X_i. The numerator represents the variance, over all possible values of X_i, of the conditional expectation of Y taken over all factors but X_i. The denominator is the unconditional variance of Y.

2. *Factor fixing* aims o simplify the model by fixing the factors which do not appreciably affect the output in their range of variation. This has to be evaluated taking into account both the first-order effect S_i, which describes the direct effect of X_i on Y, and the higher-order effects, which describe the impact of the interactions between X_i and the other input factors. The sum of all-order effects due to X_i is called the total effect S_{Ti} and represents a suitable sensitivity measure in this setting. Considering the case of a three-factor model $Y = f(X)$, where $X = (X_1, X_2, X_3)$, the first-order effect of X_1 on Y is labeled S_1; the second-order effects of X_1 on Y are S_{12} and S_{13}, respectively representing the effect of the interactions between the couples of factors (X_1, X_2) and (X_1, X_3); finally, the third-order effect S_{123} measures the impact of the interaction among all terms. The total effect of X_1 on Y is given by $S_{T1} = S_1 + S_{12} + S_{13} + S_{123}$.

3. *Factor mapping* concerns the analysis of critical regions in the output distribution, such as threshold areas. It aims at identifying the factors producing realizations of Y into the critical range, rather than those driving the variance of the model output. A useful mapping method is the so-called Monte Carlo filtering (Rose et al., 1991), which provides Monte Carlo realizations of Y corresponding to different sampled points in the input

---

[8] Other measures can also be used, e.g., entropy (Saltelli et al., 2000).

factor space. Next, it filters the realisations into two subsets depending on whether or not they belong to the critical region. Then, statistical hypothesis testing is performed to check whether the two subsets represent samples from the same distribution. An input factor is identified as important if the distribution functions of the generated samples prove to be statistically different (Saltelli et al., 2004).

4. *Metamodelling*, or model approximation, aims at identifying an approximation of the IOT function, i.e., a simple relationship between the input factors and the model output that fits the original model well enough. This simplification is due to regularity assumptions that allow to infer the value of the output at untried points in the input space, based on information from nearby sampled points. Hence, a surrogate model is identified, which contains the subset of the input factors accounting for most of the output variability. Clearly, this approach generally misses relevant high-order interaction terms and fails in the case of heavily discontinuous mapping.

In particular, Gaussian process emulators are often used as surrogate models. Emulators are particular types of meta-models: more than just an approximation, they make fully probabilistic predictions of what the actual simulation model (the simulator) will produce (Santner et al., 2003; O'Hagan, 2006; Rasmussen and Williams, 2006). Differently from regression-based meta-models, emulators are non-parametric interpolators that pass through all the training points: if asked to predict the simulator output at one of the training data points, an emulator returns the observed output with certainty. Moreover, if asked to predict the simulator output at a point that has not been sampled (and that has consequently not being used to train the emulator), an emulator returns a distribution of possible outcomes, reflecting the uncertainty over the quality of the approximation. Gaussian process emulators model this uncertainty under the assumption of Gaussian errors. Figure 7.1 depicts a standard output of an emulator, where the uncertainty is reduced as more points in the parameter space are sampled.

This list of SA strategies is not exhaustive and other strategies can be defined, depending on both the specific objective of the SA and further considerations about the model under investigation, e.g., its computational burden, the number of input factors and their theoretical interactions, and other features such as linearity, monotonicity, additivity.[9]

---

[9] Also, many software products for SA exist; Chan et al. (2000) offer a brief review of some of them.

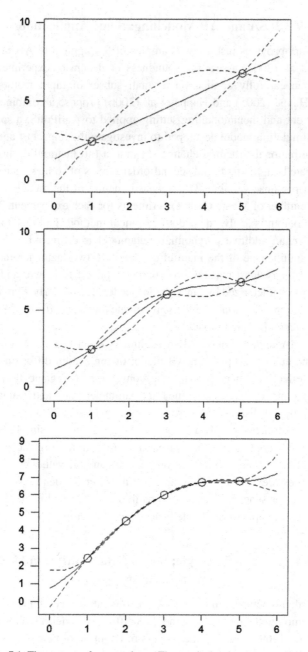

Figure 7.1 The output of an emulator. The vertical axis measures the model outcome y, the horizontal axis measures the model inputs, for instance, a parameter θ. Source: O'Hagan (2006).

7.3.3 SA and AB Modelling: Some Applications

The literature provides just a few examples of SA applied to AB modelling. Kleijnen et al. (2003) assess the soundness of design of experiments techniques when carefully applied on a small subset of input factors. As an example, Happe (2005) and Happe et al. (2006) propose a combined design of experiment and metamodelling setting applied to AgriPoliS, a spatial and dynamic simulation model developed to investigate the impact of agricultural policies on regional structural change. At first, a full factorial design is used to investigate both the first- and second-order effects of some selected factors on a target response variable. The stochastic nature of the model is faced by running a number of Monte Carlo experiments for each experiment. Then, the simulation output is analysed by both graphical methods and metamodelling. In particular, an additive polynomial metamodel is estimated to assess the statistical significance of the main effects and the two-factor interactions. A stepwise ordinary least squares procedure is applied to isolate and exclude those factors characterized by low significance levels. Similarly, Lynam (2002) adopts a fractional factorial design to investigate the mean effects of a selection of factors in a multi-agent model.

Another SA application to AB modeling is described in Deffuant et al. (2002). The authors propose an AB model of innovation diffusion to investigate the effects of incentives for the conversion to organic farming in a French department. They explore the huge parameter space and evaluate factor importance by a decision-tree approach (Breiman et al., 1984) on a composite error, which estimates the deviance between the real and the simulated data on the number of adopters and their proximity to the initial organic farmers. In particular, their SA algorithm selects the factors and the values corresponding to the smallest deviance by defining a learning set. It identifies the regions in the parameter space which are compatible with the real data. Hence, this represents an example of SA in the factor mapping setting.

7.3.4 A Simple Example: SA on a Bass Diffusion Model with Local Interaction

To gain further practical intuition in SA, we illustrate a very simple SA exercise based on a modified AB version of the Bass diffusion model. The classical Bass model (Bass, 1969) describes the process of adoption of new products by the interaction between actual and potential users. In particular, the probability of adoption for any potential user at time t depends on an innovation coefficient p, an imitation coefficient q and the cumulative distribution function of adoptions $F(t)$, i.e.,

$$Pr_t(adoption) = (f(t))/(1 - F(t)) = p + qF(t) \qquad (7.7)$$

where $f(t)$ is the probability density function of adoptions, and $p + q < 1$. The innovation coefficient p measures an external (advertising) effect, the imitation coefficient q represents the internal (word-of-mouth) effect and $F(t)$ can be interpreted as a global interaction term. In fact, this is an aggregated model describing diffusion dynamics in an homogeneous population in a fullyconnected network, where each individual is aware of and influenced by the adoption behaviour of the whole population. The model has an analytical solution,

$$f(t) = \frac{1 - e^{-(p+q)t}}{1 + \frac{q}{p}e^{-(p+q)t}} \qquad (7.8)$$

and captures the typical S-shaped adoption curve of many products. By reviewing the empirical work applying the Bass model to new products introduction, (Mahajan, Muller, Bass, 1995) find the average value of p and q to be 0.03 and 0.38, respectively, with p often less than 0.01 and q in the range $[0.3, 0.5]$.

In the original Bass model, every potential customer is linked to all the others by the function $F(t)$. Alternative formulations of the network structure yield different diffusion dynamics (Fibich and Gibori, 2010). In particular, we present the case of a small-world network characterised by an average number n of bidirectional connections per agent. Thus, the probability of adoption for the i-th potential user does not depend anymore on the global interaction term $F(t)$, but on a local interaction term $A_{i,t}$, defined as the share of individuals connected to agent i who have adopted, i.e.,

$$Pr_{i,t}(adoption) = p + qA_{i,t} \qquad (7.9)$$

The analysis of this model is particularly simple because its stochastic properties are immediate to check: the model is ergodic, with a deterministic absorbing equilibrium (everybody eventually adopts) which is achieved in finite time, given $p > 0$, irrespective of q and n. So, our interest lies in characterising how the three input parameters (p, q, n) affect the adjustment process to the equilibrium – i.e., the adoption dynamics.

The following SA exercise focuses on the effects of the parameters onto two output statistics Y: the cumulated curve of adoptions and the time of adoption of the 50th percentile of the population.

Figure 7.2 shows the sensitivity of the cumulated adoption curve at the variation of one parameter at a time around a reference parameter configuration – i.e., $p = 0.03, q = 0.4, n = 5$ on a population of 1,000 agents.

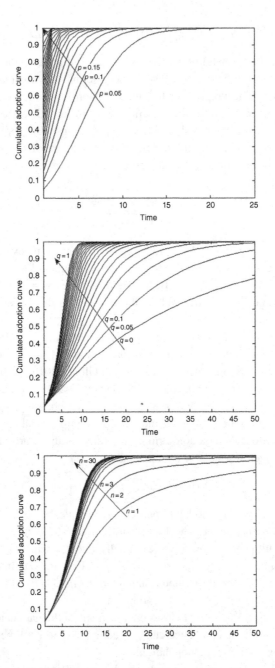

Figure 7.2 OAT analysis: average cumulated adoption curves over 50 runs, obtained by varying p in the range [0 : 0.5 : 1] (top panel), q in [0 : 0.5 : 1] (central panel), and n in [1 : 1 : 30] (bottom panel). Reference parameter configuration: $(pqn) = (0.030.45)$, 1,000 agents.

To get rid of random effects in the generation of the network, average results over 50 runs for every triple of parameters are reported. In particular, the top panel shows how adoption drastically speeds up when the effect of the external influence increases, for values of p sampled in the range $[0, 1]$ by increasing steps of 0.05; the middle panel illustrates how the adoption dynamics become more and more similar when the internal influence is higher, for values of q sampled in the range $[0, 1]$ by increasing steps of 0.05; finally, the bottom panel shows that the cumulated adoption curves are quite indistinguishable for an average number of connections per agent greater than 6, for integer values of n sampled in the range $[1, 30]$. Hence, n seems to have the weakest effect on the adoption dynamics of the population (for large n), while p somehow the strongest (for small p).

Similar results are obtained when analysing the OAT effect of the parameters on the average time of adoption of the 50th percentile over 50 runs. In fact, the bottom panel of Figure 7.3 shows a flat distribution for values of n greater than 6. Moreover, the impact on the adoption speed of high values of q is quite similar, while the 50th percentile adopts in no more than 2 periods for values of p greater than 0.2.

However, the results of an OAT analysis are local – i.e., they are generally strongly influenced by the chosen reference point – and give no information about the eventual impact of the interactions among inputs. In order to overcome this limitation, a global analysis is performed by evaluating a metamodel $Y = g(X)$ on artificial data generated by allowing all parameters to change. The metamodel imposes a relationship between the inputs X and the output Y with an arbitrary functional form g, which crucially includes interaction terms (Kleijnen and Sargent, 2000). As an example, we perform a multivariate analysis on 1,000 parameter configurations, obtained by random sampling the inputs from uniform distributions. In particular, p is sampled in the range $[0,0.2]$, q in $[0,0.8]$ and the integer n in $[1,30]$.

The preferred specification is an OLS regression of the average time of adoption of the 50th percentile on a third-order polynomial of the innovation coefficient, the imitation coefficient and the average number of connections per agent, plus the second-order interaction terms between p and q and between p and n (the remaining second-order and third-order interaction terms, qn and pqn, turn out to be nonsignificant at the 90% confidence level). Given that pq and pn are strongly significant (see Table 7.1), the OAT analysis confirms to have just local implications.

Moreover, this metamodelling exercise allows us to quantify and compare the impact of variations in the parameter values. Starting from our reference point ($p = 0.03$, $q = 0.4$, $n = 5$), a 20% increase in the value of p lowers the

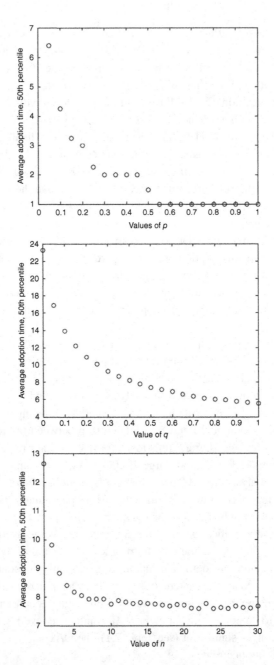

Figure 7.3 OAT analysis: average time of adoption of the 50th percentile over 50 runs, obtained by varying p in the range $[0 : 0.5 : 1]$ (top panel), q in $[0 : 0.5 : 1]$ (central panel), and n in $[1 : 1 : 30]$ (bottom panel). Reference parameter configuration: $(pqn) = (0.030.45)$, 1,000 agents.

Table 7.1 *Metamodelling: OLS regression on 1,000 different parameter configurations, obtained by random sampling from uniform distributions in the range p [0,0.2], q [0,0.8], n [1,30]. In order to get rid of random effects, the time of adoption of the 50th percentile is averaged over 50 runs. Adjusted R-squared = 0.84.*

Time_50	Coeff.	Std.Err.	
p	−417.18	11.25	***
p^2	2824.05	125.46	***
p^3	7264.88	410.95	***
q	−32.31	2.64	***
q^2	28.86	7.52	***
q^3	−14.66	6.19	
n	−0.41	0.08	***
n^2	−0.02	11.25	***
n^3	0.0003	0.0001	
pq	107.44	4.57	***
pn	0.92	0.12	***
cons	30.86	0.51	***

*** Significant at the 0.01%

average adoption time of the 50th percentile of about 11%; the same increase in n lowers the adoption time of about 2%, while a 20% increase in q causes a 8.7% variation in the output.

Furthermore, the exercise confirms a weak impact of variations in n when n is high – e.g., a 20% increase when $n = 20$ yields a 2.4% decrease in the average adoption time of the 50th percentile.

7.4 Conclusions

The discussion above should warn against the use of AB models as an 'easy' way of model building that simply allows to bypass the difficulties of deriving analytical results. Indeed, given the higher complexity of AB models (which precludes the derivation of analytical solutions), one has to expect a lot of work to understand their behaviour. To sum up, four stages are involved in the analysis of an AB model:

1. definition of the output variable(s) of interest, Y;
2. design of an appropriate experimental design, with the definition of the points in the parameter space to be explored;
3. analysis of the stationarity/ergodicity properties of the system at the chosen points;

4. sensitivity analysis of the output variables Y with respect to other variables of the model X and of the structural parameters θ.

These steps should not be necessarily undertaken in the order specified above as there may be feedbacks so that loops might become necessary; for instance, SA could be used to simplify the model structure (the model DGP), which in turn might affect the choice of the output variables Y and the design of the experiments. Similarly, finding that the system is non-ergodic might imply the need to reconsider the design of the experiments, with a higher attention to the effects of the initial conditions.

Unfortunately, such a complete analysis of the model behaviour is very rarely done in the literature. In particular, stationarity is often simply checked by visual inspection, ergodicity generally disregarded and sensitivity analysis at best implemented with a local OAT approach around a baseline configuration. True, global SA strategies with extensive testing for stationarity and ergodicity at every sampled point are very difficult to implement in large and complex models, computationally burdensome and characterised by many output variables. On the other hand, OAT designs around one central configuration (or a limited number of combinations) of the parameters are generally easier to understand, and reduce the need to test for ergodicity and stationarity, given the appropriate continuity assumptions: the tests can be performed at pre-specified intervals of the variable that is allowed to change, assuming that the results also hold for the other sampled values in between.[10]

These difficulties notwithstanding, the importance of proper formal analysis of AB models should not be downplayed, if the methodology has to gain full respectability among the scientific community. Jointly considered, the techniques reviewed here retain a fundamental role in building and analysing simulation models; they represent a compelling procedure in model development, providing tools that map the input factor space into the prediction space and back, as well as techniques to evaluate alternative model structures and the relative importance of each input factor.

---

[10] This can also be done with multi-dimensional designs; however, the identification of an adequate neighbourhood of the tested points in which the continuity assumption is supposed to hold becomes more complicated.

8

Empirical Validation of Agent-Based Models

Giorgio Fagiolo and Matteo Richiardi

8.1 Introduction

Generally speaking, validation involves a judgment over the quality of a model. How good is model A is? Is it better or worse than model B? A model can be good from a certain point of view and bad, or inadequate, from another one. Also, validation is not necessarily a 0–1 pass test: the criteria can be continuous.

The *validity* of a model can be defined as the degree of *homomorphism* between a certain system (the model) and another system that it purportedly represents (the real-world system).[1]

Model validation can be defined along different dimensions.

First of all, no model exists without an underlying theory. A first dimension of validation therefore is *concept validation*, i.e., the validation of the model relative to the theory: is the model consistent with the theory on which it is based? This is common to both analytical and computational models. The latter, however, need an additional level of validation (Stanislaw, 1986): *program validation*, i.e., the validation of the simulator (the code that simulates the model) relative to the model itself.

Second, models can be evaluated against real data. This is *empirical validation*. The aim of this chapter is to introduce the reader to the techniques of empirical validation of ABMs in economics. It requires (i) the choice of the relevant empirical indicators (so that the theoretical framework can be validated relative to its indicators) and (ii) the validation of the empirical true value relative to its indicator.

---

[1] See Vandierendonck (1975) and Bailey (1988). As the criterion for validity, homomorphism is more appropriate than isomorphism, because the goal of abstraction is to map an n-dimensional system onto an m-dimensional system, where $m < n$. If m and n were equal, the systems would be isomorphic.

Empirical validation is often the basis for *theory validation* – the validation of the theory relative to the simuland (the real-world system).[2]

Empirically validating an ABM means, broadly speaking, "taking the model to the data," in the form of empirical and/or experimental data, historical evidence or even anecdotal knowledge.[3]

Empirical validation may concern the model inputs and/or outputs. *Input validation* refers to the realism of the assumptions. There are two classes of inputs of an ABM. The first one consists of *structural assumptions* concerning the behavior of the agents or the pattern of their interactions. Examples include a particular bounded-rationality rule that we assume agents follow (e.g., a mark-up price-setting rule), or a peculiar type of network (for instance, a small-world) governing the interactions among agents.[4] Empirically validating the structural assumptions of an AB consists in using data to understand if these assumptions are in line with the behaviors and interactions of real-world agents populating the economy that we want to study (e.g., an industry or a market). Of course, the actual implementation of the model may differ according to the particular parameters that finetune the structural assumptions, e.g., the mark-up parameter or the clustering-path length ratio in a small-world network.

The second class of inputs consists of *parameters* and the *initial conditions* for all relevant micro and macro variables.

Output validation means checking whether the model generates plausible implications, that is whether the model delivers output data that resembles, in some way, real-world observations. Note that output validation is a joint test on the structure of the model and the values of the parameters. This explains why and how input and output validation are connected. Indeed, output validation can be used to refine the parameters of the model: this is called *calibration* or *Estimation*.[5] Estimation is an attempt to make the behavior of the model as

---

[2] This is not always the case. Philosophical theories for instance are often not testable in the data.

[3] A large literature has been developed on empirical validation of simulation models in other social sciences, computer science, engineering, etc. For an introduction, see Leigh Tesfatsion's web site on empirical validation at www.econ.iastate.edu/tesfatsi/empvalid.htm. For some examples of alternative empirical validation techniques in simulation models, see Klejinen (2000), Sargent (1998), and Barreteau (2003).

[4] These structural assumptions are more specific than the basic modeling choices – e.g., the type of agents that populate the model economy and the choices these agents have to make – which are the object of concept validation.

[5] In this chapter, we shall use the terms *calibration* and *Estimation* substantially as synonyms. There are however subtle and important differences in the two practices, as we will discuss in Chapter 9.

close as possible to the real behavior; output validation is a judgment on how far the two (still) are. A model where the parameters have not been properly estimated and are, for instance, simple guesses can of course be validated. However, by definition, its performance can only increase should the values of the parameters be replaced with their estimates.

This chapter mostly deals with output validation. Therefore, in what follows we shall use the term empirical validation as a shortcut to empirical validation of the outputs of an AB model, while referring specifically to input validation where appropriate.

8.2 The Methodological Basis of Empirical Validation

Models, in economics as in any other scientific discipline, isolate some features of an actual phenomenon in order to understand it and to predict its future status under novel conditions. These features are usually described in terms of causal relations and it is usually assumed that a causal (deterministic or stochastic) mechanism has generated the data that we observe in the real world.

We call this causal mechanism the real-world data-generating process (rwDGP). A model approximates portions of the rwDGP by means of a model data-generating process (mDGP). The mDGP must be simpler than the rwDGP and, in simulation models, generates a set of simulated outputs. The extent to which the mDGP is a good representation of the rwDGP is evaluated by comparing the simulated outputs of the mDGP, $\mathbf{M}$, with the real-world observations of the rwDGP, $\mathbf{R}$. In what follows, we call this procedure empirical validation.

Two remarks are in order at this point. First, $\mathbf{M}$ represents all the notional simulated outputs of the mDGP, that is those that the model can in principle generate by allowing for a full search of its parameter, initial condition, and seed spaces. Second, the main difficulty with empirical validation (and with modeling in general) is that the modeler wants to learn something about the rwDGP, but she can only observe $\mathbf{R}$, a limited number of draws (often just one) from rwDGP. The learning process has therefore to be, at this stage, inductive.

Marks (2007) formalizes the assessment of model validity as follows: a model is said to be *useful* if it can exhibit at least some of the observed historical patterns, *accurate* if it exhibits only behaviors that are compatible with those observed historically, and *complete* if it exhibits all the historically observed patterns. In particular, we can define completeness as $\mathbf{M} \cap \mathbf{R}$, and accuracy as $(\mathbf{M} - \mathbf{R})/\mathbf{M}$. Four cases are possible:

1. No intersection between **R** and **M** (**R** ∩ **M** = ⊘): the model is *useless*;
2. **M** is a subset of **R** (**M** ⊂ **R**): the model is fully accurate, but (to a certain extent) *incomplete*;
3. **R** is a subset of **M** (**R** ⊂ **M**): the model is fully complete, but (to a certain extent) *inaccurate* (or *redundant*, since the model might tell something about what could yet happen in the world);
4. **M** is equivalent to **R** (**M** ⇔ **R**): the model is fully *complete* and *accurate*.

Some key methodological issues are involved in the inductive process described above. We will discuss them in the following subsections.

8.2.1 Tractability vs. Accuracy

How can we possibly know all the different elements of the rwDGP? And even if we know them, how can we model all the different elements of the rwDGP? Serious doubts have been raised in the past (for instance by J. S. Mill and J. M. Keynes) about the possibility of building models that are fully complete and accurate. In a highly complex world, a fully complete and accurate model would be a one-to-one map of the world itself!

In order to cope with the complexity of the world, researchers proceed first by simplifying, i.e., focusing on the relationships between a very limited number of variables, and by selecting only the relevant historical behavior **R**. This process amounts to defining the criteria against which the model is to be evaluated, and leads to the identification of *stylized facts*, which are generally defined in stochastic terms. Thus, a model is eventually evaluated according to the extent to which it is able to statistically replicate the selected stylized facts. Second, scientists focus on some causal mechanisms of the rwDGP and mDGP alone, and abstract from certain entities that may have an impact on the phenomenon under examination (Mäki, 1992).

A series of open questions remains: How can we assess whether the mechanisms isolated by the model resemble those operating in the real world? In order to isolate such mechanisms, can we make assumptions that are contrary to fact, that is, assumptions that contradict our knowledge of the situation under discussion?

These dilemmas are strictly related to the *trade-off between analytical tractability and descriptive accuracy*. Indeed, the more complete and accurate are the assumptions, the higher the number of parameters in a model, the higher is the risk of failing to analytically solve the model (and derive sharp implications from our set of assumptions). By contrast, the more abstract and simplified the model, the more analytically tractable it is. The neoclassical paradigm comes down strongly on the side of analytical tractability. The AB modeling approach, on the other hand, is willing to trade-off analytical tractability with some degree of completeness and accuracy.

8.2.2 Instrumentalism vs. Realism

This brings us to the second core issue of empirical validation: *instrumentalism versus realism*. Realism, roughly speaking, claims that theoretical entities exist in reality, independent of the act of inquiry, representation, or measurement (Mäki, 1998). By contrast, instrumentalism maintains that theoretical entities are solely instruments for predictions and not true descriptions of the world. A radical instrumentalist is not much concerned with issues of empirical validation in the sense that she is not much interested in making the model resemble mechanisms operating in the world. The radical instrumentalist does not bother about input validation, by definition, and is only partially interested in output validation. Her sole goal is prediction. The ability of the model to replicate past behavior is valued only insofar as it suggests that it will continue to track the real data in the future. Indeed, a (consistent) instrumentalist is usually more willing than a realist to "play" with the assumptions and parameters of the model in order to get better predictions. Economists that have embraced the neoclassical paradigm have sometimes endorsed purely instrumentalist statements à la Friedman (1953).

8.2.3 Pluralism vs. Apriorism

The third issue is related to the choice of a *pluralist or apriorist methodology*. Methodological pluralism claims that the complexity of the subject under investigation and the limitations of our scientific representation naturally call for different levels of analysis, modeling approaches, and assumptions which may complement each other. Apriorism is a commitment to a set of *a priori* assumptions. A certain degree of commitment to a set of *a priori* assumptions is normal in science. Often these assumptions correspond to what Lakatos (1970) called the hard-core assumptions of a research program. But strong apriorism is the commitment to a set of *a priori* assumptions (possibly contrary to the facts) that are seldom exposed to empirical validation (for instance, general equilibrium and perfect rationality). Theory is considered prior to data and it is denied the possibility of interpreting the data without theoretical presuppositions. Typically, strong apriorist positions do not allow a model to be changed in the face of anomalies, and encourage the researcher to produce *ad hoc* adaptations whenever the theory in its original form is empirical refuted. Research programs in this stage of development have been labeled "degenerating" by Lakatos.

8.2.4 The Identification Problem

The fourth issue regards the *under-determination or identification problem*. In other words: What happens when different models are consistent with the same empirical data? The issue is known in the philosophy of science as the "under-determination of theory by data." In econometrics, the same idea has been formalized and labeled as "the problem of identification." As Haavelmo (1944) noted, it is impossible for statistical inference to decide between hypotheses that are observationally equivalent. He suggested to specify an econometric model in such a way that the problem of identification does not arise thanks to the restrictions derived from economic theory. The under-determination problem is also strictly connected to the so-called Duhem-Quine thesis: it is not possible to test and falsify a single hypothesis in isolation. This is because any hypothesis is inevitably tied to some auxiliary hypotheses. Auxiliary hypotheses typically include background knowledge, rules of inference, and experimental design that cannot be disentangled from the hypothesis we want to test. Thus, if a particular hypothesis is found to be in conflict with the evidence, we cannot reject the hypothesis with certainty, since we do not know if it is the hypothesis under test or one of the auxiliary hypotheses which is at odds with the evidence. Econometricians have adopted sophisticated tests which are robust to variations in the auxiliary hypotheses.[6] Nonetheless, the Duhem-Quine thesis still undermines strong apriorist methodologies that do not check the robustness of the empirical results under variations of background assumptions.

So far, we have discussed issues related to empirical validation that are common to all types of models in economics. Are there specific problems that AB modelers have to deal with in validating their models? To address this issue, we must recall from Chapter 2 some characteristics of AB models: (i) realistic assumptions about individual behavior, which often involve heterogeneity, nonlinearities, etc., (ii) non-trivial interaction among agents, (iii) interplay between the micro and the macro level, due to feedbacks between individual behavior and macro variables, and (iv) attention to the dynamic path of adjustment. Individually or collectively, these features call for a computational solution of the model. Unfortunately, they also make AB models potentially

---

[6]   See, for example, Leamer (1978).

difficult to interpret and validate. The higher the level of heterogeneity of the mDGP, the bigger the set of real-world data we need to meaningfully compare the simulated data with the observed data, as under-determination and equifinality arise: different micro structures can be consistent with the same aggregate data.

8.3 Input Validation of Agent-Based Models

Input validation of an ABM is a crucial step in model building, but so far no explicit and agreed-upon techniques have been proposed to perform such a task in a coherent way. Validating the inputs of an ABM, in a nutshell, consists of checking whether the building blocks of the model and its assumptions – concerning for instance agents' behaviors and interactions – are in line with the available evidence.

In principle, any practice that is aimed at ensuring that the fundamental conditions incorporated in the model reproduce aspects of the real system falls in the realm of input validation. For example, calibrating and estimating the parameters of the rules describing agent behaviors and interactions, as well as macroeconomic and model parameters, can be considered a way to make the model more realistic and thus validate it at the level of the inputs. However, parameter calibration and estimation can also be considered a way of validating the outputs of the model, as we will discuss in more detail. This is because performing parameter calibration or estimation often involves an assessment of how good the model performs in replicating the observed statistical regularities concerning the macro variables of interest.

Therefore, to make things simpler, we will not consider parameter calibration or estimation as an input validation technique here. What we are interested in, on the contrary, is input validation in terms of selecting assumptions about the rules of interactions and behaviors of the agents that are in line with what is observed in reality. As an example, consider a model where agents are firms that need to set the price of their output. Many different behavioral rules can be in principle considered. Neoclassical economics models would prescribe the use of a rule that comes from profit maximization, depending on the assumptions on market structure. Therefore, in standard models, the main constraint is a logic one, based on the consistency with a priori prescriptions (equilibrium, maximization, etc.). Conversely, in AB models the researcher has more flexibility in selecting behavioral rules. The main constraint is thus empirical: one should choose the rule that is closer to what the available evidence on behaviors and interactions suggests.

Note that this is (or should be) a very stringent requirement. Indeed, AB modelers often criticize standard theory because of its alleged unrealism. For instance, the building blocks of general equilibrium theory, ranging from full rationality, to the absence of direct interactions among agents and out-of-equilibrium behaviors, are known to be at odds with what empirical and experimental research suggests. This is in principle fully legitimate and in line with Friedman's instrumentalist approach, which states that assumptions are a free good: what counts is not their purported realism, which in principle is impossible to test, but their ability to successfully predict reality. In other terms, a totally unrealistic model could do its job if it is able to replicate the observed evidence. This position is harshly criticized by AB modelers, who instead maintain that good science cannot be done with wrong models. Only models that are based on assumptions close to reality should be able to reproduce it, and most of all, explain it. Indeed, suppose that one has a fully unrealistic model that is able to reproduce some stylized fact. What can we learn from it, e.g., in terms of the causal mechanisms that are behind the observed dynamics? As a result, AB models are often motivated because of their more realistic underpinnings, e.g., in terms of boundedlyrational behaviors, local direct interactions, adaptive expectations, and so on. But if AB models aim to become a strong alternative to mainstream ones, they should be grounded on behavioral assumptions that can be really more realistic – however defined – than those used in standard theory. Indeed, AB models are sometimes criticized from the neoclassical camp as being too sloppy and fragile in their behavioral assumptions, exactly along the same lines used by AB modelers in addressing the issues that plague standard models.

This leads to the foremost importance of performing a serious input validation of AB models. In absence of fully and widely accepted recipes for performing such a task, the researcher should strive to adopt assumptions about agent behaviors that are more in line with the empirical evidence than their neoclassical counterparts. But what does "more realistic assumption" really mean? Experimental evidence can give us a clue. By experiments we typically mean controlled laboratory experimentation with human subjects, with the aim of testing whether in reality humans behave according to some prescriptive behavioral rules, e.g., those suggested by the rationality paradigm. As discussed in more detail in Duffy (2006), experiments and ABM can have multiple complementarities, the most likely to be that ABM can be used to explain experimental results. Furthermore, once some stable behavioral pattern has been identified to be the norm in a certain simple environment (e.g., a prisoner dilemma game), robots programmed as artificial agents who behave according to such patterns can be employed in subsequent experiments, and play against human subjects.

However, a further and more important way in which experiments can complement AB modeling is to provide a basis for input validation. For example, perfectly rational outcomes are far from being the norm in experiments. Hence we can adopt behavioral assumptions which are inconsistent with perfect rationality and in line with what experimental evidence suggests. Experiments can also shed light on realistic interaction structures (who interacts with whom) and the functioning of organizations, markets, and institutions. Therefore, there exist two intertwined ways to have ABMs and experiments interacting (Heckbert, 2009). First, agent behaviors can be determined using the results of experiments, so as to create populations of simulated agents that behave consistently with the participants to the experiment. Second, experiments can help choose between possible sets of decision-making algorithms, whenever the modeler does not have any particular idea on which one should be preferred and does not want to introduce additional degrees of freedom in her/his model. Indeed, as argued in Duffy (2006), "[C]hoosing simple, parsimonious adaptive learning rules that also compare favorably with the behavior of human subjects in controlled laboratory settings would seem to be a highly reasonable selection criterion," which may also be a natural way to comply with a "keep-it-simple-stupid" (KISS) principle in model building, namely the suggestion not to over-parametrize the model.

As discussed in D'Orazio and Silvestri (2014), the practice to employ results from lab experiments as an input to ABM building is still in its infancy. Some notable examples include the work of Cars Hommes, Thomas Lux and coauthors (see, e.g., Hommes and Lux, 2013). Using lab experiments, they show that human subjects tend to display heterogeneous expectations when asked to forecast price dynamics. Using this piece of evidence, they build a number of ABMs when agents are endowed by heterogeneous expectations mimicking those exhibited by human subjects in the experiments, and show that their interactions can replicate much of the existing evidence on price dynamics at both micro and macro levels.

Another useful source of information in designing agents' behaviors and interactions are of course casestudies and empirical data collected at the micro level (studies on firms and consumption behaviors, etc.). Management science can often help the researcher to identify realistic routines as far as firms and entrepreneurial activity is concerned.

All these sources of information may be employed in building models where individual behaviors and interactions are – at the very least – more realistic than those usually assumed in standard models. This could help the researcher to understand to what extent the results of standard models depend on such over-simplifying assumptions.

8.4 Output Validation of Agent-Based Models

A number of ABMs mostly engage in purely qualitative theorizing, and are not empirically validated in any meaningful sense. In a sense they are *thought experiments*. There is little rationale in testing such models against existing empirical data. Notable examples are evolutionary game-theoretic models (Vega-Redondo, 1996), and Polya urn models (Arthur, 1988, 1994): only a weak relationship can be established between the micro-macro variables/ parameters of these models and their empirically observed counterparts. The focus of such models is the emergence of qualitative aggregate patterns, such as the emergence of coordination and cooperation. Forecasting exercises are possible, but they typically yield unpredictability. For example, we can state with certainty that users will lock into one of the competing technologies in Arthur's (1994) Polya urn model but it is impossible to know *ex ante* which of the competing technologies will be selected. Therefore models belonging to this class are not frequently taken to the data. Sometime, however, appropriate extensions/modifications of this model can be empirically tested. For example, the predictions of an appropriately modified Schelling segregation model can be matched with real-world segregation indicators. Similarly, the outputs of simple technological adoption models based on coordination games may be compared to existing data about market shares of competing technologies in a certain market.

Even when the model is suited for empirical validation, some basic issues arise.

A first issue concerns the quality of the empirical data: the most common reason for under-determination in economics is the incompleteness of the available data sets.[7] Sometimes a model is disregarded on the basis of existing empirical data, but other types of data could provide a better test and potentially support the model, if they had been collected. There is a strong conservative tendency in empirical validation to support established theories and models for which empirical data is readily available, while putting at a disadvantage new theories and models for which empirical research has not yet caught up

---

[7] The problem of data availability is made worse by the large degrees of freedom AB models often have. Two points are sufficient to identify a straight line; more data are needed to discriminate between alternative, nonlinear specifications.

and discouraging the study of qualitative phenomena that are either difficult to measure or are inherently nonmeasurable by their very nature.

Kaldor observed that, when hampered by a lack of large, high-quality data sets, we should use stylized facts or statistical regularities to evaluate models (Kaldor, 1961; Kwasnicki, 1998). By emphasizing the reproduction (explanation) or prediction of a set of stylized facts, one hopes to circumvent problems of data availability and reliability. However, in order for empirical validation to be effective, the stylized facts of interest should not be too stylized, or too general. Otherwise, they might not necessarily represent a difficult test for the model: the model might pass the validation procedure without providing any effective explanation of the phenomena of interest. This parallels Brock's (1999) discussion of "unconditional objects" (another aspect of the under-determination problem). Empirical regularities need to be handled with care because they often contain information only on the stationary (unconditional) properties of the process of interest. They often provide little information on the dynamics of the stochastic processes that actually generated them. In this respect, replication does not necessary imply explanation. For example, many evolutionary growth models can generate similar outputs on differential growthrates between countries, technology leadership, and catch-up, even though they differ significantly with respect to agents' behavior and learning schemes (Windrum, 2007). Similarly, the Nelson and Winter (1982) model replicates highly aggregated data on time paths for output (GDP), capital, labor inputs, and wages (labor share in output), but these facts can also be replicated by conventional neoclassical growth models. In the same vein, there might be many different stochastic processes (and therefore models of industry dynamics) that are able to generate, in the stationary state, a power-law distribution of firm size.[8]

Supposing the available real data are good enough, the first step in output validation is the selection of appropriate statistics as summary measures for both artificial and real data. Subsets of the parameter space are then identified where the statistics computed on artificial data (which depend on the values of the parameters) are close enough to those computed on the observed data.

Adopting the terminology introduced in Chapter 5, let Y_t be some aggregate statistics computed on the state of the simulated system, in a transient or absorbing equilibrium, say the unemployment rate. Assume that the mechanics of the model imply, for a given value of the parameters θ, a probability of

---

[8] One way out of the unconditional objects critique is to validate not only the macro-economic output of the model, but also its micro-economic structure. This however requires even greater data requirements.

being unemployed for any individual worker equal to $u(\boldsymbol{\theta})$. Given that being employed/unemployed is a Bernoulli random variable, its variance is equal to $\sigma_u^2 = u(\boldsymbol{\theta})(1 - u(\boldsymbol{\theta}))$.

By the properties of the sample mean (the central limit theorem), in large populations of size N the expected value of the unemployment rate at time t is normally distributed with mean $E_N(Y_t) = u$, and variance equal to $V_N(Y_t) = \frac{\sigma_u^2}{N}$. (In small samples, the unemployment rate follows a binomial distribution with mean u and variance σ_u^2.) In other words, given the stochastic elements of the model, the unemployment rate at time t is a random variable, with different realizations in different periods and in different simulation runs. If we want Y to be representative of the model output, so that we can use it as a summary measure for comparison with the real output, we must therefore choose N high enough. Alternatively, if the model is ergodic, we can use the average of the unemployment rate over M simulation runs, $\bar{Y}_M$, which is equivalent to using the unemployment rate of a single run with $M \cdot N$ agents.

In this simple case, focusing on the state of the system at one specific point in time t poses no problems, as the employment status shows no persistence, hence the unemployment rate bears no memory whatsoever of past values. More in general however, it could be the case that even if the system is at an absorbing equilibrium, the distribution of Y is not constant over time. Indeed, as we have seen in Chapter 5, (weak) stationarity is defined as the distribution of Y_t having a constant mean and variance, and an autocorrelation structure that depends only on the number of the lags and not on t. Hence, the unconditional mean is constant, but the mean of the distribution of Y at time t conditional on the past realizations $Y_{t-1}, Y_{t-2}, \cdots$ is not constant.[9] In this case, focusing on a specific period t might introduce an idiosyncrasy: to characterize the system then one has to compute an average over many periods, $\bar{Y}$, where the length of the observation period is determined in order to get rid of the autocorrelation structure in the statistics of interest. This turns out to be a crucial difference between calibration and estimation, as we shall see.

Once we have the summary measures for both the simulated (Y) and real (Y_R) output, we must compare them. The second step is therefore the definition of a *distance metric* $d(Y, Y_R)$. This is the loss function for the modeler, that is it contains the judgment about "how good" the model is. A common choice for this function is the quadratic form $d(Y, Y_R) = (Y - Y_R)^2$, which increasingly penalizes the performances of the model as they are more distant from the observed data. However, the summary measure chosen may well be

---

[9] In addition, given the definition of stationarity, moments other than the first and the second could be time variant.

multidimensional, that is $Y' = \{Y_1, Y_2, \cdots, Y_K\}$. In the example above, we might be interested in the average income, in the poverty rate, in the Gini coefficient of income, etc., in addition to the unemployment rate. The distance function must then specify appropriate *weights* for the different summary measures. A natural choice is to use weights that are inversely proportional to the variability of each statistics, so that more volatile statistics, being less informative on the model behavior, count less. Given that the variability of the statistics computed on the simulated data can be decreased at will, as we have seen above, the weights are generally computed on the real data.

The distance function then becomes

$$d(Y, Y_R) = (Y - Y_R)'W(Y - Y_R) \tag{8.1}$$

where W is best chosen to be a consistent estimate of $V(Y_R)^{-1}$, as in the White covariance matrix or, in a time series context, the appropriate Newey-West covariance matrix.

Recall that Y depends on θ. The distance d provides a measure of the quality of the model, conditional on the values of the parameters. However, unless some acceptance/refusal criteria are specified that explicitly define the biggest distance the modeler is willing to accept, it is of little use *per se*. But it immediately leads to the comparison of different models, or of different specifications of the same model. In this case, the question that the validation exercise is supposed to answer is not how good a model is, but rather is one model better or worse than another model. If we compare different instances of the model with different values of the parameters, this validation method offers a natural way for the selection of the best values of the parameters, that is calibration or estimation. This will be the focus of the next chapter, where we dig into details of the issue of how one can use data to tune the parameters of the model.

The issue concerning the ergodicity of the rwDGP (with respect to outcomes Y_t) is crucial. If the underlying rwDGP is non-ergodic (as well as the theoretical mDGP described in the ABM), initial conditions matter. In theory, to compare the real and simulated data the modeler should identify the true set of initial conditions in the empirical data, generated by the rwDGP, in order to correctly set the initial parameters of the model. Even if perfect data existed (which is unlikely), this would be a hard task, as few real processes have a clearly defined starting point. How far in the past does one need to go in order to identify the correct set of initial values for the relevant micro and macro variables? Possibly well before the data started to be collected.[10]

---

[10] One can still be interested in building a model that describes the particular history of the non ergodic rwDGP observable in the data.

But even when the mDGP and rwDGP are ergodic and stationary, the problem of correctly setting the time span for analyzing the simulated data remains. The underlying rwDGP may generate a number of different regimes (transient equilibria); for instance, the same macroeconomic structure may generate a diverse set of outcomes that include economic depression, full employment, inflation, hyper-inflation, and even stagflation. If this is the case, then one is faced with the problem of which sub-sample of the simulated and observed timeseries should be compared in order to carry out model validation. By incorrectly setting the period over which the model output is analyzed, one can generate a set of simulated output data that describes a different regime than that found in the empirical data. In this case, one may incorrectly reject a true model. Moreover, if – as it is frequently the case – the modeler sets the simulated data to start at a point where the model reaches a stationary behavior, one is implicitly assuming that the empirical evidence comes from a stationary DGP. This may, or may not, be the case.

As a final note of care, we should stress that if the model is to be used for prediction or policy analysis (that is, in most cases) empirical validation should not be confused with model acceptance. Is the model able to make good predictions out of sample? Does it take into consideration that changes in the economic environment (for instance, policy changes) might modify the way individuals behave? Real economic agents not only think in statistical terms based on past experience (adaptive expectations) but use current data to forecast the future. In this way, agents are able to respond to exogenous economic shocks. This intuition was the basis for the rational expectations critique of Keynesian behavioral models: exogenous shocks alter individual behavior, even when leaving the underlying structure of the economy unchanged. As a consequence, Keynesian theories seriously mis-predict the consequences of shocks, whereas models that explicitly take into consideration the micro fundamentals – individual production functions and utility functions – don't. The Lucas critique (Lucas, 1976) applies even to empirically validated models. Only structurally correct models should be given a structural interpretation. The fact that a model is able to replicate the observed data does not guarantee that it will perform well even when tracing future data or counterfactual data.

8.5 Qualitative Output Validation Technqiues

We now turn to the issue of choosing the value of the structural parameters in order to get a good fit with the real data. Here, output validation is not a goal, but a mean for the calibration/estimation of the parameters. As already noticed, what we would like to do here is compare (possibly an infinite number of) instances of the model with different parameter values and choose the one that best fits the data.

As we will be discussing in more detail in the next chapter, we almost never aim to calibrate or estimate a model by means of a unique optimal choice for all the parameters. We rather look for confidence intervals or ranges of the relevant parameters. Indeed, a point estimate or calibration of all parameters is useful for predictive purposes, though probabilistic assessments of likely outcomes based on estimates of the uncertainty about the "true value" of the parameters should be preferred. On the other hand, when the goal is more descriptive, we rather aim at identifying a reasonable (and relatively small) subset of the parameter space where counter-factual types of questions can be asked.

Furthermore, the fact that a given parameter set leads to the best fit does not mean that the model is empirically validated: it can be the case that even the best fit is not good enough, according to the criteria of acceptance for the model. In other words, even a wrong model can be calibrated/estimated.

One of the main purposes of calibration/estimation is to address the over-parametrization problem of many ABMs by reducing the space of possible worlds explored by an ABM (Kwasnicki, 1998). This is done through the use of empirical data, such that the model mDGP resembles as closely as possible the actual rwDGP that we observe.[11]

In the rest of this chapter, and in the one that follows, we review the most influential approaches to calibration and estimation developed in the AB literature so far and assess their strengths and weaknesses. Each approach attempts to put restrictions on the parameters so that the model output resembles the real output of interest as closely as possible. However, they do this in different ways.

A rough but useful distinction is between approaches that are mostly qualitative and those that instead rely on a battery of quantitative methods to estimate/calibrate the parameters. Whereas the former are based on observed qualitative similarities between real-world and model outputs, the latter try to identify the most-likely parameter ranges based on optimization techniques employing, e.g., explicit metrics between rwDGP and mDGP, as well as sophisticated search algorithms.

In the remaining part of this chapter we will briefly review some of the most-employed qualitative estimation/calibration techniques, whereas in the next chapter we will deal in details with quantitative approaches.

---

[11] For a notable example of calibration on ABMs, see Bianchi et al. (2007, 2008).

The history-friendly approach constrains parameters, interactions, and decision rules of the model in line with a specific, empirically observable history of a particular industry.

8.5.1 The Indirect Calibration Approach

Drawing upon a combination of stylized facts and empirical data sets, many AB modelers have been developing a pragmatic four-step approach to empirical validation, typically referred to as the *Indirect Calibration Approach*. This qualitative procedure can be interpreted as a calibration exercise with respect to unique historical evidence. The indirect calibration approach aims to replicate some relevant statistical regularities or stylized facts. In the first step, the modeler identifies a set of stylized facts that she is interested in reproducing and/or explaining with her model. Stylized facts typically concern the macro-level (as an example, the relationship between unemployment rate and GDP growth) but can also concern cross-sectional regularities (for instance, the shape of the distribution of firm size). In the second step, the researcher builds the model in a way that keeps the microeconomic description as close as possible to empirical and experimental evidence about microeconomic behavior and interactions. This step entails gathering all possible evidence about the underlying principles that inform real-world behaviors (of firms, workers, consumers, etc.) so that the microeconomic level is modeled in a realistic fashion. In the third step, the empirical evidence on stylized facts is used to restrict the space of parameters, and the initial conditions if the model turns out to be non-ergodic.

Suppose, for example, that the Beveridge curve is one of the statistical regularities to be investigated. The model must be able to replicate a relationship in which unemployment rates decrease with vacancy rates in the labor market.[12] The researcher should restrict her analysis to all (and only) parameter combinations under which the model does not reject that hypothesis (at some confidence level). This step is the most sensible because it involves a fine sampling of the parameter space. It is also computationally demanding and requires the use of Monte Carlo techniques. Indeed, for any given point in the parameter space, one must generate a distribution for the statistics summarizing the stylized facts of interest (for instance, the slope of the relationship between unemployment and vacancy rate), and test the null hypothesis that the empirically observed valued can be generated by our model under that particular parameter combination.

---

[12] See Fagiolo et al. (2004b) and Richiardi (2006).

In the fourth and final step, the researcher should deepen her understanding of the causal mechanisms that underlie the stylized facts and/or explore the emergence of new stylized facts (statistical regularities that are different to the stylized facts of interest) which the model can validate *ex post*. This might be done by further investigating the subspace of parameters that resist to the third step, those consistent with the stylized facts of interest. For example, one might study how the absolute value of the Monte Carlo average of the slope of the unemployment-vacancy rate relation varies with some macro-parameter (if any) that governs wage setting and/or union power in the model. This can shed light on the causal mechanism underlying the emergence of a Beveridge curve. Similarly, one can ask whether business cycle properties (for instance, average and volatility of growth rates) change with the slope of the Beveridge relation. If this is the case, a fresh implication generated by the model (under empirically plausible parameters) can be taken to the data – and further provide support for the AB model under scrutiny.

Although appealing, the indirect calibration approach is open to criticism in at least two important respects. First, notice that no attempt is made to quantitatively set model parameters using their empirical counterparts. This is mostly because, due to the difficulties of qualitatively matching theoretical and empirical observations, one is bounded to be as agnostic as possible as to whether the details of a model (variables, parameters) can be really compared with empirically observable ones. However, in order for this indirect, qualitative, calibration procedure to be effective, the empirical phenomena of interest should not be very general. Otherwise, they might not necessarily represent a difficult test for the model. If this is the case, the model might pass the validation procedure without providing any effective explanation of the phenomena of interest (e.g., no restrictions on the parameter space would be made). Here the fundamental issue of discriminating between the descriptions and explanations of reality pops up once more.

The second problem is far subtler, and has to do with the interpretation of the points belonging to the sub-region of the parameter space (and initial conditions) that resist the sort-of exercise in plausibility that one performs in the third step of the procedure. After a suitable sub-region of the parameter space (and initial conditions) has been singled out – according to the capability of the model to replicate the set of stylized facts of interests in that sub-region – how should one interpret all comparative exercises that aim at understanding what happens when one tunes the parameters within that sub-region? This boils down to the problem of interpreting the different parameter configurations as counterfactuals.

A stream of recent ABM contributions to the fields of industry and market-dynamics has been strongly rooted in the four-step empirical validation procedure just outlined. For example, Fagiolo and Dosi (2003b) study an evolutionary growth model that is able to reproduce many stylized facts about output dynamics, such as I(1) patterns of GNP growth, growth-rates autocorrelation structure, and the absence of size-effects, while explaining the emergence of self-sustaining growth as the solution of the trade-off between exploitation of existing resources and exploration of new ones. Similarly, in a number of papers exploring the properties of the "Keynes meets Schumpeter" (K+S) model (Dosi et al., 2006, 2010, 2015), an indirect calibration approach is used to show that the KS model is able to successfully replicate a huge number of stylized facts related to firm dynamics, the business cycle, and the financial side of the economy.

8.5.2 The History-Friendly Approach

The history-friendly approach offers an alternative to the problem of over-parametrization. Like the indirect calibration approach discussed above, it seeks to bring modeling more closely in line with the empirical evidence and thereby reduce the dimensionality of a model. The key difference is that this approach uses the specific historical case study of an industry to model parameters, agent interactions, and agent decision rules. In effect, it is a calibration approach which uses particular historical traces in order to calibrate a model.

In this approach a good model is one that can generate multiple stylized facts observed in an industry. The approach has been developed in a series of papers, in particular Malerba et al. (1999) and Malerba and Orsenigo (2002). In the first of these papers, the authors outlined the approach and then applied it to a discussion of the transition in the computer industry from mainframes to desktop PCs. In the latter, the approach was applied to the pharmaceutical industry and the role of biotech firms therein. Here we shall keep the description of the approach succinct. Through the construction of industry-based AB models, detailed empirical data on an industry informs the researcher in model building, analysis, and validation. Models are to be built upon a range of available data, from detailed empirical studies to anecdotal evidence to histories written about the industry under study. This range of data is used to assist model building and validation. It should guide the specification of agents (their behavior, decision rules, and interactions), and the environment in which they operate. The data should also assist the identification of initial conditions and parameters on key variables likely to generate the observed history. Finally, the data is to be used to empirically validate the model by comparing its output (the simulated trace history) with the actual history of the industry. It is this latter step that truly distinguishes the history-friendly approach from other approaches. Previous researchers have used historical case studies to guide the specification of agents and environment, and to identify possible key parameters. The authors of the history-friendly approach suggest that, through a process of backward induction, one can arrive at a satisfactory approximation of structural assumptions, parameter settings, and initial conditions. Having identified the approximated set of history-replicating parameters, one can carry on and conduct sensitivity analysis to establish whether (in the words of the proponents of this methodology) history divergent results are possible.

The history-friendly approach raises a set of fundamental methodological issues.[13] First, the approach to empirical validation that is advocated involves comparing the output traces of a simulated model with detailed empirical studies of the actual trace history of an economic system. This does not move us much further on from ascertaining whether a model is capable of generating an output trace that resembles an empirically observed trace. It is not a very strong test. As we have seen, an individual simulated trace may, or may not, be typical of the model.

A second issue is the ability to infer backward the "correct" set of structural assumptions, parameter settings, or initial conditions from a set of traces – even if we have a model that generates an appropriate distribution of output traces. Simply stated, there are, in principle, a great many combinations of alternative parameter settings that can produce an identical output trace. We cannot deduce which combination of parameter settings is correct, let alone the appropriate set of structural assumptions.

A third issue is the possibility to build counterfactual histories (although the authors do not themselves engage in this in their papers). For example, we need to be able to construct a world in which IBM did not enter the PC market. This poses a very serious question. Could the PC market have developed in much the same way had IBM not invented the PC? Can we meaningfully construct a counterfactual history? As Cowan and Foray (2002) discuss, it is exceedingly difficult in practice to construct counterfactual histories because economic systems are stochastic, non-ergodic, and structurally evolve over time.

Finally, a fourth key methodological issue concerns the meaning of history. To what extent can we actually rely on history to be the final arbiter of

---

[13] Interested readers are referred to Windrum (2007) for a detailed critique of history-friendly modeling.

theoretical and modeling debates? To pose the question another way, can simulations, in principle, be guided by history? In practice, it is unlikely that we will be able to appeal to history, either to bear witness, or to act as a final arbiter in a dispute. This is because history itself is neither simple nor uncontested, and any attempt to develop a historically based approach to modeling faces deep level methodological problems.[14]

[14] A well-known example of the contestability of history is evidenced by the ongoing debate about whether inferior quality variants can win standards battles (Liebowitz and Margolis, 1990; Arthur, 1988). As Carr (1961) observed in his classic work, history can be contestable at more fundamental and unavoidable levels.

9

Estimation of Agent-Based Models

Matteo Richiardi

'How absurdly simple!' I cried.

'Quite so!' said he, a little nettled.

'Every problem becomes very childish when once it is explained to you.'

Arthur Conan Doyle. *The Adventure of the Dancing Men.*

9.1 Introduction

The ultimate test of a theory is its empirical validity, so the question whether a model 'fits the data well' is crucial. In the last chapter, we introduced some of the many issues involved in model evaluation. Here, we dig into the problem of tuning the values of the parameters. Moreover, we are also interested in the values of the estimated parameters for interpreting the model behaviour and to perform what-if type counterfactual (e.g., policy) evaluation exercises. Agent-based (AB) models are in general complex non-linear models, and can therefore display many different behaviours depending on the region of the parameter space being sampled. Assessing the performances of the model in the right region of the parameter space is therefore important for model evaluation. Once this region has been identified and the model deemed appropriate for its scopes, lessons can be learned about what might happen in the real world if some of the parameters changed, either as a consequence of some unforeseen developments (*scenario analysis*) or due to some specific actions purposefully implemented (*policy analysis*).

Our goal, broadly speaking, is comparing (possibly an infinite number of) instances of the model with different parameter values and select those that fits the data better.

Before going on, a first remark is necessary. Generally, we do not aim at calibrating or estimating a model by getting to a single optimal choice for all the parameters. In a frequentist approach, we rather look at confidence intervals – that is, ranges where the 'true' value of the parameters, assuming the model is correctly specified, is likely to lie – while in a Bayesian approach we focus on the posterior probability distributions for the parameters – reflecting our uncertainty about the parameters values given our prior knowledge and the information contained in the data. In this chapter we will provide examples of both approaches.

A second remark is about the fact that it is always possible to find some parameter set leading to the best fit with the real data, but this does not mean that the model is empirically validated: it can be that even the best fit is not good enough, according to the criteria of acceptance for the model. In other words, even a wrong model can be calibrated/estimated.

Third, there is the issue of the invariance of parameters. What if the observed micro and macro parameters are time dependent? One needs to be sure that the calibrated/estimated parameters are at least slow changing variables (and, hence, can reasonably be treated as fixed within the time scale explored by the model). If they are significantly time dependent, then the researcher needs to go back to the specification of the model and endogenise some of the parameters or, if he prefers to remain agnostic about how they change, employ appropriate inference techniques which allow time-varying parameters, as particle filters (not discussed here).

A fourth remark concerns the difference between calibration and estimation. This has been overly debated, with researchers arguing that calibration (to which different people give a different meaning) is something different from estimation, while others stress that the two things are basically the same thing.[1] The issue boils down to a matter of convenience. For our discussion, it is helpful to distinguish calibration and estimation along the following lines: *calibration* aims at maximising the fitness of the model with the observed data in a distance metric arbitrarily chosen by the modeller, without bothering about the 'true' value of the parameters of the real world data generating process (rwDGP), or the uncertainty surrounding them; *estimation* aims at learning about the 'true' value of the parameters of the rwDGP by evaluating the fitness of the model with the observed data in a carefully chosen distance metric, such that the estimator has well known (at least asymptotically) properties. Roughly speaking, maximisation of the fitness is a goal in calibration, a mean in estimation. Calibration is meant to show that the model is *plausible* – that

---

[1] See Dawkins et al. (2001) for an overview.

is, it resembles the real world – and aims at reducing the number of possible worlds, one for each combination of the parameters, that have to be explored in order to understand the behaviour of the system; estimation assumes that the model is at least approximately *correct* – that is, well specified – to make inference about the true rwDGP.

While some calibration techniques have been presented in the previous chapter, here we focus only on estimation.

The rest of the chapter is organised as follows: Section 9.2 discusses how we can choose the real and simulated data on which we perform estimation, and the basic principles and properties of the data and the model that estimation relies upon. Section 9.3 describes how AB models can be simulated by means of simulated minimum distance techniques, in a frequentist approach. Section 9.4 introduces the main issues and techniques in Bayesian estimation of AB models. Section 9.5 concludes.

9.2 Taking the Model to the Data

9.2.1 Comparing Apples with Apples

This section is of crucial importance, but it can be kept very short. Let's assume that our model is a good description of the unknown rwDGP, for the specific purposes that we have in mind: that is, the model has passed a preliminary validation stage (see Chapter 8). The behaviour of the model, however, is dependent on the values of the parameters and on the initial conditions, which amount to the initial state of the system and the random seed: $y_{t+1} = g_t(X_0, s, \theta)$. Estimation is all about comparing the artificial data produced by the model with the real data, but the model is in principle able to produce much more data than what is available in the observations. So, a preliminary choice has to be made with respect to what data to select from the simulated time series.

If we could run the model starting from the same initial conditions X_0 as observed in the real data, we could simply compare the first T simulated periods with the corresponding real-world observations. However, it is often very difficult to initialise the model with real-world data, especially as these can be available only in aggregate form. Therefore, a direct, one-to-one relationship between the artificial data and the real data is lost: there is not a simulated day $t = 16$ September 2015 to be compared with the actual data for 16 September 2015. The best we can do is therefore select subsamples of the artificial time series that *qualitatively* resemble the real series, and then look at the values of the parameters that make the two series also *quantitatively* similar. This is often reduced to focusing on some stationarity properties of the observed data, and selecting the simulation output so that those stationarity properties also hold in the artificial data. Loosely speaking, this ensures that the data for 16 September 2015 are not particularly special – they look not too different from the data for 15 or 17 September – so that they can be meaningfully matched to the selected artificial data, provided these are also not too special. In other words, the initialisation problem can be overcome by focusing on the *equilibrium properties* of both the real and the simulated data, whereby equilibrium we mean statistical equilibrium, that is stationarity. Focusing on stationary regimes has also an additional advantage. Stationary data are, to some extent, interchangeable. It does not really matter if September 15 is considered before or after September 17, if they both come from a stationary distribution.[2] This means that we can easily summarise them, for instance by taking their mean (on the contrary, two non-stationary series might have the same mean, but very different behaviour – for instance, one might trend upwards, while the other might trend downwards).

Ergodicity (or lack thereof) is also an important property which should be considered before turning to the data. In particular, mistakenly considering a model as ergodic, when in fact it is not, might lead to a significant underestimation of the uncertainty surrounding the estimates. As an example, think of a non-ergodic model with a long run equilibrium at $\mu^* = r\theta$, where r is a random variable with mean 1, whose actual value is determined at model setup – that is, by the random seed. At the risk of being redundant, let us make clear what this means. The model produces an outcome y_t, that after an adjustment phase becomes stationary with mean μ^*. Note that in the stationary state, y_t keeps fluctuating around μ^* (with a correlation structure that depends only on the number of lags and not on time). The model is non-ergodic insofar as the mean μ^* differs across simulation runs, for the same value of θ. Suppose now that the model is correctly specified, and that the specific universe that we observe has a value of $r \neq 1$. If we ignore the non-ergodic nature of the model when estimating it, we would infer that $\hat{\theta} = \mu_R$, while in facts the true value of θ is μ_R/r.[3] While the rwDGP can generate many parallel universes distributed around a central universe with $\mu^* = \mu_R/r$, we are treating it as if it were capable to produce only one universe, centred at μ_R. Given that we only observe μ_R, we cannot remove a bias towards this particular value, but

---

[2] Stationary data can be serially correlated, but this can often be neglected in estimation, at the cost of increasing the error of the estimates – see next section.

[3] We assume for simplicity that the observed time series is long enough to drive the sampling error to 0 (the mean μ_R is insensitive to new observations).

we should at least recognise that the true value of θ could be different from μ_R, knowing that the model is non-ergodic.[4] Devising a policy based on a precise but biased estimate of θ might lead to inaccurate predictions. On the contrary, taking fully into account the non-ergodic nature of the model helps recognise that there is an extra source of uncertainty on top of sampling error, arising from the fact that we do not know from what universe the data we are observing come from. Moreover, by simulating the effects of the policy and taking into account the full uncertainty around the parameters, we might discover that the policy is able to move permanently the system to a different equilibrium, which persists even when the initial conditions are restored (i.e., the policy is abandoned). To summarise, non-ergodic models are trees which are able to produce a whole variety of apples, and we should expect many different trees (instances of the model with different values of the parameters) to produce something that closely resembles the specific apple that we observe in the data.

9.2.2 Preliminary Tests

Operationally, the discussion of the previous section amounts to say that we need to understand the properties of a model *and* the properties of the data before engaging in estimation. Stationarity can be easily tested in the observed data, using one of the many tests available in the literature. If the data are not stationary, an attempt to make them stationary by looking at appropriate transformations should be made. Stationarity greatly simplifies the choice of the artificial data to be considered as the model outcome in the estimation process, as we can run the model until an appropriate stationary state (statistical equilibrium) is found, and then disregard the initial adjustment path. On the other hand, if the observations are not stationary, we often do not know when to stop the simulation, as the model might in principle be able to produce something that resembles the observations in the future.

Ergodicity, on the contrary, cannot in general be tested in the real data, unless we observe many instances of the process. For instance, consider the diffusion of rival technologies with strong network externalities. By observing many adoption trajectories for different products, we can infer whether they always lead to the selection of one dominant technology, which drives the others out of the market. The irreversibility of the process, together with its

---

[4] Indeed, we can do better than this, and estimate a distribution for the parameter, though this distribution will be centred on μ_R and not on μ_R/r. We will discuss this in more detail in Section 9.3.2.

stochastic nature, implies non-ergodicity: each technology has in principle some chances of winning the race, so that outcomes can be very different even if the initial conditions are the same.

A classic example is the battle between Sony's Betamax and JVC's VHF video standards that started in the mid-1970s. For around a decade these two standards battled for dominance, while in the end VHF became dominant, and Betamax disappeared. Presumably, the process is non-ergodic, meaning that if we could rewind history and repeat the competition again starting from exactly the same conditions, we might end up with a very different outcome, e.g., Betamax winning, or both standards coexisting in the market.[5]

Note again that the non-ergodic nature of the process lies in the fact that it has more than one long-run equilibrium (which presupposes that the process is stochastic, to allow the selection of different long-run equilibria).

Quite obviously then, the possibility of learning about the non-ergodic nature of the process depends on our ability to observe more than one realisation of the process. If we observe only one equilibrium, we cannot learn about the existence of other equilibria. In turn, observing more realisations requires considering more technologies, under the assumption that they are all governed by the same law (that is, they are all instances of the same stochastic process). This might actually be a problematic assumption. Can we claim that the battle for internet search engines follows the same process as the VHF-Betamax war? Google has come close to dominating the market, with about 2/3 of all searches, but Bing has climbed up to a 10% despite being a latecomer, and Yahoo! still has another 10% market share. It can be argued that network externalities are lower for search engines than for video formats: it is therefore possible that the process for search engines is ergodic, while the one for video formats was not.[6] But what about operating systems (OS)? Under the assumption that the diffusion of video formats and OS (and possibly of many more technologies) are instances of the same process, and that the initial

---

[5] The reason why VHF won the war has been the subject to intense debate. Arguably, Betamax was a slightly better technology; however, VHF had a slicker marketing. Other explanations have pointed to licensing problems between Sony and other companies, VHF machines being simpler, Sony giving inadvertently a help to its competitors by revealing key aspects of Betamax technology which were then incorporated into VHS, and even the fact that pornography was not available on Betamax. Perfectly 'explaining' why VHF won would reduce the adoption process to a deterministic one; following our discussion, it would be similar to controlling for the random seed. The whole issue of determining whether the process is ergodic or not would then be pointless, as deterministic processes are ergodic by nature.

[6] We should stress that the fact that there is not a single search engine that has eaten up all the market does not mean by itself that the process is ergodic: it might be the case that if history was given a second chance, given the same initial conditions, Yahoo! might end up having a bigger market share than Google.

conditions are approximately the same (e.g., all alternatives appear at the same time, and no one is drastically better than the other in terms of performances or costs), we could test for ergodicity by comparing the equilibrium market shares in the different markets.[7] For OS, the market is dominated by Microsoft, but Mac has a fairly stable share (over the past few years) of about 10%. We would then find that the (unique) diffusion process is non-ergodic, as in the video formats case there is only one firm who gets all the market, while in the OS there is a coexistence of many firms.

The lesson from this discussion is that it is very hard to test for ergodicity in the real data, as history never exactly repeats itself. The assumption that two observed trajectories are instances of the same underlying process, and that the initial conditions are the same, is likely not to hold. On the other hand, ergodicity can easily be tested in the simulated data, as multiple simulation runs can be performed by keeping all the parameters and initial conditions fixed and changing only the random seed. If we had a model of product adoption in the presence of network externalities, we could test it for ergodicity, for the appropriate initial conditions (e.g., the different technological features and costs of rival video formats), and reasonable values of the unknown parameters (e.g., users' preferences). If the results of the test were pointing to ergodicity, we could then fix a random seed and proceed with estimation. If, on the other hand, non-ergodicity was detected, we should take this information into consideration in the estimation process, as discussed in Sections 9.3.2 and 9.4.4.

9.2.3 Simulation-Based Estimation

In AB modelling everything, from solving a model to estimating it, must be done numerically. However, AB models generally involve many parameters and non-linearities, and this implies that the computational methods that need to be used are often particularly burdensome. As LeBaron and Tesfatsion (2008, p. 249) put it, 'the very properties that make ACE [Agent-based Computational Economics] models so interesting to study can cause empirical headaches when estimating them'. This has so far deterred estimation, and harmed the diffusion of the methodology. Fortunately, the development of computational techniques and the increasing availability of computer power have made the problem more manageable.

---

[7] A nonparametric test for ergodicity is proposed in Grazzini (2012), and rests on an application of the Wald-Wolfowitz Runs test for testing whether two samples come from the same population.

The diffusion of simulation-based techniques is rather a recent trend in econometrics, but it is rooted in a long history of developments of computational methods.[8] Three periods can be identified in this process. During the first period, before the 1960s, models and estimation methods were assumed to lead to analytical expressions for the estimators. The techniques employed made use of linear models with associated least-square approach, multivariate linear simultaneous equations with associate instrumental variables approach, exponential families for which maximum likelihood techniques are suitable.

In the second period, during the 1970s and 1980s, numerical optimization algorithms were introduced to derive the estimates and their precision without knowing the analytical form of the estimators. Among the techniques employed were nonlinear models as limited dependent variable models, duration models, ARCH, GARCH, etc., with optimization of some non-quadratic criterion functions (log likelihood, pseudo-log likelihood, etc.). These different approaches, however, still require a tractable form of the criterion function.

Simulation-based methods were introduced only in the third period, dating back to the 1990s, to deal with criterion functions without simple analytical expression (for instance, because of integrals of large dimensions in the probability density function or in the moments).

The basic idea with simulation-based econometrics is to replace the evaluation of analytical expressions about theoretical (model) quantities with their numerical counterparts computed on the simulated data. The (simulated) theoretical quantities, which are functions of the parameters to be estimated, can then be compared with those computed on the real (observed) data as in any estimation procedure. If the model is correctly specified – and some technical conditions hold – for large samples, the observed quantities tend to the theoretical quantities, at the 'true' values of the parameters. Because the simulated quantities also tend to the theoretical quantities, the observed quantities converge to the simulated quantities.

As for econometrics in general, two families of approaches can then be followed. In a frequentist approach, we look at the values of the parameters that minimize the distance between the simulated and the observed quantities. The procedure is known in general as *simulated minimum distance* (SMD). The method of simulated moments (MSM), indirect inference (II) and simulated maximum likelihood (SML), among other techniques, all fall in this general class. The task of comparing real and artificial data involves the computation of some statistics y both in the real and in the artificial data, and then aggregated in a unique measure of distance. Clearly, these statistics have to be computed

---

[8]   See Gouriéroux and Monfort (1996) and Stern (1997, 2000).

just once in the real data (which do not change), and once every iteration until convergence in the artificial data, which depend on the value of the structural parameters. The change in the value of the parameters of each iteration is determined according to some optimisation algorithm, with the aim to minimise the distance.[9]

The other approach is Bayesian. In Bayesian analysis, one starts with a prior knowledge (sometimes imprecise) expressed as a distribution on the parameter space and updates this knowledge according to the posterior distribution given the data. Classical Bayesians still believe in an unknown 'true' model, as in the frequentist approach. However, rather than aiming at identifying the 'true' values of the parameters (or a corresponding confidence interval), they use the information contained in the data to update the subjective beliefs about them. On the other hand, subjective Bayesians do not believe in such true models and think only in terms of the predictive distribution of a future observation.

For frequentists (and classical Bayesians), parameters are assumed to be fixed (at least within a group or condition) and inference is based on the sample space of hypothetical outcomes that might be observed by replicating the experiment many times. For subjective Bayesians, on the other hand, parameters are treated as random quantities, along with the data, and inference is based on posterior distributions.

9.2.4 Consistency

An important feature that is sought after when choosing an estimation method is *consistency*. This property states that as the sample size increases indefinitely, the estimates converge in probability to the true value of the parameters, assuming the model is correctly specified: the distribution of the estimates becomes more and more concentrated, so that the probability of the estimator being arbitrarily close to the true value converges to one. From a classical Bayesian perspective, consistency means that the updated knowledge becomes more and more accurate and precise as data are collected indefinitely.[10]

As such, consistency can be evaluated with respect to different dimensions: *consistency in size* means that the estimates converge to their true value as

---

[9] Minimisation requires that the same series of random draws is used for each iteration of the simulated model, in order to insulate from the stochastic component of the model. Lacking this, the minimisation algorithm might well get stuck in cycles. Many optimization algorithms can be used, from simple grid search to genetic algorithms, etc. – see Nocedal and Wright (1999) for an excellent reference book on the topic.

[10] Consistency is important to subjective Bayesians, too, for whom it is equivalent to *intersubjective agreement*, meaning that two Bayesian should ultimately have very close predictive distributions, as the number of observations grows indefinitely.

the observed population grows bigger; *consistency in time* means that the estimates converge to their true value as the length of the observation period increases; *consistency in replications* means that the estimates converge to their true value as more occurrences of the same stochastic process are observed. With reference to an abstract observations space, consistency in size (cross-sectional) refers to the height, consistency in time (longitudinal) refers to the length, consistency in replications refers to the width.

In order to obtain consistency, some conditions have to be met.[11] Without providing all the details, the basic requirements are (i) that the statistics used *identify* the parameters of interest (that is, there is a one-to-one relationship between the theoretical values of the statistics and the values of the parameters) and (ii) that the simulated values of the statistics *converge* to their theoretical values.

9.2.5 Calibration vs. Estimation

As we have seen, taking a model to the data is always done in terms of some *summary statistics* which are computed in the data and obtained from the model, be they some specific data points, cross-sectional averages, longitudinal averages, estimated coefficients of some meta-model which is superimposed both to the real data and to the simulated data. These statistics are fixed in the data, and are possibly dependent on the structural parameters, the initial conditions and the random seed in the model.

The constraints placed on the statistics used for bringing the model to the data is what distinguish estimation for calibration. When doing estimation, we are concerned with the properties of the estimators, and in particular we care about consistency. With calibration, these issues get overlooked. In a sense, we could say that estimation is nothing else than more conscious calibration.

For instance, given that the output of interest is a time series, a natural criteria would be to compare the two paths $y_t(\theta)$ (simulated) and $y_{R,t}$ (real), where $\theta^\star$ is the true value of the parameter θ governing the real and model DGP. Indeed, this is the essence of the history-friendly approach to calibration, but it does not guarantee consistency. To see why, consider that this *path estimator* is

$$\hat{\theta} = \arg\min_{\theta} \sum_{t=1}^{T} [y_t(\theta) - y_{R,t}]^2 \qquad (9.1)$$

---

[11] See Grazzini and Richiardi (2015) for a thorough discussion of the issues involved in estimating AB models.

where we assume for simplicity that both the real and artificial time series are observed for T periods.

Under the usual regularity conditions, the estimator tends asymptotically to the solution $\hat{\theta}_\infty$ of the limit problem:

$$\hat{\theta}_\infty = \arg\min_\theta \lim_{T \to \infty} \frac{1}{T} \sum_{t=1}^T [y_t(\theta) - y_{R,t}]^2$$

$$= \arg\min_\theta E[y(\theta) - y_R]^2 \qquad (9.2)$$

$$= \arg\min_\theta \{V(y) + V(y_R) + [E(y) - E(y_R)]^2\}$$

Consistency requires $\hat{\theta}_\infty = \theta^\star$, a condition that is not satisfied in general. For instance, suppose that y is exponentially distributed, with $f(y) = \frac{1}{\theta} e^{-\frac{1}{\theta} y}$, for $y > 0$. Then $E(y) = \theta$, $V(y) = \theta^2$, and

$$\hat{\theta}_\infty = \arg\min_\theta [\theta^2 + \theta^{*2} + (\theta - \theta^*)^2] = \theta^*/2 \neq \theta^* \qquad (9.3)$$

The reason why the path estimator is inconsistent is that by targeting the idiosyncrasies in the data, it goes after the noise, as well as after the signal. If the noise is highly skewed (as in the case of the exponential distribution of the example), this results in wrong inference. The problem is exacerbated if deviations from expected values are big (again, this is the case of the exponential distribution), whenever the weighting procedure in the distance measure is not linear in the difference between simulated and real data (in our example, the loss function is quadratic in the prediction errors). By appropriately constructing the likelihood of observing the data, rather than simply taking the distance between the real and simulated the data, the problem is solved (see Section 9.4); sometimes, the devil is in the details.

This example illustrates the difference between estimation and calibration. Comparing the real and simulated paths is a convenient way to calibrate a model, but not to estimate it.

Also, the common approach to comparing real and simulated distributions *at a given point in time* is in general inconsistent. To see why, let us consider a simple example. Let y_t be some aggregate statistics computed on the state of the simulated system, in a transient or long-run equilibrium – say the unemployment rate. Assume that the mechanics of the model imply, for a given value of the parameters θ, a probability of being unemployed for any individual worker equal to $u(\theta)$. Given that being employed/unemployed is a Bernoulli random variable, its variance is equal to $\sigma_u^2 = u(\theta)(1 - u(\theta))$.

By the properties of the sample mean (the central limit theorem), in large populations of size N the expected value of the unemployment rate at time t is normally distributed with mean $E_N(y) = u$, and variance equal to $V_N(y) = \frac{\sigma_u^2}{N}$. (In small samples, the unemployment rate follows a binomial distribution with mean u and variance σ_u^2.) In other terms, given the stochastic elements of the model, the unemployment rate at time t is a random variable, with different realizations in different periods and in different simulation runs. If we want y to be representative of the model output, so that we can use it as a summary measure for comparison with the real output, we must therefore choose N high enough. Alternatively, if the model is ergodic, we can use the average of the unemployment rate over M simulation runs, $\bar{y}_M$, which is equivalent to using the unemployment rate of a single run with $M \cdot N$ agents.

In this simple case, focusing on the state of the system at one specific point in time t poses no problems, as the employment status shows no persistence – hence, the unemployment rate bears no memory whatsoever of past values. More in general however, it could be the case that even if the system is at a long-run equilibrium, the distribution of y is not constant over time. Indeed, (weak) stationarity is defined as the distribution of y_t having a constant mean and variance, and an autocorrelation structure that depends only on the number of the lags and not on t. Hence, the unconditional mean is constant, but the mean of the distribution of y at time t *conditional* on the past realizations $y_{t-1}, y_{t-2}, \cdots$ is not constant.[12] In this case, focusing on a specific period t might introduce an idiosyncrasy.

Suppose for instance that the unemployment rate displays some degree of persistence, that is $Cov(y_t, y_{t+h}) \neq 0$. This implies that the observed unemployment rate at any time t – even if we assume that the real world is in the long-run equilibrium – is influenced by the past unemployment rate. The conditional mean and variance of the distribution – conditional on the past realizations – are different from the unconditional values. If we match the simulated unemployment rate with the observed rate, we get inconsistent estimates for the structural parameters θ. If we increase the sample size of the simulated population, or increase the number of simulation runs, our estimate of the theoretical unemployment rate $u(\theta)$ will become more and more precise, but the value of θ matching the observed unemployment rate will converge to something different from the real, unobserved parameter of the rwDGP. This is, in essence, the problem of many indirect calibration exercises, indeed of all

---

[12] In addition, given the definition of stationarity, moments other than the first and the second could be time variant.

calibration exercises which involve matching cross-sectional moments.[13] Even when the model is correctly specified, they lead to inconsistent estimates of the parameters of interest.[14]

To correctly characterise the system, then one has to compute an average over many periods, $\bar{y}$, where the length of the observation period is determined in order to get rid of the autocorrelation structure in the statistics of interest. This turns out to be a crucial difference between calibration and estimation.

9.3 Simulated Minimum Distance

9.3.1 The Method of Simulated Moments

A solution, to properly characterise both the model output and the real data, rests on considering *longitudinal means* of the selected statistics, in our example the mean of the unemployment rate. Rather than seeking consistency in *sample size*, consistency in *time* is achieved: by increasing the length of the observation period, both for the real and the simulated data, the estimates become more and more precise and they converge toward the true value of the parameters.

This is the method of simulated moments (MSM). With the usual notation, the moment estimator is:

$$\hat{\theta} = \arg \min_{\theta}[\mu^*(\theta) - \mu_R]'\mathbf{W}^{-1}[\mu^*(\theta) - \mu_R] \qquad (9.4)$$

where $\mathbf{W}$ is a positive definite matrix of weights.

More generally in the MSM, as in the simulated general method of moments, different order of moments of the time series of interest are used, and then weighted to take into account their uncertainty.[15] The intuition behind this is to allow parameters estimated with a higher degree of uncertainty to count less in the final measure of distance between the real and artificial data (Winker et al., 2007). Having different weights (or no weights at all) impinges on the efficiency of the estimates, not on their consistency. If the number of moments is equal to the number of structural parameters to be estimated, the model is just-identified. The minimized distance, for the estimated values of the parameters, is therefore 0 in the limit (as the sample size grows bigger),

---

[13] A common example is the exponent of the Pareto distribution of firm size.
[14] True, one has often to live with incorrectly specified models, for which consistency is not even an issue. Still, focusing on cross-sectional statistics is suboptimal.
[15] We stress again that while the uncertainty regarding the simulated moments can be reduced by increasing the number of simulation runs, the uncertainty in the estimation of the real, population moment on the basis of real sample data cannot be avoided.

supposing the model is correctly specified. If the number of moments is higher than the number of parameters, the model is over-identified and the minimized distance is always positive. If it is lower it is under-identified.

However, consistency in *time* is conceptually attainable only at a *long-run equilibrium*, where the regularities that we exploit for estimation remain stable indefinitely. By contrast, in a *transient equilibrium*, any regularity will eventually dissolve, and looking for an asymptotic behavior as the observation period grows larger becomes meaningless. Consistency in sample *size* can be achieved in a transient equilibrium if the individual observations are independent, so that any autocorrelation structure wipes out in the aggregate for large sample sizes. Consistency in replications can also be achieved in a transient equilibrium if reality itself offers many instances of the process, so that the idiosyncrasies of some specific trajectories are balanced by opposite idiosyncrasies of other trajectories.

As an example, let us focus for simplicity on a situation which can be described analytically, and suppose the rwDGP is such that individuals exit a given state (say, unemployment), at time t, at a rate

$$h(t) = p\lambda t^{p-1} \tag{9.5}$$

This is a Weibull duration model, and the survival function is

$$S = exp(-\lambda t^p) \tag{9.6}$$

with λ as a scale factor. The hazard rate, for different values of the parameter p, is depicted in Figure 9.1.

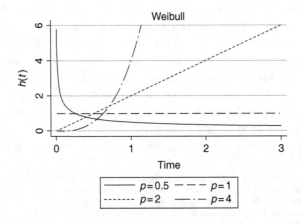

Figure 9.1 Example plot of Weibull hazard functions.

Let us assume that the true value of the parameter p is $p^\star = 2$.[16] Suppose that we have a model for this process that happens to be correct, i.e., well specified. We want to estimate the parameter p of our model.[17]

If the model is well specified, the theoretical mean time to failure (MTTF) is:[18]

$$E[T_i] = \frac{1}{\lambda^{1/p}} \Gamma\left(1 + \frac{1}{p}\right) \tag{9.7}$$

Note that this simple model has only one long-run equilibrium: sooner or later, everybody exits the state. As such, the long-run equilibrium carries no information on which estimation can be performed. On the other hand, the MTTF is computed in the adjustment process, and therefore defines a transient equilibrium – that is, an equilibrium that will eventually disappear (the MTTF is not defined anymore once everybody has exited the state.) The relationship between the value of the parameter and the summary measure is stable (more formally, the MTTF is ergodic) and can be exploited for estimation. Consistency can be obtained in our case both over time, as individual hazards are independent of each other, and over replications, if the process is commonly observed in the real data.

Equation 9.7 is a moment condition. As an estimate for $E[T_i]$, we take the average observed time to failure, $\bar{T}_R$. Since in general the expression for the theoretical mean on the r.h.s. is not known, or it cannot be inverted in order to get an estimate for p, the MSM prescribes to simulate it. Hence, the moment condition becomes

$$E[T_i(p) - \bar{T}_R] = 0 \tag{9.8}$$

which implies

$$\hat{p} = \arg\min|\bar{T}(p) - \bar{T}_R| \tag{9.9}$$

However, the choice of the MTTF as our summary statistics is not a good one. The reason is that the moment used for estimation does not identify the parameter: more than one value of p can lead to the same MTTF. Figure 9.2 exemplifies this. The intuition is that very high values of p (low values of $1/p$ in the graph) imply a very small exit probability for small durations; however, the

---

[16] This implies positive duration dependence: the hazard rate (linearly) increases with the elapsed duration. We assume for simplicity that we observe all durations.
[17] Here we consider for simplicity a model that leads to a (well-known) closed form solution. The model would therefore be better estimated by applying the appropriate (Weibull) duration model technique. The ideas exemplified here however also apply, as discussed in the text, to more complex models, possibly involving more parameters.
[18] Failure being, in our example, not a bad thing at all as it implies finding a job and exiting unemployment.

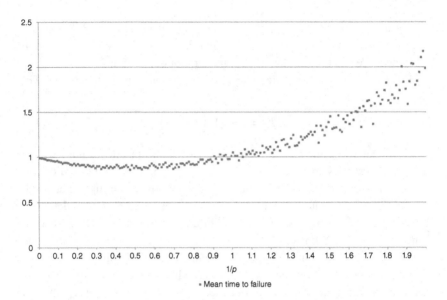

Figure 9.2 Mean time to failure for Weibull model, $\lambda = 1$. Simulation over 1,000 individuals.

hazard rate increases quickly, so that very long durations are also very unlikely. On the other hand, somewhat lower values of p imply a higher probability of observing very short durations, but also a higher probability of observing very long durations. The two effects, for appropriate values of p, counterbalance perfectly, so that the mean is the same.

The second order moment σ_T^2, on the other hand, is monotonic in p (Figure 9.3).

The latter moment is then used for estimation. To give more weight to big mistakes, the following summary statistics is used:

$$\hat{p} = \arg \min \left[\sigma_T^2(p) - \sigma_{T,R}^2\right]^2 \tag{9.10}$$

The estimation procedure is tested by means of a Montecarlo experiment. Pseudo-true data are extracted from a Weibull distribution with $p^\star = 2$, and the variance of time to failure is recorded. Then, the Weibull model is simulated for different values of the parameter p, until the distance between the pseudo-true and the simulated variance of time to failure is minimised.[19] The iterated call to the simulation model all share the same pseudo-random numbers, which are different from those used to extract the pseudo-true observations.

---

[19] The Brent algorithm is used for minimisation.

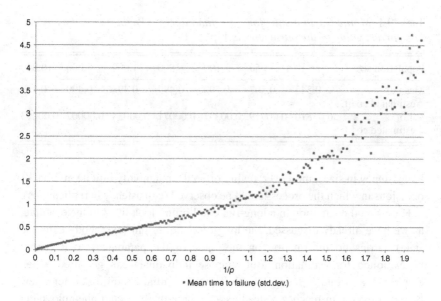

Figure 9.3 Standard deviation of time to failure for Weibull model, $\lambda = 1$.
Simulation over 1,000 individuals.

This procedure is repeated – with different pseudo-random numbers for the pseudo-true and the simulated data – 100 times, in order to compute the mean and the standard deviation of the estimates. The results, for a simulated population of 10–10,000 individuals, are reported in Table 9.1.

The fact that the estimates are always centred around the true value 0.5 shows that the estimation procedure is unbiased. This is because the moment function (the standard deviation of the time to failure) is approximately linear around the true value of the parameter $1/p = 09.5$.[20] Consistency (in size) is shown by the reduction in the variability of the estimated coefficients as the sample size increases: when the population size doubles, the variance halves.

The distribution of the estimator is asymptotically normal. Hence, confidence intervals can be constructed from the standard deviation of the (bootstrapped) estimated coefficients.

Finally, at the risk of being redundant, let us stress that obtaining consistent estimates of the parameters in a transient equilibrium was possible only because individual observations were independent, in our example

---

[20] With nonlinear moments we get a small sample bias, of predictable direction (which depends on the curvature of the moment). The bias decreases as the sample size (number of agents) increases. See Grazzini et al. (2012).

Table 9.1 *Monte Carlo results for the estimation of a Weibull model by MSM.
The correct value of the parameter is $1/p^\star = 0.5$.*

Population size	10	50	100	500	1,000	5,000	10,000
Mean of estimated coeff.	0.543	0.507	0.500	0.499	0.498	0.499	0.499
Var of estimated coeff.	0.03870	0.00919	0.00397	0.00071	0.00034	0.00007	0.00003

(consistency in size); moreover, reality offered a potentially infinite number of occasions in which the process could be observed (consistency in replications).

How would estimation in a long-run equilibrium look like? In the example, as we have already discussed, the long-run equilibrium (everybody exits the state) carries no information on the value of the parameter, so it cannot be exploited for estimation. But suppose individuals can get fired, when employed, at a rate δ. Independently from the initial conditions, after a few periods the system reaches a steady state where the expected unemployment rate is a function of p and δ.[21] We now have two parameters to estimate, and estimation can be performed by exploiting both the moment condition in the transitory equilibrium (the MTTF) and the moment condition in the long run equilibrium (the unemployment rate).

Indirect Inference

In the indirect inference (II) method, the basic idea is to use the coefficients of an *auxiliary model*, estimated both on the real and on the simulated data, to describe the data, that is as summary statistics on the original model. Hence, the method prescribes the following steps:

1. simulate the model for a candidate parameters vector $\boldsymbol{\theta}_i$ and obtain artificial data;
2. estimate the parameters $\boldsymbol{\beta}$ of a (possibly misspecified) auxiliary model $y_t = f(\boldsymbol{\beta}, \mathbf{z}_t)$, where *mathbfz* are the explanatory variables;
3. change the structural parameters $\boldsymbol{\theta}$ of the original model until the distance between the estimates of the auxiliary model using real and artificial data is minimized:

$$\hat{\boldsymbol{\theta}} = \arg\min_{\boldsymbol{\theta}}[\hat{\boldsymbol{\beta}}(\boldsymbol{\theta}) - \hat{\boldsymbol{\beta}}_R]'\mathbf{W}^{-1}[\hat{\boldsymbol{\beta}}(\boldsymbol{\theta}) - \hat{\boldsymbol{\beta}}_R] \qquad (9.11)$$

where $\mathbf{W}$ is a positive definite matrix of weights.

---

[21] For instance, with $p = 2$, $\delta = 0.1$ and a scale factor $\lambda = 0.2$ the equilibrium unemployment rate is about 15.3%.

Table 9.2 *Monte Carlo results for the estimation of a Weibull model by II, with an exponential auxiliary model. The correct value of the parameter is* $1/p^\star = 0.5$.

Population size	10	50	100	500	1,000	5,000	10,000
Mean of estimated coeff.	0.298	0.421	0.436	0.489	0.463	0.475	0.459
Var of estimated coeff.	0.07344	0.05805	0.05874	0.02262	0.01596	0.00877	0.00508

Note that MSM can be thought of as an instance of II, where the meta-model is just a constant: $\mathbf{y_t} = \mu + \mathbf{u}_t$. Indeed, the auxiliary model can be overly simple and misspecified; however, the estimates are more efficient if it is a good statistical description of the data, that is a bona fide reduced form version of the model.[22]

As in the method of simulated moments, if the number of the parameters of the auxiliary model is equal to the number of parameters in the original model, the original model is just-identified, and the distance between the estimated coefficients on the real and on the simulated data, if the model is correctly specified, goes in the limit to zero. If the number of parameters in the auxiliary model is bigger than the number of parameters in the original model, the original model is over-identified, and the distance between the estimated coefficients remain positive. If the number of parameters in the auxiliary model is smaller than the number of parameters in the original model, the original model is under-identified.

In the Weibull example of the previous section, it could be tempting to opt for a very simple auxiliary model in the form of an exponential model. Exponential models are particular cases of the Weibull models, with $p = 1$. This implies a constant hazard rate. Inference in this case is theoretically possible by comparing the scaling factor λ in the pseudo-true and in the simulated data. However, a Monte Carlo experiment similar to the one already described shows that the exponential model is too poor a description of the Weibull model, for $p^\star = 2$: the estimation procedure is not able to recover the pseudo-true value (Table 9.2).

The log-logistic specification appears to be a better choice for our auxiliary model. In the log-logistic model, the hazard and the survival functions are respectively

---

[22] The properties of II methods, however, crucially depend on a correct specification of the structural model. Some semiparametric methods have been proposed that make II more robust to the structural model specification (Dridi and Renault, 2000).

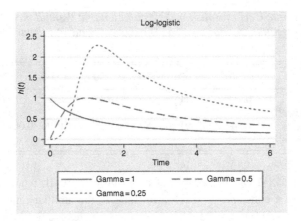

Figure 9.4 Example plot of Weibull hazard functions.

$$h(t) = \frac{\lambda^{1/\gamma} t^{1/\gamma-1}}{\gamma[1 + (\lambda t)^{1/\gamma}]^2} \tag{9.12}$$

$$S(t) = [1 + (\lambda t)^{1/\gamma}]^{-1} \tag{9.13}$$

Figure 9.4 depicts the shape of the hazard rate of the log-logistic model, for different values of the parameter γ. As a proxy for the Weibull, it immediately appears more apt than the exponential.

In the estimation procedure, the γ coefficients for the auxiliary model estimated on the (pseudo-)real and the simulated data are compared, and used to infer the true value of the parameter b, in the (correctly specified) original Weibull model. The Monte Carlo experiment confirms that the choice is correct: although the log-logistic model is misspecified, the estimated parameters for p are centered around the true value, with a variance that declines at the usual rate with sample size (Table 9.3).[23]

While the usual strategy, as followed in the earlier example, is to choose a simple auxiliary model with a number of parameters comparable to that of the structural model, and whose estimation is relatively straightforward, another approach is to introduce an auxiliary model with a large number of parameters, providing a good description of the real DGP. The idea is to gain in asymptotic efficiency. However, with large auxiliary models, indirect inference can be very computationally demanding, as the summary statistics $\tilde{\beta}(\theta)$ have to be evaluated for each value of θ appearing in the numerical optimization

---

[23] Note that consistency in sample size is attainable, in this example, because observations are independent. Note also that the efficiency of the MSM estimates and the II estimates, as measured by the variance of the estimates, is similar.

Table 9.3 *Monte Carlo results for the estimation of a Weibull model by II,*
with a log-logistic auxiliary model. The correct value of the parameter is 0.5.

Population size	10	50	100	500	1,000	5,000	10,000
Mean of estimated coeff.	0.523	0.497	0.495	0.502	0.499	0.499	0.500
Var of estimated coeff.	0.03901	0.00627	0.00367	0.00071	0.00038	0.00009	0.00004

algorithm. This has led to the development of a variant to II, the so-called
Efficient Method of Moments, which makes use of a score generator to define
the matching conditions.[24]

9.3.2 Ergodicity and an Application to a Simple AB Model

In the sections above, we have used, to highlight the mechanics of the
estimation procedure, a simple analytical model. We now apply the Method of
Simulated Moments to a simple AB model, Thomas Schelling's Segregation
model (Schelling, 1969).[25] This application is also used to illustrate the effects
of non-ergodic behaviour, and to suggest a way to take this into account.

The model considers an idealised interaction between individuals having
to choose where to live, on a finite grid. Individuals are initially located at
random on the grid, with one cell being occupied at most by one agent.
Because each cell has eight adjacent cells, individuals can have at most eight
immediate neighbours.[26] There are two types of individuals, say black and
white. Individuals are characterised by a tolerance level, that is the minimum
fraction of same-colour neighbours they can accept. If the composition of
their immediate neighbourhood does not satisfy this condition, individuals
become unsatisfied and they search for another location (empty cell) where
the share of same-colour neighbours is above the threshold. For simplicity, an
homogeneous tolerance level is assumed. As an example, suppose the tolerance
level is 30%, that is, individuals want to have at least 30% of their neighbours
of the same colour as they are. A black individual with eight neighbours (no
empty cells around him) would move away if less than three of his neighbours
are black. The model then shows that even when the thresholds are pretty low
(corresponding to high levels of tolerance), the equilibrium outcome where

---

[24] Gallant (1996).
[25] For further examples of estimation of AB models by Simulated Minimum Distance, see
Grazzini and Richiardi (2015).
[26] To avoid boundary effects, it is supposed that cells on one edge of the grid are adjacent to cells
on the other edge (so that the grid is effectively a torus).

everybody is happy and nobody is willing to move is highly segregated, with the formation of ghettoes possibly surrounded by empty locations. This is because of two externalities that are in place. When a black individual moves out because there are too many white individuals around him, he affects the composition of his original neighbourhood, making other black people more likely to become unsatisfied (there is one black individual less around). At the same time, when he settles down to a new location with a high enough presence of black people, he makes white people in the area more likely to become unsatisfied, as there is one more black individual around. Because initial locations are random, even with homogeneous tolerance thresholds – and even if the threshold is low (high tolerance) – there will be some individuals who happen to be unhappy with their location. They then move out, and this triggers a chain reaction that leads to highly segregated outcomes.

The model is clearly very stylized, and nobody would think of taking it seriously to the data. However, for the sake of our argument, let us assume that this is a good-enough description of some real-world situation. We observe the size of the city, the density of houses and where individuals live, and we want to make inference about their tolerance threshold. We assume that the real world is in equilibrium – that is, every observed individual is happy about his or her location and does not want to move. We also abstract from demographic processes, job mobility, house prices and other factors that might affect location choices: the population is fixed and only neighbourhood composition matters. For each individual, we compute the fraction of same-colour neighbours, and we characterise the system with the average fraction of same-colour neighbours, a measure of segregation.

Note that, given there are enough empty cells so that movers can find a new suitable location, the model always settles down to a situation where everybody is happy, and nobody wants to move. Such an equilibrium is an absorbing state of the model. Because no further relocations take place in the absorbing state, the level of segregation (average share of same-colour neighbours, or similarity) does not vary.

Also, note that, with a finite grid size, the outcome depends on the initial (random) location of agents. For the same tolerance threshold, different levels of segregation can be obtained depending on the initial conditions, which are in turn determined by the random seed. Because the final level of segregation of each run is constant (it has a degenerate distribution with 0 variance), there is no chance that the outcomes of two different runs can be thought to be drawn from the same theoretical distribution, unless they exactly coincide. If we obtain a level of similarity of 68.2% in one run, and of 69.8% in another run, we must treat those two numbers as irreducibly different. Said differently,

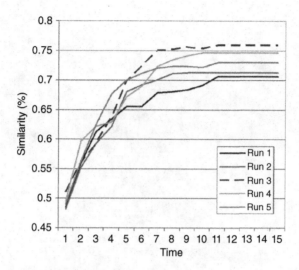

Figure 9.5 Evolution of segregation in the Schelling model, different random seeds. The vertical axis measure the average share of neighbours of the same colour (similarity). Tolerance threshold is 0.3. Grid size is 15 × 15. Density is 0.9.

the model is non-ergodic, and no statistical test is needed to confirm this. Figure 9.5 exemplifies.

Due to its non-ergodic nature, rather than having one long-run equilibrium (absorbing state), the model has a distribution of long-run equilibria (figure 9.6).[27]

However, as the grid size grows, the different outcomes get closer and closer: the effects of the initial conditions (random seed) matter less and less, and the distribution of equilibrium segregation levels shrinks. In the limit, the model becomes ergodic, with only one equilibrium for given values of the parameters.

Here, to illustrate the point about non-ergodicity, we consider a small grid size. We assume that we observe data coming from one real village composed of 15 × 15 = 225 houses, inhabited by approximately 200 individuals (density is 0.9). The level of segregation in this hypothetical village is 0.7. We wish to estimate how tolerant its inhabitants are.

We first fix the random seed. Because of the limited number of neighbours one individual can have, the individual responsiveness to changes in the tolerance threshold is a step function (Figure 9.7).

The accuracy of the estimates cannot go beyond the distance between those steps. Optimisation is therefore easily achieved by a simple grid search: the

---

[27] In general, the distribution of long-run equilibria needs not to be normal.

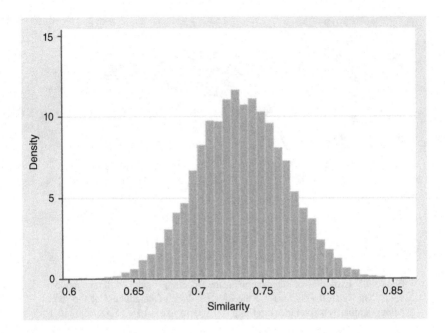

Figure 9.6 Distribution of equilibrium segregation levels in the Schelling model, different random seeds. The horizontal axis measure the average share of neighbours of the same colour (similarity), in equilibium. Tolerance threshold is 0.3. Grid size is 15 × 15. Density is 0.9. 10,000 runs are performed; those where an equilibrium is not reached after 250 iterations are discarded. Normal density is superimposed.

model is simulated for all values of the parameter in the range [0,1], with an interval equal to 0.01 (which is big enough to discriminate between different steps). Figure 9.8 shows how our summary statistics $\mu^*(\theta)$ – or *moment function* – responds to changes in the value of the parameter θ, the tolerance threshold.[28]

The moment is monotonic in the parameter: as we have seen, with only one parameter this is a sufficient condition for identification.[29] Note that so far we have only looked at the model, in order to construct the moment function $\mu^*(\theta)$. We now compare this moment function with the observed value m^D, which we assume to be 70%. By inverting the moment function at the observed value, we get our estimate of the parameter. In our case, a

[28] Because the level of segregation is constant in the stationary state, we do not actually need to compute a longitudinal average to estimate the theoretical moment; we can simply look at the level of segregation that occurs at the first point in simulated time where everybody is happy.

[29] See also Grazzini and Richiardi (2015).

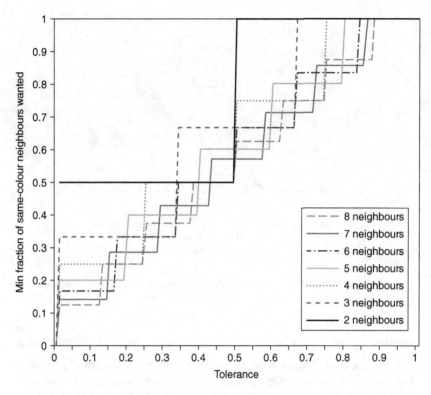

Figure 9.7 Individual choices in the Schelling model: minimum fraction of same-colour neighbourhood wanted for different levels of tolerance. In the limit, for an infinitely large neighbourhood, the function would be a straight 45° line.

linear interpolation between the two values of the parameters, which give a level of segregation respectively immediately below and immediately above 70%, gives our point estimate of 0.289. Because there is no variation in the steady state (by assumption), there is no sampling error, and the theoretical moment (given the random seed) is estimated with precision: consequently, the standard error of the estimate is 0.

On the contrary, if there were some stochastic factor that exogenously forced relocation, like birth and death, we would have obtained a stationary state where the level of segregation fluctuates around the long-term mean μ^*. We would then need to estimate the moments, both in the real and in the simulated data. Such an estimate is nothing other that the sample mean m, computed in the stationary state. The Central Limit Theorem tells us that the sample mean is asymptotically normally distributed with mean $E[m] = \mu^*$ and standard

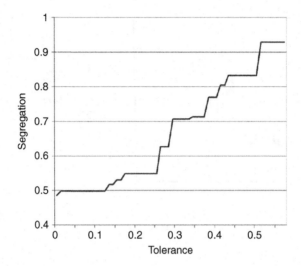

Figure 9.8 The effects of tolerance on segregation in the Schelling model.

deviation $\sigma_m = \dfrac{\sigma}{\sqrt{n}}$, where σ is the standard deviation of the underlying statistics (the level of segregation in our case), and n is the number of periods of observation. The simulated moment $\mu^*(\theta)$ can then be computed, for any θ, to any desired degree of accuracy, given that we can simulate an arbitrarily large number of periods in the steady state. The real moment μ^D, however, can only be estimated in the available data. Due to this *sampling error*, our estimates for θ are also subject to uncertainty. To obtain the standard error of the estimates, we can simply bootstrap the observed moment from its estimated distribution (a normal distribution with mean m^D and variance σ_m^2). The simulated moments are then inverted, giving a distribution of estimates. The standard deviation of this distribution is the standard error of the estimates.

Until now, we have kept the random seed fixed. However, we have seen that for finite city sizes, the model is non-ergodic, so that different levels of segregation are obtained for the same value of the parameter due to different initial conditions. A simple way to take non-ergodicity into account is to repeat the estimation for different random seeds. This gives us a distribution of estimates, even in the simple case of constant segregation in the steady state. The amplitude of this distribution measures the uncertainty that originates from the non-ergodic nature of the model: we do not know what random seed God used to produce the real data, and whether the real data are a low draw (like run #1 in Figure 9.5) or a high draw (like run #3). Note that this uncertainty is

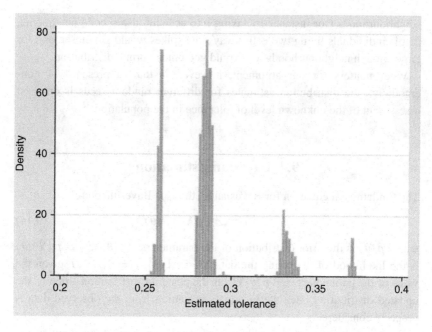

Figure 9.9 Distribution of estimates in the Schelling model. 10,000 random seeds are tested; the parameter space is regularly sampled on the interval [0,1] at 0.01 intervals. The assumed observed level of segregation is 70%.

different from sampling error: even if we enlarge the period of observation, we cannot learn about the random seed used to produce the real data. Hence, the uncertainty coming from non-ergodicity does not vanish over time.

To illustrate the issue, we construct the theoretical moments for 10,000 different random seeds, and invert them at the observed level of segregation to obtain a distribution of estimates. This is depicted in Figure 9.9. The distribution is multimodal, which might look at first surprising, given the beautiful normal distribution of Figure 9.6. However, Figure 9.6 depicts the distribution of segregation levels that can be obtained for a given level of tolerance, while Figure 9.9 relates to the inverse problem, the distribution of tolerance levels that are consistent with a given level of segregation. The reason for its multimodal nature can be understood by a closer inspection of Figure 9.7. The spikes in the distribution of estimates result from different possible combinations of tolerance level and neighbourhood composition of individuals with different number of neighbours.[30] If we considered larger

---

[30] In the range of values of the tolerance threshold which are relevant for the exercise (that is, leading to a segregation level around 70%), individuals with exactly 8 neighbours change their

neighbourhoods (for instance by taking into account also second neighbours, that is individuals living two cells away), the spikes would get closer, and for large enough neighbourhoods, we would get a nice normal distribution.

What matters for our argument, however, is that in presence of non-ergodicity, the distribution estimates for different random seeds is our best assessment of the unknown level of tolerance in the population.[31]

9.4 Bayesian Estimation

The fundamental equation for Bayesian methods is Bayes theorem:

$$p\left(\boldsymbol{\theta}|\mathbf{Y}^R\right) \propto \mathscr{L}\left(\boldsymbol{\theta};\mathbf{Y}^R\right)p\left(\boldsymbol{\theta}\right) \tag{9.14}$$

where $p\left(\boldsymbol{\theta}\right)$ is the prior distribution of the parameters, $\mathscr{L}\left(\boldsymbol{\theta};\mathbf{Y}^R\right) \equiv p\left(\mathbf{Y}^R|\boldsymbol{\theta}\right)$ is the likelihood of observing the data $\mathbf{Y}^R \equiv \left\{\mathbf{y}_t^R\right\}$, $t = 1, \cdots, T$ given the value of the parameters, and $p\left(\boldsymbol{\theta}|\mathbf{Y}^R\right)$ is the posterior distribution – that is, the updated distribution once the information coming from the observed data is properly considered.

Bayesians give a prior distribution of the parameters as an input to the estimation process, and get back a posterior distribution: knowledge gets updated by the information contained in the data. The prior distribution typically comes from other studies or subjective evaluations. A uniform distribution in the allowed range of the parameters is often used as a way to introduce uninformative priors, though no such a thing as an uninformative prior actually exists (Bernardo, 1997). What matters, the prior is a distribution, which through application of Bayes theorem produces another distribution as an output.

The difference with SMD techniques can be evaluated by comparing the Bayesian approach with Maximum Likelihood (ML), an instance of SMD methods which entails maximising the likelihood $\mathscr{L}\left(\boldsymbol{\theta};\mathbf{Y}^R\right)$ with respect

---

behaviour only as the required number of same-colour neighbours passes 25% (below, they require two neighbors of the same colour; above, they require three neighbours of the same colour) or 37.5% (below, three same-colour neighbours; above, four same-colour neighbors). Individuals with exactly 7 neighbors change their behaviour only at 28.6% (from two to three same-colour neighbors) or 42.9% (from three to four). Individuals with exactly 6 neighbors change their behavior only at 33.3% (from two to three same-colour neighbors). Individuals with exactly 5 neighbours change their behaviour only at 20% (from one to two same-colour neighbors) or 40% (from two to three). Given the assumed density (0.9), there are very few individuals with 4 neighbours, and it practically never happens that there are individuals with less than 4 neighbours.

[31] With sampling errors, each estimate would carry its own (bootstrapped) standard error.

to θ: (i) in the Bayesian approach, there is no maximisation involved; (ii) rather than obtaining a point estimate for the parameters (plus an estimate for the standard error which, if the distribution of the estimator is known, at least asymptotically, allows computation of confidence intervals) we get a distribution; (iii) prior knowledge can be incorporated.[32]

Sampling the posterior distribution $p\left(\theta | \mathbf{Y}^R\right)$ involves two computationally intensive steps: (i), for given values of θ, obtaining an estimate for the likelihood $\mathscr{L}$; (ii) iterating over different values of θ. In the next section we elaborate on the first issue, while in Section 9.4.2 we discuss the latter.

9.4.1 Estimating the Likelihood

Estimation of the likelihood (the probability of observing the data, given the current values of the parameters) can be done when its analytical derivation is not feasible, by repeatedly sampling from the model output. For instance, in a long-run equilibrium, the outcome fluctuates around a stationary level $\mu(\theta)^* = E[\mathbf{y}_t(\theta)|t > \bar{T}]$. If we collect the artificial data produced by the model in such a long-run equilibrium, we can construct a probability distribution around μ^*, and therefore evaluate the density at each observed data point y_t^R. If the outcomes $\mathbf{y}(\theta)$ were discrete, we would only have to count the frequency of occurrence of each observed value y_t^R. With continuous $\mathbf{y}(\theta)$, the likelihood has to be estimated either non-parametrically or parametrically, under appropriate distributional assumptions. A traditional *non-parametric* method is kernel density estimation (KDE), which basically produces histogram-smoothing: the artificial data are grouped in bins (the histogram), and then a weighted moving average of the frequency of each bin is computed.[33] The approximation bias introduced by KDE can be reduced by using a large number of very small bins, but then the variance in the estimate of the density grows. To see this,

---

[32] We have not considered ML in our review of SMD methods as obtaining an estimate of the likelihood can be computationally heavy, as we shall see. For the same reason, we will not dwell into this problem here, and we will focus on likelihood-free approximate Bayesian methods instead.

[33] More formally, kernel density estimation (KDE), given a simulated time series $\mathbf{y}(\theta) \equiv \{y_s\}$, $s = 1 \cdots S$, approximates the density $f(y_t^R, \theta)$, for each observed data point y_t^R, with:

$$\tilde{f}(y_t^R|\theta) = \frac{1}{Sh} \sum_{s=1}^{S} \mathscr{K} \frac{\sqrt{\sum_{k=1}^{K} \sum_{s=1}^{S} \left(y_{ks}^S - y_{kt}^R\right)^2}}{h} \tag{9.15}$$

where $\mathscr{K}$ is a kernel function that places greater weight on values y_{ks} that are closer to y_{kt}^R, is symmetric around zero and integrates to one, and h is the bandwidth. Algorithms for KDE are available in most statistical packages.

think of estimating the probability density function (PDF) when the data comes from any standard distribution, like an exponential or a Gaussian. We can approximate the true PDF $f(x)$ to arbitrary accuracy by a piecewise-constant density (that is, by constructing an histogram), but, for a fixed set of bins, we can only come so close to the true, continuous density.

The main problem with KDE is however its computational cost. A (faster) alternative is to assume a *parametric* distribution for the density, around $\mu^*(\theta)$. Imposing additional information about the distribution of the simulation output can help generate better estimates from a limited number of simulation runs. On the other hand, those estimates may increase the bias if the assumed distribution does not conform to the true density of the model output. Such an assumption can of course be tested in the artificial data, for specific values of θ, and should be tested in the relevant range (i.e., where the estimated coefficients lie). Use of parametric methods leads to *synthetic likelihood* or *pseudo-likelihood* estimation (Wood, 2010; Hartig et al., 2011).

For instance, Grazzini et al. (2015) estimate a stock market model with one behavioural parameter determining how traders react to a difference between the target price and the current price p_{it}, and assume a Gaussian distribution of the price level around its long-run stationary level. Under this assumption, they derive a close-form expression for the likelihood function. Figure 9.10 shows that the assumption is violated at the estimated value of the parameter, given that prices are much more concentrated around the theoretical equilibrium value. However, the shape of the distribution is symmetric and not too far from Gaussian, except for the spike at the theoretical equilibrium. Monte Carlo experimentation with the new posterior suggests that it performs very well, saving significant computational time.

The parametric and non-parametric methods discussed above use the output variability that is predicted by the model, and use this information for inference. However, it is possible that the model shows much less variability than the data. This is due to fundamental *specification errors* (the model is only a poor approximation of the real process, so that the mean model predictions do not fit to the data), *simplification errors* (the model is a good approximation of the real process, but there are additional stochastic processes that have acted on the data and are not included in the model) or *measurement errors* (there is uncertainty about the data). While the first type of errors calls for a respecification of the model, the latter types could in principle be dealt with by including additional processes that explain this variability within the model. 'However, particularly, when those processes are not of interest for the scientific question asked, it is simpler and more parsimonious to express this unexplained variability outside the stochastic simulation. One way to do this is

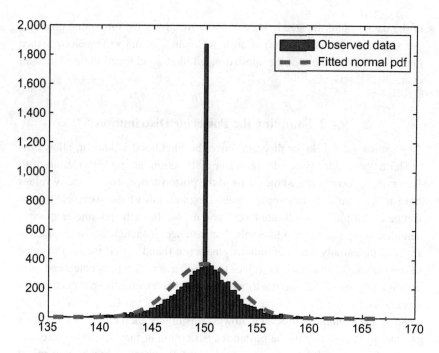

Figure 9.10 Price distribution in the long-run stationary state at the pseudo-true value of the coefficient. Source: Grazzini and Richiardi (2015).

adding an *external error model* with a tractable likelihood on top of the results of the stochastic simulation'. (Hartig et al., 2011). Again, the validity of such a strategy depends on the quality of the assumption about the distribution of these external errors, given the model and the data. This assumption cannot be tested *per se*, as the variability in the real data comes both from the *explained* components (i.e., the model) and from the *unexplained* ones (i.e., the external errors), the external errors being defined as a residual.

The two parametric strategies (modelling the variability of model outcome and modelling external errors that might affect the real data in the stationary state) are often explored separately. For instance, most studies that use the augmentation by external errors approach then treat the model outcome as deterministic, in the stationary state, whilst most studies that employ a synthetic likelihood do not consider external errors. However, it is in principle possible to combine the two approaches together, and determine explicit distributional assumptions for both the model outcomes and the external errors. It is also possible to be agnostic about the origin of the variability (whether the model or the external errors) and consider a single parametric distribution of the data around the steady state.[34] Moreover, for most inferential purposes the amplitude of the distribution does not matter, as the variance-covariance matrix is integrated out of the approximated likelihood function (see Grazzini et al., 2015).

9.4.2 Sampling the Posterior Distribution

Application of the Bayes theorem, once the likelihood is known, allows the model to get a density for the posterior distribution, at one given value of θ. However, to recover the whole shape of the posterior distribution, many values have to be sampled. In simple models, exploration of the parameter space can be accomplished by 'brute force' grid exploration: the parameter space is sampled at regular (small) intervals. For instance, if there are two parameters that can potentially vary continuously between 0 and 1, and we set the value of the step to 0.1, we have 11 values to consider for each parameter, and their combination gives 121 points to sample: by discretising the parameters, we have reduced the size of the parameters space from $\mathbb{R}^2$ to 121 points.

Such a systematic grid search, however, is highly inefficient, as it involves evaluating the density of the posterior distribution at many points where it is practically zero, while more likely values of θ, where a finer search might be valuable, are sampled with the same probability. Multi-level grid search, where the grid is explored at smaller intervals in ranges of the parameter space on the bases of the results of previous, looser, grid explorations, can of course be devised. However, as soon as the number of parameters increases, the computational limits of this approach become evident.

There are four main classes of *efficient sampling schemes*, to obtain samples from a function of θ, the *target distribution* (the posterior, in our case), which is unknown analytically but can be evaluated point-wise for each θ: (i) rejection sampling, (ii) importance sampling, (iii) Markov chain Monte Carlo and (iv) sequential Monte Carlo. Here we provide only an intuition of how they work, drawing extensively from the excellent survey by Hartig et al. (2011).[35]

Rejection Sampling*
The simplest possibility of generating a distribution that approximates $\mathscr{L}(\theta)$ is to sample random parameters θ and accept those proportionally to their

---

[34] Given that the data does not allow to disentangle model errors from external errors, these two approaches are equivalent.

[35] The entries marked with * are excerpt from Hartig et al. (2011), where we have replaced ϕ in their notation with θ, in order to maintain consistency. The entries marked with ** are based on Hartig et al. (2011), appropriately integrated.

(point-wise approximated) value of $\mathscr{L}(\theta)$. This approach can be slightly improved by importance sampling or stratified sampling methods such as the Latin hypercube design, but rejection approaches encounter computational limitations when the dimensionality of the parameter space becomes larger than typically 10–15 parameters.

Importance Sampling

The intuition behind importance sampling is to to study the distribution $\mathscr{L}(\theta) = p(\theta|\mathbf{y})$ while sampling from another, simpler distribution $q(\theta)$ (called *importance distribution*). This technique was born as a variance reduction technique, aimed at increasing the likelihood to sample from an important but small region by sampling from a different distribution that overweights the important region (hence the name). Having oversampled the important region, we have to adjust our estimate somehow to account for having sampled from this other distribution. This is done by reweighting the sampled values by the adjustment factor $p(\theta)(q(\theta))$. Importance sampling and rejection sampling are similar as both distort a sample from one distribution in order to sample from another. They also share the limitation that they do not work well in high dimensions.

Markov chain Monte Carlo (MCMC)**

MCMC sampling is a process that filters proposed values for θ to arrive at a sample of values drawn from the desired distribution. MCMC algorithms construct a Markov chain of parameter values (θ_1, θ_n), where the next parameter combination θ_{i+1} is chosen by proposing a random move conditional on the last parameter combination θ_i, and accepting conditional on the ratio of $\mathscr{L}(\theta_{i+1})/\mathscr{L}(\theta_i)$. There are a number of MCMC samplers, the most popular of which is the Metropolis–Hastings algorithm. In its simplest form, the *random-walk Metropolis-Hastings*, a candidate $\theta^c \sim \mathscr{N}\left(\theta^{(s)}, \mathbf{V}\right)$ is drawn in each period, given the current value $\theta^{(s)}$. The candidate is accepted with probability

$$\min\left\{1, \frac{p\left(\theta^c|\mathbf{y}_R\right)}{p\left(\theta^{(s)}|\mathbf{y}_R\right)}\right\} \tag{9.16}$$

in which case we set $\theta^{(s+1)} = \theta^c$; else, we set $\theta^{(s+1)} = \theta^{(s)}$ and we repeat the previous candidate.

Given that certain conditions are met (see, e.g., Andrieu et al., 2003), the Markov chain of parameter values will eventually converge to the target distribution $\mathscr{L}(\theta)$. The advantage of an MCMC is that the time needed to obtain acceptable convergence is typically much shorter than for rejection sampling, because the sampling effort is concentrated in the areas of high likelihood or posterior density.

Sequential Monte Carlo Methods (SMC)*

Particle filters or sequential Monte Carlo methods (SMCs) also try to concentrate the sampling effort in the areas of high likelihood or posterior density based on previous samples. Unlike MCMCs, however, each step of the algorithm contains not a single θ, but N parameter combinations θ_i (particles), that are assigned weights ω_i proportional to their likelihood or posterior value $\mathscr{L}(\theta_i)$ (see Arulampalam et al., 2002). When starting with a random sample of parameters, many particles may be assigned close to zero weights, meaning that they carry little information for the inference (degeneracy). To avoid this, a resampling step is usually added where a new set of particles is created based on the current weight distribution [...]. The traditional motivation for a particle filter is to include new data in each filter step, but the filter may also be used to work on a fixed dataset or to subsequently add independent subsets of the data.

9.4.3 Approximate Bayesian Computation

As we have seen in section 9.4.1, obtaining a non-parametric estimate of the likelihood can be computationally heavy. Turning to parametric estimates, assuming of a fixed distributional form of the variable of interest around a long-term stationary state predicted by the model – where the variability is produced either by model uncertainty or external errors – can sometimes be too restrictive. Originating from population genetics (Fu and Li, 1997; Tavaré et al., 1997), where the task of estimating the likelihood of the observed changes in DNA is impervious, a new set of methods have appeared in the last fifteen years to produce approximations of the posterior distributions without relying on the likelihood. These methods are labelled likelihood-free methods, and the best-known class is approximate Bayesian computation (ABC).[36]

In standard Bayesian methods, it is the likelihood function that provides the fit of the model with the data – describing how plausible a particular parameter set θ. The likelihood is, however, often computationally impractical to evaluate. The basic idea of ABC is to replace the evaluation of the likelihood with a 0-1 indicator, describing whether the model outcome is close enough to the observed data. To allow such an assessment, the model outcome and the data must first be summarised. Then, a distance between the simulated and the real data is computed. The model is assumed to be close enough to the data

---

[36] See Marin et al. (2011) and Turner and Zandt (2012).

if the distance falls within the admitted tolerance. As such, there are three key ingredients in ABC: (i) the selection of *summary statistics*, (ii) the definition of a *distance measure*, (iii) the definition of a *tolerance threshold*. The choice of a distance measure is usually the least controversial point (the Euclidean distance or weighted Euclidean distance, where the weights are given by the inverse of the standard deviation of each summary statistics, is generally used). The choice of a tolerance threshold, as we shall see, determines the trade-off between *sampling error* and *approximation error*, given computing time. The choice of summary statistics is the most challenging, and we will discuss it in greater detail.

The basic ABC algorithm works as follows:

1. a candidate vector θ_i is drawn from a prior distribution;
2. a simulation is run with parameters vector θ_i, obtaining simulated data from the model density $p(y|\theta_i)$;
3. the candidate vector is either retained or dismissed depending on whether the distance between the summary statistics computed on the artificial data $S(y(\theta))$ and summary statistics computed on the real data $S(y_R)$ is within or outside the admitted tolerance h: $d(S, S_R) \leq h$.

This is repeated N times; the retained values of the parameters define an empirical approximated posterior distribution. KDE can then be applied to smooth out the resulting histogram, and obtain an estimate of the theoretical approximated posterior. Approximation error refers to the fact that the posterior is approximated; sampling error refers to the fact that we learn about the approximated posterior from a limited set of data.

It is easy to see where the approximation error comes from. While the true posterior distribution is $p(\theta|y = y_R)$, in ABC we get $p(\theta|S(y) \approx S(y_R))$.

If we set the tolerance threshold $h = 0$, and our statistics were *sufficient summary statistics*[37], we would get back to standard Bayesian inference, and sample from the exact posterior distribution. However – and this is the whole point – because of the complexity of the underlying model, the likelihood of observing the real data is tiny everywhere, so that acceptances are impossible, or at least very rare. When h is too small, the distribution of accepted values of θ is closer to the true posterior, and the approximation error is smaller; however, the number of acceptances is usually too small to obtain a precise estimate of the (approximated) posterior distribution, hence, the sampling error

---

[37] A summary statistic is said to be sufficient if 'no other statistic that can be calculated from the same sample provides any additional information as to the value of the parameter' (Fisher, 1922). Sufficient statistics satisfy $p(\theta|S(y_R)) = p(\theta|y_R)$.

increases. On the other hand, when h is too large, the precision of the estimate improves because we have more accepted values (the sampling error goes down), but the approximation error gets bigger. In other words, we obtain a better estimate of a worse object.

An alternative to choosing h in advance is to specify the number of acceptances k required (e.g., $k = 500$); then, h is chosen (after the distance for every draw is computed) in order to achieve that number of acceptances. Finally, note that the tradeoff between sampling error and approximation error is for a given number of draws (hence, a given computing time). Drawing more candidates allows to reduce the approximation error (by decreasing h) without increasing the sampling error. Stated more formally, ABC converges to true posterior as $h \to 0, N \to \infty$.

The choice of summary statistics is at the same time the weak point of ABC and a great source of flexibility. For instance, by choosing the moments $\mu(\mathbf{y})$ or the coefficients β of an appropriate auxiliary model as summary statistics, it allows us to embed the method of simulated moments and indirect inference in a Bayesian setting, incorporating prior information. Also, an appropriate choice of the summary statistics allows to make *conditional forecasts* about the evolution of the real world. Suppose an extreme case where we only condition on the state of the system at time t: we wish to project the likely evolution of a system given $\mathbf{y}_t$. We can then simply set our summary statistics $\mathbf{S}(\mathbf{y}) = \mathbf{y}_{R,t}$; the ABC algorithm will retain any simulated trajectory that passes for $\mathbf{y}_t$, producing not only a (quite poor, in this case) approximation of the posterior, but also conditional projections about future states.[38]

Any condition can in principle be used as summary statistics; of course, the lower the informational content of the condition, the poorer the approximation (and the bigger the dispersion of the projections). However, there is also a drawback in increasing the informational content of the summary statistics, and it comes again from the trade-off between sampling error and approximation error. As Beaumont et al. (2002, p. 2026) put it, 'A crucial limitation of the ... method is that only a small number of summary statistics can usually be handled. Otherwise, either acceptance rates become prohibitively low or the tolerance ... must be increased, which can distort the approximation.' This is because the asymptotic rate of converge of ABC to the true posterior

---

[38] The case when it is possible to kill two birds (inference and conditional statements) with one stone is of course quite a lucky one. More generally, when the condition in the conditional statement is too poor to allow for good inference, we should keep the two problems separate: first, get a good approximation of the posterior (by selecting appropriate summary statistics); then, sample from the estimated posterior and select the trajectories that fulfil the condition.

distribution, as $h \to 0, N \to \infty$, worsens with dim(S). The problem with choosing appropriate *low-dimensional* summary statistics that are informative about θ is an open issue in ABC. 'The insidious issue is that it is rarely possible to verify either sufficiency or insufficiency. Furthermore, if they are insufficient, it is usually not possible to determine how badly they have distorted results. Said another way, you know you are probably making errors, but you don't know how large they are' (Holmes, 2015).

The topic is an active area of research. Recent years have seen the development of techniques that provide guidance in the selection of the summary statistics (see, e.g., Fearnhead and Prangle, 2012). Also, post-processing of the results can improve the quality of the approximation by correcting the distribution of θ by the difference between the observed and simulated summary statistics (Beaumont et al., 2002). Finally, new methods have appeared that require no summary statistics, external error terms or tolerance thresholds, at a computational cost (Turner and Sederberg, 2013).

Two final notes on ABC concern efficiency.

The standard scheme for ABC is, as we have seen, rejection sampling. Candidates are drawn from the prior distribution, and only those that perform well are retained. This is not very efficient, especially if the prior distribution differs significantly from the posterior. However, it is possible to employ ABC with more efficient sampling schemes (see Sisson et al., 2016). For instance, rather than sampling from the prior, one could sample from an importance distribution $q(\theta)$. Candidates are then accepted if $d(S, S_R) \leq h$, with a weight $p(\theta)(q(\theta))$. SMC methods can then be employed to adaptively refine both the threshold and the importance distribution. MCMC methods can also be employed, where new candidates depend on the current value of θ and are accepted with a modified Metropolis-Hastings rule.

Efficiency can also be improved in an ABC setting by assigning a *continuation probability* to each simulation. The idea is to stop premature simulations that are likely to end up in a rejection, and has originated the *lazy ABC* approach (Prangle, 2016).

9.4.4 ABC Estimation of the Segregation Model

As an illustration of the ABC approach, we estimate the Schelling model. As in Section 9.3.2, we assume to observe a segregation level of 70% (the average share of same-colour neighbours). The parameter to estimate is the individual (homogeneous) tolerance level, that is the minimum share of same-colour neighbours that a person is willing to accept before deciding to move out of the current location. Our prior is a uniform distribution between 0 and 1.

We then follow the simple rejection algorithm discussed in Section 9.4.3: we perform random sampling from the prior distribution, run the simulation with the sampled value of the parameter until an equilibrium configuration is obtained where nobody wants to move, compute the distance d between the observed level of segregation (70%) and the simulated one and retain only the values of the parameters where $d \leq h$, with different thresholds h.

When sampling from the prior distribution, we do not need to keep the random seed constant. Note that we could indeed fix the random seed: we would then obtain a posterior distribution reflecting the uncertainty net of non-ergodicity.[39] Then we could repeat, as with SMD, the estimation exercise many times for different random seeds, and obtain a *distribution of distributions*. Comparing the variance of the posterior distributions obtained with fixed seeds with the variance of the overall posterior distribution would permit to disentangle the uncertainty coming from the limited information contained in the data, plus the imprecise information underpinning our priors, from the uncertainty coming from non-ergodicity.

But disentangling these sources of uncertainty is not really relevant for Bayesians. This is because the main object of interest for Bayesians – the posterior – is already a distribution, which reflects the intrinsic uncertainty about the value of the parameter; for subjective Bayesians, such things as 'true' values of the parameters simply do not exist. Non-ergodicity however still matters for interpreting and using the estimates: when simulating a non-ergodic model, we should realize that multiple statistical equilibria exist for the same values of the parameters. This might be important for prediction and for policy analysis, as discussed in Section 9.2.

Figure 9.11 depicts the posteriors obtained in the Schelling model, for different levels of h. The prior for the individual tolerance threshold is a uniform distribution between 0 and 0.45. Over 2 million draws are taken from the prior. With $h = 10$ percentage points, the shape of the posterior is detectable, but the distribution stretches over a wide range of values. Decreasing the value of h to 5 percentage points reduces the range of admitted values, a sign that the approximation improves. However, decreasing h further seems to provide no additional benefits, at the cost of reducing sample size.

---

[39] In the Schelling model, because the long-run stationary state is just a constant value for the segregation level, for h low enough we would simply get a uniform posterior between the two values which give a level of segregation respectively immediately below and immediately above the observed level of 70%. See Figure 9.7.

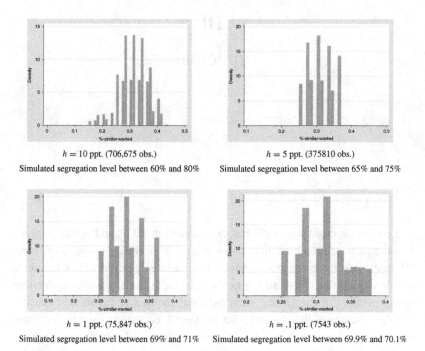

$h = 10$ ppt. (706,675 obs.)

Simulated segregation level between 60% and 80%

$h = 5$ ppt. (375810 obs.)

Simulated segregation level between 65% and 75%

$h = 1$ ppt. (75,847 obs.)

Simulated segregation level between 69% and 71%

$h = .1$ ppt. (7543 obs.)

Simulated segregation level between 69.9% and 70.1%

Figure 9.11 Posterior distributions in the Schelling model. 2,300,000 draws from a Uniform prior in (0,0.45).

9.5 Conclusions

Estimation of AB models has been so far confined to a few, relatively simple, cases. This is surely bound to change as the field gets more mature, and the challenge of empirical validation is taken seriously. Basically, the main difference between estimation of AB models and more standard applications lies in the higher computational complexity of AB models. This means that likelihood-based methods are in general impractical, unless very few parameters are involved. Likelihood-free methods like approximate Bayesian computation, which embed simulated minimum distance techniques in a Bayesian framework, seem therefore promising, especially coupled with the use of efficient Monte Carlo sampling.

10

Epilogue

The economic crisis the world has experienced in 2007, and is still ongoing in some parts of the globe, has been also a crisis of the economic profession. "Over the past three decades, economists have largely developed and come to rely on models that disregard key factors – including heterogeneity of decision rules, revisions of forecasting strategies, and changes in the social context – that drive outcomes in asset and other markets. It is obvious, even to the casual observer that these models fail to account for the actual evolution of the real-world economy... In our hour of greatest need, societies around the world are left to grope in the dark without a theory" (Colander et al., 2009).

This predicament was not new. Back in 1995, Frank Hahn and Robert Solow fiercefully argued against the new classical basic methodological principle according to which "the only appropriate micro model is Walrasian ... based exclusively on inter-temporal utility maximization subject to budget and technological constraints ... [This model] proposes that the actual economy can be read as it is ... approximating the infinite time discounted utility maximizing program of a single immortal representative agent ... There is simply no possibility of coordination failures ... Of course that is the economy of Dr. Pangloss and it bears little relation to the world" (Hahn, 1995, p.2). Since then, some developments of economic thought have gone in the right direction, but overall their criticisms have gone largely unnoticed. The straight jacket of axiomatic Walrasian micro-foundations has limited the scope of the research for alternatives.

Walrasian micro-foundations should be considered the wrong answer to a right research question, the most stimulating question since the very beginning of economic thought: How does a completely decentralized economy composed of myriads of self-interested agents manages to coordinate individual actions?

Agent-based models provide a promising tentative answer to this question. There is still a long way to go, but the path has been traced. These elements present and discuss the basic toolkit for researchers interested in building ABMs.

If the reader arrives so far in this book, we will be happy. If, from now on, it is we who will follow the reader's progress, we will be blissfully happy.

Bibliography

Aiyagari, S. R. (1994). Uninsured idiosyncratic risk and aggregate saving. *Quarterly Journal of Economics*, 109(3):659–684.

Albin, P. S. (1998). *Barriers and Bounds to Rationality: Essays on Economic Complexity and Dynamics in Interactive Systems*. Princeton University Press, Princeton, NJ.

Anderson, P., Arrow, K., and Pines, D., editors (1988). *The Economy as an Evolving Complex System*. SFI Studies in the Sciences of Complexity. Addison-Wesley Longman, Redwood City, CA.

Anderson, P. W. (1972). More is different. *Science*, 177(4047):393–396.

Andrieu, C., de Freitas, N., Doucet, A., and Jordan, M. (2003). An introduction to mcmc for machine learning. *Machine Learning*, 50(1):5–43.

Aoki, M. and Yoshikawa, H. (2006). *Reconstructing Macroeconomics*. Cambridge University Press.

Arrow, K. J. (1982). Risk perception in psychology and economics. *Economic Inquiry*, 20(1):1–9.

Arthur, W. (1988). Competing technologies: An overview. In Dosi, G., Freeman, C., Nelson, R., Silverberg, G., and Soete, L., editors, *Technical Change and Economic Theory*, pages 590–607, London. Pinter.

Arthur, W. (1990). *Emergent Structures: A Newsletter of the Economic Research Program*. The Santa Fe Institute, Santa Fe, NM.

Arthur, W. (1991). On designing economic agents that behave like human agents: A behavioural approach to bounded rationality. *American Economic Review*, 81:353–359.

Arthur, W. (1994). Inductive reasoning and bounded rationality. *American Economic Review*, 84:406.

Arthur, W., Durlauf, S., and Lane, D., editors (1997). *The Economy as an Evolving Complex System II*. Addison-Wesley Longman, Reading, MA.

Arthur, W. B. (2006). Out-of-equilibrium economics and agent-based modeling. In *Handbook of Computational Economics*, volume 2, pages 1551–1564. Elsevier.

Arulampalam, M., Maskell, S., Gordon, N., and Clapp, T. (2002). A tutorial on particle filters for online nonlinear/non-gaussian bayesian tracking. *IEEE Transactions on Signal Processing*, 50:174–188.

Askenazi, M., Burkhart, R., Langton, C., and Minar, N. (1996). The swarm simulation system: A toolkit for building multi-agent simulations. *Santa Fe Institute Working Paper no.* 96-06-042.

Assenza, T., Delli Gatti, D., and Grazzini, J. (2015). Emergent dynamics of a macroeconomic agent based model with capital and credit. *Journal of Economic Dynamics and Control*, 50(1):5–28.

Attal, S. (2010). Markov chains and dynamical systems: The open system point of view. *Communications on Stochastic Analysis*, 4:523–540.

Axtell, R. (2000). Why agents? On the varied motivations for agent computing in the social sciences. In *Proceedings of the Workshop on Agent Simulation: Applications, Models and Tools*. Argonne National Laboratory, IL.

Bailey, K. (1988). The conceptualization of validity: Current perspectives. *Social Science Research*, 17:117–136.

Bak, P., Chen, K., Scheinkman, J., and Woodford, M. (1993). Aggregate fluctuations from independent sectoral shocks: Self-organized criticality in a model of production and inventory dynamics. *Ricerche Economiche*, 47(1):3–30.

Baker, W. E. (1984). The social structure of a national securities market. *American Journal of Sociology*, 89(4):775–811.

Banerjee, A. (1992). A simple model of herd behaviour. *Quarterly Journal of Economics*, 108:797–817.

Barabasi, A. L. and Albert, R. (1999). Emergence of scaling in random networks. *Science*, 286:509–512.

Barreteau, O. (2003). Our companion modeling approach. *Journal of Artificial Societies and Social Simulation*, 6(1).

Bass, F. M. (1969). A new product growth for model consumer durables. *Management Science*, 15(5):215–227.

Beaumont, M. A., Zhang, W., and Balding, D. J. (2002). Approximate bayesian computation in population genetics. *Genetics*, 162(4):2025–2035.

Benzion, U., Rapoport, A., and Yagil, J. (1989). Discount rates inferred from decisions: An experimental study. *Management Science*, 35(3):270–284.

Bergmann, B. R. (1974). A microsimulation of the macroeconomy with explicitly represented money flows. *Annals of Economic and Social Measurement*, 3(3): 475–489.

Bergmann, B. R. (1990). Micro-to-macro simulation: A primer with a labor market example. *The Journal of Economic Perspectives*, 4:99–116.

Bergmann, B. R., Eliasson, G., and Orcutt, G. H., editors (1977). *Micro Simulation–Models, Methods, and Applications: Proceedings of the Symposium on Micro Simulation Methods, Stockholm, September 19–22.*

Bernanke, B., Gertler, M., and Gilchrist, S. (1999). The financial accelerator in a quantitative business cycle framework. In Woodford, M. and Taylor, J., editors, *Handbook of Macroeconomics*, volume 1, chapter 21, pages 1341–1393. North-Holland.

Bianchi, C., Cirillo, P., Gallegati, M., and Vagliasindi, P. A. (2007). Validating and calibrating agent-based models: A case study. *Computational Economics*, 30: 245–264.

Bianchi, C., Cirillo, P., Gallegati, M., and Vagliasindi, P. A. (2008). Validation in agent-based models: An investigation on the cats model. *Journal of Economic Behavior and Organization*, 67:947–964.

Bianconi, G. and Barabasi, A. L. (2001). Bose – Einstein condensation in complex networks. *Physical Review Letters*, 86:5632–5635.

Bikhchandani, S., Hirschleifer, D., and Welch, I. (1992). A theory of fads, fashion, custom and cultural change as informational cascades. *Journal of Political Economy*, 100:992–1026.

Blume, L. and Durlauf, S., editors (2006). *The Economy as an Evolving Complex System, III: Current Perspectives and Future Directions*. Santa Fe Institute in the Science of Complexity. Oxford University Press, Oxford, UK.

Booker, L. B., Goldberg, D. E., and Holland, J. H. (1989). Classifier systems and genetic algorithms. *Artificial Intelligence*, 40:235–282.

Box, G. E. P., Hunter, W. G., and Hunter, J. S. (1978). *Statistics for Experimenters: An Introduction to Design, Data Analysis and Model Building*. Wiley, New York.

Brailsford, S. (2014). Discrete-event simulation is alive and kicking. *Journal of Simulation*, 8(1):1–8.

Breiman, L., Freidman, J. H., Olshen, R. A., and Stone, J. H. (1984). *Classification and Regression Trees*. Chapman & Hall, New York,.

Brock, W. A. and Hommes, C. H. (1997). A rational route to randomness. *Econometrica*, 65:1059–1160.

Buiter, W. (1980). The macroeconomics of Dr. Pangloss: A critical survey of the new classical macroeconomics. *Economic Journal*, 90:34–50.

Bullard, J. (1994). Learning equilibria. *Journal of Economic Theory*, 64:468–485.

Caballero, R. J. (2010). Macroeconomics after the crisis: Time to deal with the pretense-of-knowledge syndrome. *Journal of Economic Perspectives*, 24:85–102.

Calvo-Armengol, A. and Jackson, M. O. (2004). The effects of social networks on employment and inequality. *American Economic Review*, 94(3):426–454.

Carr, E. (1961). *What Is History?* London, Macmillan.

Catania, J. A., Coates, T. J., Kegels, S., and Fullilove, M. T. (1997). Condom use in multi-ethnic neighborhoods of San Francisco: The population-based amen (Aids in multi-ethnic neighborhoods) study. *American Journal of Public Health*, 82:284–287.

Chan, K., Scott, E. M., and Andres, T. (2000). Software for sensitivity analysis – a brief review. In Saltelli, A., Chan, K., and Scott, E. M., editors, *Sensitivity Analysis*. John Wiley & Sons Ltd., Chichester.

Chew, S. H., Karni, E., and Safra, Z. (1987). Risk aversion and the theory of expected utility with rank-dependent probabilities. *Journal of Economic Theory*, 42:370–81.

Chew, S. H. and MacCrimmon, K. R. (1979). Alpha-nu choice theory: A generalization of expected utility theory. *Working paper, University of British Columbia, Vancouver*, 669.

Chiarella, C., Iori, G., and Perello, J. (2009). The impact of heterogeneous trading rules on the limit order book and order flows. *Journal of Economic Dynamics and Control*, 33(3):525–553.

Chu, D., Strand, R., and Fjelland, R. (2003). Theories of complexity. *Complexity*, 8(3):19–30.

Colander, D., Follmer, H., Haas, A., Goldberg, M., Juselius, K., Kirman, A., Lux, T., and Sloth, B. (2009). The financial crisis and the systemic failure of academic economics. *Kiel working paper*.

Collins, A. G. and Frank, M. J. (2012). How much of reinforcement learning is working memory, not reinforcement learning? A behavioral, computational, and neurogenetic analysis. *European Journal of Neuroscience*, 35:1024–1035.

Conlisk, J. (1996). Why bounded rationality. *Journal of Economic Literature*, 34(2): 669–700.

Cowan, R. and Foray, D. (2002). Evolutionary economics and the counterfactual threat: On the nature and role of counterfactual history as an empirical tool in economics. *Journal of Evolutionary Economics*, 12(5):539–562.

Cukier, R., Fortuin, C. M., Schuler, K. E., Petschek, A. G., and Schaibly, J. H. (1973). Study of the sensitivity of coupled reaction systems to uncertainties in the rate coefficients: I theory. *Journal of Chemical Physics*, 59:3873–3878.

Damasio, A. (1994). *Descartes' Error: Emotion, Reason and the Human Brain*. Avon Books, New York.

Daniel, C. (1973). One-at-time plans. *Journal of the American Statistical Association*, 68:353–360.

David, P. (1985). Clio and economics of qwerty. *American Economic Review Proceedings*, 75:332–337.

Daw, N. D., Niv, Y., and Dayan, P. (2005). Uncertainty-based competition between prefrontal and dorsolateral striatal systems for behavioral control. *Nature Neuroscience*, 8:1704–1711.

Dawid, H., Gemkow, S., Harting, P., van der Hoog, S., and Neugart, M. (2013). Agent-based macroeconomic modeling and policy analysis: The eurace@unibi model. In Chen, S.-H. and Kaboudan, M., editors, *Handbook on Computational Economics and Finance*. Oxford University Press, Oxford, UK.

Dawid, H., Gemkow, S., Harting, P., van der Hoog S., and Neugart, M. (2012). The eurace@unibi model: An agent-based macroeconomic model for economic policy analysis. *Working paper, University of Bielefeld*.

Dawkins, C., Srinivasan, T., and Whalley, J. (2001). Calibration. In Heckman, J. and Leamer, E., editors, *Handbook of Econometrics. Vol. 5.*, pages 3653–3703. Elsevier.

Dayan, P. and Berridge, K. (2014). Model-based and model-free pavlovian reward learning: Revaluation, revision, and revelation. *Cognitive, Affective, and Behavioral Neuroscience*, 14:473–492.

Dayan, P., Niv, Y., Seymour, B. J., and Daw, N. D. (2006). The misbehavior of value and the discipline of the will. *Neural Networks*, 19:1153–1160.

Deffuant, G., Huet, S., Bousset, J. P., Henriot, J., Amon, G., and Weisbuch, G. (2002). Agent-based simulation of organic conversion in allier départment. In Janssen, M. A., editor, *Complexity and Ecosystem Management*. Edward Elgar, Cheltenham.

Delli Gatti, D., Desiderio, S., Gaffeo, E., Cirillo, P., and Gallegati, M. (2011). *Macroeconomics from the Bottom-Up*. Springer-Verlag, Mailand.

Delli Gatti, D., Di Guilmi, C., Gaffeo, E., Giulioni, G., Gallegati, M., and Palestrini, A. (2005). A new approach to business fluctuations: Heterogeneous interacting agents, scaling laws and financial fragility. *Journal of Economic Behavior and Organization*, 56(4):489–512.

Delli Gatti, D., Gallegati, M., Greenwald, B., Russo, A., and Stiglitz, J. (2006). Business fluctuations in a credit-network economy. *Physica A*, 370(1):68–74.

Delli Gatti, D., Gallegati, M., Greenwald, B., Russo, A., and Stiglitz, J. (2008). Financially constrained fluctuations in an evolving network economy. *NBER Working paper*, 14112.

Delli Gatti, D., Gallegati, M., Greenwald, B., Russo, A., and Stiglitz, J. (2010). The financial accelerator in an evolving credit network. *Journal of Economic Dynamics and Control*, 34(9):1627–1650.

DeMarzo, P., Vayanos, D., and Zwiebel, J. (2003). Persuasion bias, social inauence, and unidimensional opinions. *Quarterly Journal of Economics*, 118(3):909–968.

Di Guilmi, C., L. S. G. M. (2016). *Interactive Macroeconomics*. Cambridge University Press, Cambridge, UK.

Diamond, D. and Dybvig, P. (1983). Bank runs, deposit insurance, and liquidity. *Journal of Political Economy*, 91(3):401–419.

Diamond, P. (1989). Search theory. In Eatwell, J., Milgate, M., and Newman, P., editors, *The New Palgrave: A Dictionary of Economics*, pages 273–279. Macmillan, London.

Dickinson, A. and Balleine, B. (2002). The role of learning in the operation of motivational systems. In Gallistel, R., editor, *Stevens' Handbook of Experimental Psychology*, pages 497–534. Wiley, Vol. 3. New York, NY.

Dolan, R. J. and Dayan, P. (2013). Goals and habits in the brain. *Neuron*, 80:312–325.

D'Orazio, P. and Silvestri, M. (2014). The empirical microstructure of agent-based models: Recent trends in the interplay between ace and experimental economics. In Omatu, S., Bersini, H., Corchado, M. J., Rodríguez, S., Pawlewski, P., and Bucciarelli, E., editors, *Distributed Computing and Artificial Intelligence, 11th International Conference*, pages 85–90. Springer International Publishing, Cham.

Dorogovtsev, S. N. and Mendes, J. F. F. (2001). Effect of the accelerating growth of communications networks on their structure,. *Physical Review E*, 63:25–101.

Dosi, G., Fagiolo, G., Napoletano, M., Roventini, A., and Treibich, T. (2015). Fiscal and monetary policies in complex evolving economies. *Journal of Economic Dynamics and Control*, 52(C):166–189.

Dosi, G., Fagiolo, G., and Roventini, A. (2006). An evolutionary model of endogenous business cycles. *Computational Economics*, 27(1):3–34.

Dosi, G., Fagiolo, G., and Roventini, A. (2010). Schumpeter meeting keynes: A policy-friendly model of endogenous growth and business cycles. *Journal of Economic Dynamics and Control*, 34(9):1748–1767.

Dosi, G., Marengo, L., and Fagiolo, G. (2005). Learning in evolutionary environments. In Dopfer, K., editor, *Evolutionary Principles of Economics*. Cambridge University Press.

Dosi, G. and Nelson, R. (1994). An introduction to evolutionary theories in economics. *Journal of Evolutionary Economics*, 4:153–172.

Dridi, R. and Renault, E. (2000). Semi-parametric indirect inference. *Working Paper* 396, London School of Economics – Suntory Toyota, Econometrics.

Duffy, J. (2006). Agent-based models and human subject experiments. In Tesfatsion, L. and Judd, K. L., editors, *Handbook of Computational Economics*, volume 2, chapter 19, pages 949–1011. Elsevier.

Edmonds, B. (1999). The evolution of complexity. In Heylighen, F. and Aerts, D., editors, *What Is Complexity? – The Philosophy of Complexity per se with Application to Some Examples in Evolution*. Kluwer, Dordrecht.

Eliasson, G. (1977). Competition and market processes in a simulation model of the swedish economy. *The American Economic Review*, 67:277–281.

Eliasson, G., Olavi, G., and Heiman, M. (1976). A micro-macro interactive simulation model of the swedish economy. *IUI Working Paper*, (7).

Epstein, J. (1999). Agent-based computational models and generative social science. *Complexity*, 4(5):41–60.

Epstein, J. (2006a). Remarks on the foundations of agent-based generative social science. In Tesfatsion and Judd (2006).

Epstein, J. and Axtell, R. (1996). *Growing Artificial Societies: Social Science from the Bottom Up*. The MIT Press, Cambridge, MA.

Epstein, J. M. (2006b). *Generative Social Science: Studies in Agent-Based Computational Modeling*. Princeton University Press, Princeton, NY.

Epstein, J. M. (2008). Why model? *Journal of Artificial Societies and Social Simulation*, 11(4).

Evans, G. W. and Honkapohja, S. (2001). *Learning and Expectations in Macroeconomics*. Princeton University Press, Princeton.

Fagiolo, G. (1998). Spatial interactions in dynamic decentralised economies. In Cohendet, P., Llerena, P., Stahn, H., and Umbhauer, G., editors, *The Economics of Networks: Interaction and Behaviours*. Springer Verlag, Berlin Heidelberg.

Fagiolo, G. and Dosi, G. (2003a). Exploitation, exploration and innovation in a model of endogenous growth with locally interacting agents. *Structural Change and Economic Dynamics*, 14:237–273.

Fagiolo, G. and Dosi, G. (2003b). Exploitation, exploration and innovation in a model of endogenous growth with locally interacting agents. *Structural Change and Economic Dynamics*, 14(3):237–273.

Fagiolo, G., Dosi, G., and Gabriele, R. (2004a). Matching, bargaining, and wage setting in an evolutionary model of labor market and output dynamics. *Advances in Complex Systems*, 7:157–186.

Fagiolo, G., Dosi, G., and Gabriele, R. (2004b). Matching, bargaining, and wage setting in an evolutionary model of labor market and output dynamics. *Advances in Complex Systems*, 07(2):157–186.

Farmer, J. D. and Foley, D. (2009). The economy needs agent-based modelling. *Nature*, 460:685–686.

Fearnhead, P. and Prangle, D. (2012). Constructing summary statistics for approximate bayesian computation: Semi-automatic approximate bayesian computation. *Journal of the Royal Statistical Society: Series B (Statistical Methodology)*, 74(3):419–474.

Feldman, A. M. (1973). Bilateral trading processes, pairwise optimality, and pareto optimality. *The Review of Economic Studies*, 40:463–473.

Feller, W. (1957). *An Introduction to Probability Theory and Its Applications*. John Wiley and Sons Inc.

Feyerabend, P. (1975). *Against Method*. Verso, London.

Fibich, G. and Gibori, R. (2010). Aggregate diffusion dynamics in agent-based models with a spatial structure. *Operations Research*, 58(5):1450–1468.

Fisher, R. (1922). On the mathematical foundations of theoretical statistics. *Philosophical Transactions of the Royal Society A*, 222:309–368.

Föllmer, H. (1974). Random economies with many interacting agents. *Journal of Mathematical Economics*, 1:51–62.

Forrester, J. (1971). Counterintuitive behavior of social systems. *Technology Review*, 73(3):52–68.

Friedman, M. (1953). *Essays in Positive Economics*. University of Chicago Press.

Fu, Y. and Li, W. (1997). Estimating the age of the common ancestor of a sample of dna sequences. *Molecular Biology and Evolution*, 14(2):195–199.

Gabszewicz, J. and Thisse, J. F. (1986). Spatial competition and the location of firms. In Lesourne, J. and Sonnenschein, H., editors, *Location Theory*, pages 1–71. Harwood Academic Publishers, London.

Gaffeo, E., Delli Gatti, D., Desiderio, S., and Gallegati, M. (2008). Adaptive microfoundations for emergent macroeconomics. *Eastern Economic Journal*, 34:441–463.

Gallant, A.R. and Tauchen, G. (1996). Which moments to match? *Econometric Theory*, 12:657–681.

Gardner, M. (1970). Mathematical games: The fantastic combinations of John Conway's new solitaire game "Life." *Scientific American*, 223:120–123.

Gigerenzer, G. and Selten, R., editors (2001a). *Bounded Rationality: The Adaptive Toolbox*. The MIT Press, Cambridge, MA.

Gigerenzer, G. and Selten, R. (2001b). *Bounded Rationality: The Adaptive Toolbox*. The MIT Press, Cambridge.

Gigerenzer, G., Todd, P. M., and the ABC Research Group (1999). *Simple Heuristics that Make Us Smart*. Oxford University Press, New York.

Gilles, R. P. and Ruys, P. H. M. (1989). Relational constraints in coalition formation. *Research Memorandum Tilburg University*, 371.

Gleick, J. (1987). *Chaos: Making a New Science*. Penguin Books, New York.

Gleick, J. (1992). *Genius: The Life and Science of Richard Feynman*. Pantheon Books, New York.

Glimcher, P. W., Camerer, C. F., Fehr, E., and Poldrack, R. A. (2009). *Neuroeconomics: Decision Making and the Brain*. Academic Press, New York.

Gouriéroux, C. S. and Monfort, A. (1996). *Simulation-Based Econometric Methods*. Oxford University Press, New York.

Granovetter, M. (1985). Economic action and social structure: The problem of embeddedness. *American Journal of Sociology*, 91:481–510.

Grazzini, J. (2012). Analysis of the emergent properties: Stationarity and ergodicity. *Journal of Artificial Societies and Social Simulation*, 15(2).

Grazzini, J. and Richiardi, M. (2015). Estimation of agent-based models by simulated minimum distance. *Journal of Economic Dynamics and Control*, 51:148–165.

Grazzini, J., Richiardi, M., and Sella, L. (2012). Small sample bias in msm estimation of agent-based models. In Teglio, A., Alfarano, S., Camacho-Cuena, E., and Giné-Vilar, M., editors, *Managing Market Complexity: The Approach of Artificial Economics*. Lecture Notes in Economics and Mathematical Systems. Springer.

Grazzini, J., Richiardi, M., and Tsionas, M. (2015). Bayesian inference in ergodic agent-based models. Institute for New Economic Thinking, University of Oxford.

Grilli, R., Tedeschi, G., and Gallegati, M. (2012). Markets connectivity and financial contagion. *Journal of Economic Interaction and Coordination*, 10(2):287–304.

Haavelmo, T. (1944). The probability approach in econometrics. *Econometrica*, 12(Supplement):1–118.

Hahn, F., S. R. (1995). *A Critical Essay on Modern Macroeconomic Theory*. MIT Press, Cambridge.

Haken, H. (1983). *"Synergetics." Non-equilibrium Phase Transitions and Social Measurement*. Springer-Verlag, Berlin, 3rd edition.

Happe, K. (2005). Agent-based modeling and sensitivity analysis by experimental design and metamodeling: An application to modeling regional structural change. In *Proceedings of the XI International Congress of the European Association of Agricultural Economists*.

Happe, K., Kellermann, K., and Balmann, A. (2006). Agent-based analysis of agricultural policies: An illustration of the agricultural policy simulator agripolis, its adaptation, and behavior. *Ecology and Society*, 11(1).

Hartig, F., Calabrese, J. M., Reineking, B., Wiegand, T., and Huth, A. (2011). Statistical inference for stochastic simulation models: Theory and application. *Ecology Letters*, 14:816–827.

Heathcote, J., S. K. V. G. (2009). Quantitative macroeconomics with heterogeneous households. *Annual Review of Economics*, 1:319–354.

Heckbert, S. (2009). Experimental economics and agent-based models. 18th World IMACS/MODSIM Congress, Cairns, Australia.

Hendry, D. F. (1980). Econometrics-alchemy or science? *Economica*, 47(188): 387–406.

Higgins, E. T. (1996). Knowledge activation: Accessibility, applicability, and salience. In Higgins, E. T. and Kruglanski, A. W., editors, *Social Psychology: Handbook of Basic Principles*, pages 133–168. The Guilford Press, New York.

Hildenbrand, W. (1971). On random preferences and equilibrium analysis. *Journal of Economic Theory*, 3:414–429.

Hinkelmann, F., Murrugarra, D., Jarrah, A. S., and Laubenbacher, R. (2011). A mathematical framework for agent based models of complex biological networks. *Bulletin of Mathematical Biology*, 73(7):1583–1602.

Hodgson, G. M. (2007). Meanings of methodological individualism. *Journal of Economic Methodology*, 14(2):211–226.

Holcomb, J. H. and Nelson, P. S. (1992). Another experimental look at individual time preference. *Rationality and Society*, 4:199–220.

Holland, J. H. (1986). A mathematical framework for studying learning in classifier systems. *Physica D*, 22:307–317.

Holmes, W. R. (2015). A practical guide to the probability density approximation (pda) with improved implementation and error characterization. *Journal of Mathematical Psychology*, 68–69:13–24.

Hommes, C. and Lux, T. (2013). Individual expectations and aggregate behavior in learning-to-forecast experiments. *Macroeconomic Dynamics*, 17:373–401.

Hommes, C. H. (2006). Heterogeneous agent models in economics and finance. In Tesfatsion and Judd (2006), chapter 23, pages 1109–1186.

Hommes, C. H. (2009). Bounded rationality and learning in complex markets. In Rosser, J. B. J., editor, *Handbook of Research on Complexity*, chapter 5. Edward Elgar, Cheltenham.

Horgan, J. (1995). From complexity to perplexity. *Scientific American*, 272(6):104.

Horgan, J. (1997). *The End of Science: Facing the Limits of Knowledge in the Twilight of the Scientific Age*. Broadway Books, New York.

Howitt, P. and Clower, R. (2000). The emergence of economic organization. *Journal of Economic Behavior and Organization*, 41(1):55–84.

Ioannides, Y. M. (1994). Trading uncertainty and market form. *International Economic Review*, 31:619–638.

Iori, G., de Masi, G., Precup, O., Gabbi, G., and Caldarelli, G. (2008). A network analysis of the italian overnight money market. *Journal of Economic Dynamics and Control*, 32:259–278.

Izquierdo, L. R., Izquierdo, S. S., Galán, J. M., and Santos, J. I. (2009). Techniques to understand computer simulations: Markov chain analysis. *Journal of Artificial Societies and Social Simulation*, 12(1):6.

Jackson, M. O. (2008). *Social and Economic Networks*. Princeton University Press, Princeton & Oxford.

Janssen, M. C. W. (1993). *Microfoundations: A Critical Inquiry*. Routledge.

Jones, R. H. (2000). *Reductionism: Analysis and the Fullness of Reality*. Associated University Press, London.

Kahneman, D. and Tversky, A. (1974). Judgment under uncertainty: Heuristics and biases. *Science*, 185(4157):1124–31.

Kahneman, D. and Tversky, A. (1979). Prospect theory: An analysis of decision under risk. *Econometrica*, 47(2):263–291.

Kakade, S. M., Kearns, M., Ortiz, L. E., Pemantle, R., and Suri, S. (2004). Economic properties of social networks. In *Proceedings of Neural and Information Processing Systems, (NIPS)*.

Kaldor, N. (1961). *Capital Accumulation and Economic Growth*. MacMillan, London.

Kelso, J. A. S. and Engstrom, D. (2006). *The Complementarity Nature*. MIT Press, Cambridge.

Keynes, J. M. (1937). The general theory of employment. *The Quarterly Journal of Economics*, 51(2):209–223.

Kirman, A. (1993). Ants, rationality, and recruitment. *The Quarterly Journal of Economics*, 108:137–156.

Kirman, A. (2010). Complex economics: Individual and collective rationality. In *The Graz Schumpeter Lectures (Eds)*.

Kirman, A. and Vriend, N. (2001). Evolving market structure: An ace model of price dispersion and loyalty. *Journal of Economic Dynamics and Control*, 25:459–502.

Kirman, A. P. (1983). On mistaken beliefs and resultant equilibria. In Frydman, R. and Phelps, E., editors, *Individual Forecasts and Aggregate Outcomes*. Cambridge University Press, Cambridge.

Kirman, A. P. (1994). Economies with interacting agents. *Santa Fa Institute Working Papers*, 1994 – 30.

Kleijnen, J. P. C., Sanchez, S. M., Lucas, T. W., and Cioppa, T. M. (2003). A user's guide to the brave new world of designing simulation experiments. CentER Discussion paper, Tilburg University.

Kleijnen, J. P. C. and Sargent, R. G. (2000). A methodology for the fitting and validation of metamodels in simulation. *European Journal of Operational Research*, 1:14–29.

Kleijnen, J. P. C. and van Groenendaal, W. (1992). *Simulation: A Statistical Perspective*. John Wiley & Sons Ltd., New York,.

Klejinen, J. (2000). Validation of models: Statistical techniques and data availability. In *Proceedings of 1999 Winter Simulation Conference*, pages 647–654.

Knight, F. (1921). *Risk, Uncertainty and Profits*. Houghton Mifflin, Boston and New York.

Koppl, R. (2000). Policy implications of complexity: An austrian perspective. In Colander, D., editor, *The Complexity Vision and the Teaching of Economics*, pages 97–117. Edward Elgar, Cheltenham.

Koza, J. R. (1992). *Genetic Programming: On the Programming of Computers by Means of Natural Selection*. The MIT Press, Cambridge.

Krusell, P., and Smith, A. (1998). Income and wealth heterogeneity, portfolio choice and equilibrium asset returns. *Journal of Political Economy*, 106(5):867–896.

Kwasnicki, W. (1998). Simulation methodology in evolutionary economics. In Schweitzer, F. and Silverberg, G., editors, *Evolution und Selbstorganisation in der konomie*. Duncker and Humblot, Berlin.

Lakatos, I. (21970). Falsification and the methodology of scientific research programmes. In Lakatos, I. and Musgrave, A., editors, *Criticism and the Growth of Knowledge*. Cambridge University Press, Cambridge, UK.

Leamer, E. (1978). *Specification Searches: Ad Hoc Inference with Nonexperimental Data*. John Wiley, New York.

LeBaron, B. (2006). Agent-based computational finance. In Tesfatsion, L. and Judd, K. L., editors, *Handbook of Computational Economics, Vol 2*. North-Holland/ Elsevier, Amsterdam.

LeBaron, B. and Tesfatsion, L. (2008). Modeling macroeconomies as open-ended dynamic systems of interacting agents. *American Economic Review: Papers & Proceedings*, 98(2):246–250.

Liebowitz, S. J. and Margolis, S. E. (1990). The fable of the keys. *Journal of Law and Economics*, 4(1):1–25.

Ljungqvist, L., S. T. (2004). *Recursive Macroeconomic Theory*. MIT Press, Cambridge, Mass.

Loewenstein, G. F., Weber, E. U., Hsee, C. K., and Welch, E. S. (2001). Risk as feelings. *Psychological Bulletin*, 127(2):267–286.

Loomes, G. and Sugden, R. (1982). Regret theory: An alternative theory of rational choice under uncertainty. *Economc Journal*, 92:805–24.

Lucas, R. (1976). Econometric policy evaluation: A critique. In Brunner, K. and Meltzer, A., editors, *The Phillips Curve and Labor Markets*, number 1 in Carnegie-Rochester Conference Series on Public Policy, pages 19–46. American Elsevier, New York.

Luenberger, D. (1979). *Introduction to Dynamic Systems: Theory, Models, and Applications*. Wiley, New York.

Lux, T. and Marchesi, M. (2002). Special issue on heterogeneous interacting agents in financial markets. *Journal of Economic Behavior and Organization*, 49(2):143–147.

Lynam, T. (2002). Scientific measurement and villagers' knowledge: An integrative multi-agent model from the semi-arid areas of zimbabwe. In Janssen, M. A., editor, *Complexity and Ecosystem Management*, pages 188–217. Edward Elgar, New York.

M. Aoki, H. Y. (2011). *Reconstructing Macroeconomics: A Perspective from Statistical Physics and Combinatorial Stochastic Processes*. Cambridge University Press, Cambridge.

Macal, C. M. (2010). To agent-based simulation from system dynamics. In *Proceedings of the 2010 Winter Simulation Conference*, pages 371–382.

Machina, M. J. (1982). Expected utility analysis without the independence axiom. *Econometrica*, 50:277–323.

Mackintosh, N. (1983). *Conditioning and Associative Learning*. Oxford University Press, New York.

Mäki, U. (1992). On the method of isolation in economics. In Dilworth, C., editor, *Idealization IV: Intelligibility in Science*, Poznan Studies in the Philosophy of the Sciences and the Humanities. Rodopi.

Mäki, U. (1998). Realism. In Davis, J., Hands, D. W., and Maki, U., editors, *The Handbook of Economic Methodology*. Cheltenham, UK.

Malerba, F., Nelson, R., Orsenigo, L., and Winter, S. (1999). History-friendly' models of industry evolution: The computer industry. *Industrial and Corporate Change*, 8(1):3–40.

Malerba, F. and Orsenigo, L. (2002). Innovation and market structure in the dynamics of the pharmaceutical industry and biotechnology: Towards a history friendly model. *Industrial and Corporate Change*, 11(4):667–703.

Manson, S. M. (2006). Bounded rationality in agent-based models: Experiments with evolutionary programs. *International Journal of Geographical Information Science*, 9(20):991–1012.

Marin, J.-M., Pudlo, P., Robert, C. P., and Ryder, R. J. (2011). Approximate bayesian computational methods. *Statistics and Computing*, 22(6):1167–1180.

Marks, R. E. (2007). Validating simulation models: A general framework and four applied examples. *Computatational Economics*, 30(3):265–290.

Martini, A. and Trivellato, U. (1997). The role of survey data in microsimulation models for social policy analysis. *Labour*, 11(1):83–112.

Milgram, S. (1967). The small-world problem. *Psychology Today*, 2:60–67.

Miller, J. H. and Page, S. E. (2006). *Complex Adaptive Systems: An Introduction to Computational Models of Social Life*. Princeton University Press, Princeton, NY.

Muth, J. F. (1961). Rational expectations and the theory of price movements. *Econometrica*, 29(3):315–335.

Nelson, R. R. and Winter, S. (1982). *An Evolutionary Theory of Economic Change*. Belknap Press of Harvard University Press, Cambridge.

Neugart, M. (2008). Labor market policy evaluation with ace. *Journal of Economic Behavior and Organization*, 67:418–430.

Newman, M. E. J. (2003a). Ego-centered networks and the ripple effect. *Social Networks*, 25:83–95.

Newman, M. E. J. (2003b). Mixing patterns in networks. *Physical Review E*, 67.

Newman, M. E. J. (2003c). Random graphs as models of networks. In Bornholdt, S. and Schuster, H. G., editors, *Hand-book of Graphs and Networks*, pages 35–68. Wiley-VCH, Berlin.

Newman, M. E. J. (2010). *Networks: An Introduction*. Oxford University Press, New York.

Nicolis, G. and Prigogine, I. (1989). *Exploring Complexity: An Introduction*. Springer-Verlag, New York.

Nocedal, J. and Wright, S. J. (1999). *Numerical Optimization*. Springer.

O'Hagan, A. (2006). Bayesian analysis of computer code outputs: A tutorial. *Reliability Engineering and System Safety*, 91:1290–1300.

Orcutt, G. (1957). A new type of socio economic system. *Review of Economics and Statistics*, 58:773–797.

Orcutt, G. H. (1990). The microanalytic approach for modeling national economies. *Journal of Economic Behavior and Organization*, 14:29–41.

Orcutt, G. H., Greenberger, M., Korbel, J., and Rivlin, A. M. (1961). *Microanalysis of Socioeconomic Systems: A Simulation Study*. Harper & Brothers, London.

Palmer, S. E. (1999). Gestalt perception. In Wilson, R. A. and Keil, F. C., editors, *The MIT Encyclopedia of the Cognitive Sciences*. MIT Press, Cambridge.

Pender, J. L. (1996). Discount rates and credit markets: Theory and evidence from rural india. *Journal of Development Economics*, 50:257–296.

Phelan, S. (2001). What is complexity science, really? *Emergence*, 3(1):120–136.

Potts, J. (2000). *The New Evolutionary Microeconomics*. Edward Elgar, Cheltenham – Northampton.

Prangle, D. (2016). Lazy ABC. *Statistics and Computing*, 26(1–2):171–185.

Price, D. J. d. S. (1965). Networks of scientific papers. *Science*, 149:510–515.

Prigogine, I. and Stengers, I. (1984). *Order out of Chaos: Man's New Dialogue with Nature*. Bantam Books, New York.

Pyka, A. and Fagiolo, G. (2007). Agent-based modelling: A methodology for neo-schumpetarian economics. In Hanusch, H. and Pyka, A., editors, *Elgar Companion to Neo-Schumpeterian Economics*, chapter 29, pages 467–487.

Quiggin, J. (1982). A theory of anticipated utility. *Journal of Economic Behavior and Organization*, 3:323–343.

Quiggin, J. (1993). *Generalized Expected Utility Theory: The Rank-Dependent Expected Utility Model*. Kluwer-Nijhoff, Amsterdam.

Rangel, A., Camerer, C., and Montague, M. (2008). A framework for studying the neurobiology of value-based decision-making. *Nature Reviews Neuroscience*, 9:545–556.

Rasmussen, C. E. and Williams, C. K. I. (2006). *Gaussian Processes for Machine Learning*. MIT Press, Cambridge, MA.

Rescorla, R. A. and Wagner, A. R. (1972). A theory of pavlovian conditioning: The effectiveness of reinforcement and non-reinforcement. In Black, A. H. and Prokasy, W. F., editors, *Classical Conditioning II: Current Research and Theory*, pages 64–69. Appleton-Century-Crofts, New York.

Resnick, M. (1994). *Turtles, Termites and Traffic Jams: Explorations in Massively Parallel Microworlds*. The MIT Press, Cambridge, MA.

Riccetti, L., Russo, A., and Gallegati, M. (2014). An agent based decentralized matching macroeconomic model. *Journal of Economic Interaction and Coordination*, 10:305–332.

Richiardi, M. (2006). Toward a non-equilibrium unemployment theory. *Computational Economics*, 27:135–160.

Richiardi, M. (2013). The missing link: Ab models and dynamic microsimulation. In Leitner, S. and Wall, F., editors, *Artificial Economics and Self Organization*, volume 669 of *Lecture Notes in Economics and Mathematical Systems*. Springer, Berlin.

Richiardi, M. G. (2005). On the virtues of the shame lane. *Topics in Economic Analysis & Policy*, 5(1):Article 8.

Rios-Rull, J. (1995). Models with heterogeneous agents. In Cooley, T., editor, *Frontiers of Business Cycles Research*. Princeton University Press.

Rose, K. A., Smith, A. P., Gardner, R. H., Brenkert, A. L., and Bartell, S. M. (1991). Parameter sensitivities, Monte Carlo filtering, and model forecasting under uncertainty. *Journal of Forecasting*, 10:117–33.

Rosser, J. B. J. (1999). On the complexities of complex economic dynamics. *The Journal of Economic Perspectives*, 13(4):169–192.

Rosser, J. B. J. (2010). How complex are the Austrians? In Koppl, R., Horwitz, S., and Desrochers, P., editors, *What Is so Austrian about Austrian Economics?*, pages 165–179. Emerald Group Publishing Limited.

Roth, A. E. and Ever, I. (1995). Learning in extensive-form games: Experimental data and simple dynamic models in the intermediate term. *Games and Economic Behavior*, 8(1):164–212.

Russo, A., Catalano, M., Gaffeo, E., Gallegati, M., and Napoletano, M. (2007). Industrial dynamics, fiscal policy and r&d: Evidence from a computational experiment. *Journal of Economic Behavior and Organization*, 64:425–440.

Saltelli, A. (2000). Fortune and future of sensitivity analysis. In Saltelli, A., Chan, K., and Scott, E. M., editors, *Sensitivity Analysis*. John Wiley & Sons Ltd., Chichester, West Sussex England.

Saltelli, A., Chan, K., and Scott, E. M. (2000). *Sensitivity Analysis*. Jonh Wiley & Sons Ltd., Chichester, West Sussex England.

Saltelli, A., Ratto, M., Andres, T., Campolongo, F., Cariboni, J., Gatelli, D., Saisana, M., and Tarantola, S. (2008). *Global Sensitivity Analysis: The primer*. John Wiley & Sons, Ltd., Chichester, West Sussex England.

Saltelli, A., Tarantola, S., Campolongo, F., and Ratto, M. (2004). *Sensitivity Analysis in Practice: A Guide to Assessing Scientific Models*. John Wiley & Sons, Ltd., Chichester.

Santner, T. J., Williams, B. J., and Notz, W. I. (2003). *The Design and Analysis of Computer Experiments*. Springer, New York.

Sargent, R. P. (1998). Verification and validation of simulation models. In *Proceedings of 1998 Winter Simulation Conference*.

Sargent, T. J. (1993). *Bounded Rationality in Macroeconomics*. Clarendon Press, Oxford.

Savage, L. (1954). *The Foundations of Statistics*. John Wiley, New York.

Schelling, T. (1969). Models of segregation. *American Economic Review*, 59(2): 488–493.

Schelling, T. (1971). Dynamic models of segregration. *Journal of Mathematical Sociology*, 1:143–186.

Schelling, T. C. (2006). Some fun, thirty-five years ago. In Tesfatsion and Judd (2006), chapter 37, pages 1639–1644.

Schumpeter, J. (1909). On the concept of social value. *The Quarterly Journal of Economics*, 23(2):213–232.

Seymour, B. J. and Dolan, R. (2008). Emotion, decision making, and the amygdala. *Neuron*, 58:662–671.

Siebers, P. O., Macal, C. M., Garnett, J., Buxton, D., and Pidd, M. (2010). Discrete-event simulation is dead, long live agent-based simulation! *Journal of Simulation*, 4(3):204–210.

Simon, H. (1981). *The Sciences of the Artificial*. MIT Press, Cambridge.

Simon, H. A. (1955). On a class of skew distribution functions. *Biometrika*, 42: 425–440.

Simon, H. A. (1987). Using cognitive science to solve human problems. In Farley, F. and Null, C. H., editors, *Using Psychological Science: Making the Public Case*. The Federation of Behavioral, Psychological and Cognitive Sciences, Washington, DC.

Sisson, S. A., Fan, Y., and Beaumont, M., editors (2016). *Handbook of Approximate Bayesian Computation*. Taylor & Francis.

Slovic, P., Finucane, M. L., Peters, E., and MacGregor, D. G. (2002). The affect heuristic. In Gilovich, T., Griffin, D., and Kahneman, D., editors, *Heuristics and Biases: The Psychology of Intuitive Judgment*, pages 397–420. Cambridge University Press, New York.

Stanislaw, H. (1986). Tests of computer simulation validity: What do they measure? *Simulation and Games*, 17:173–191.

Stern, S. (1997). Simulation based estimation. *Journal of Economic Literature*, 35(4):2006–2039.

Stern, S. (2000). Simulation-based inference in econometrics: Motivation and methods. In Mariano, R., Schuermann, T., and Weeks, M. J., editors, *Simulation-Based Inference in Econometrics: Methods and Applications*. Cambridge University Press.

Stiglitz, J. E. and Greenwald, B. (2003). *Towards a New Paradigm in Monetary Economics*. Cambridge University Press, Cambridge.

Story, G., Vlaev, I., Seymour, B., Darzi, A., and Dolan, R. (2014). Does temporal discounting explain unhealthy behavior? A systematic review and reinforcement learning perspective. *Frontiers in Behavioral Neuroscience*, 8:76.

Sutton, R. S. (1988). Learning to predict by the methods of temporal difference. *Machine Learning*, 3:9–44.

Sutton, R. S. and Barto, A. G. (1998). *Reinforcement Learning: An Introduction*. Cambridge University Press, Cambridge.

Talmi, D., Seymour, B., Dayan, P., and Dolan, R. (2008). Human pavlovian-instrumental transfer. *Journal of Neuroscience*, 28:360–368.

Tavaré, S., Balding, D. J., Griffiths, R. C., and Donnelly, P. (1997). Inferring coalescent times from DNA sequence data. *Genetics*, 145:505–518.

Tedeschi, G., Iori, G., and Gallegati, M. (2009). The role of communication and imitation in limit order markets. *European Physical Journal B*, 71(4):489–497.

Tedeschi, G., Iori, G., and Gallegati, M. (2012). Herding effects in order driven markets: The rise and fall of gurus. *Journal of Economic Behavior and Organization*, 81:82–96.

Tesfatsion, L. (2006). Agent-based computational economics: A constructive approach to economic theory. In Tesfatsion, L. and Judd, K. L., editors, *Handbook of Computational Economics*, volume 2, chapter 16, pages 831 – 880. North-Holland.

Tesfatsion, L. and Judd, K., editors (2006). *Handbook of Computational Economics.*, volume 2 of *Handbook in Economics 13*. North-Holland.

Thaler, R. (1981). Some empirical evidence on dynamic inconsistency. *Economics Letters*, 8(3):201–207.

Turner, B. M. and Sederberg, P. B. (2013). A generalized, likelihood-free method for posterior estimation. *Psychonomic Bulletin & Review*, 20(5):227–250.

Turner, B. M. and Zandt, T. V. (2012). A tutorial on approximate bayesian computation. *Journal of Mathematical Psychology*, 56:69–85.

Tversky, A. and Kahneman, D. (1981). The framing of decisions and the psychology of choice. *Science*, 211(4481):453–458.

Tversky, A. and Kahneman, D. (1986). Rational choice and the framing of decisions. *Journal of Business*, 59(4):251–278.

Vandierendonck, A. (1975). Inferential simulation: Hypothesis-testing by computer simulation. *Nederlands Tijdschrift voor de Psychologie*, 30:677–700.

Vaughn, K. (1999). Hayek's theory of the market order as an instance of the theory of complex adaptive systems. *Journal des economists et des Etudes humaines*, 9:241–256.

Vega-Redondo, F. (1996). *Evolution, Games, and Economic Behavior*. Oxford University Press, Oxford.

Vega-Redondo, F. (2007). *Complex Social Networks*. Cambridge University Press, Cambridge.

Vlaev, I. and Dolan, P. (2015). Action change theory: A reinforcement learning perspective on behaviour change. *Review of General Psychology*, 19:69–95.

von Hayek, F. A. (1948). *Individualism and Economic Order*. University of Chicago Press, Chicago.

von Hayek, F. A. (1967). The theory of complex phenomena. In *Studies in Philosophy, Politics, and Economics*, pages 22–42. University of Chicago Press, Chicago.

von Neumann, J. and Burks, A. W. (1966). *Theory of Self-Reproducing Automata*. University of Illinois Press, Urbana, IL.

Voon, V., Derbyshire, K., Rück, C., Irvine, M. A., Worbe, Y., Enander, J., Schreiber, L. R., Gillan, C., Fineberg, N. A., Sahakian, B. J., Robbins, T. W., Harrison, N. A., Wood, J., Daw, N. D., Dayan, P., Grant, J. E., and Bullmore, E. T. (2015). Disorders of compulsivity: A common bias towards learning habits. *Molecular Psychiatry*, 20:345–352.

Vriend, N. (1994). Self-organized markets in a decentralized economy. *Santa Fa Institute Working Papers*, 1994–13.

Vriend, N. (2000). An illustration of the essential difference between individual and social learning, and its consequences for computational analyses. *Journal of Economic Dynamics & Control*, 24:1–19.

Vriend, N. J. (2002). Was hayek an ace? *Southern Economic Journal*, 68(4):811–840.

Vriend, N. J. (2006). Ace models of endogenous interaction. In Tesfatsion, L. and Judd, K. L., editors, *Handbook of Computational Economics, Vol. 2*, pages 1047–1079. North-Holland/Elsevier, Amsterdam.

Waldrop, M. (1992). *Complexity: The Emerging Science at the Edge of Order and Chaos*. Touchstone, New York.

Watts, D. J. and Strogatz, S. H. (1998). Collective dynamics of small-world networks. *Nature Reviews Neuroscience*, 393:440–442.

Watts, H. W. (1991). An appreciation of guy orcutt. *Journal of Economic Perspectives*, 5(1):171–179.

Weber, M. (1922 (1968)). *Economy and Society*. University of California Press, Berkeley.

Welch, I. (2000). Herding among security analysts. *Journal of Financial Economics*, 58:369–396.

White, H. C. (1981). Where do markets come from? *Advances in Strategic Management*, 17:323–350.

Wilensky, U. (1998). Netlogo segregation model. Technical report, Center for Connected Learning and Computer-Based Modeling, Northwestern University, Evanston, IL. http://ccl.northwestern.edu/netlogo/models/Segregation.

Wilhite, A. W. (2001). Bilateral trade and small-world networks. *Computational Economics*, 18(1):49–64.

Wilhite, A. W. (2006). Economic activity on fixed networks. In Tesfatsion, L. and Judd, K. L., editors, *Handbook of Computational Economics, Vol. 2*. North-Holland/Elsevier, Amsterdam.

Williams, D. R. and Williams, H. (1969). Auto-maintenance in the pigeon: Sustained pecking despite contingent non-reinforcement. *Journal of the Experimental Analysis of Behavior*, 12:511–520.

Windrum, P. (2007). Neo-schumpeterian simulation models. In Hanusch, H. and Pyka, A., editors, *The Elgar Companion to Neo-Schumpeterian Economics*, chapter 26. Edward Elgar, Cheltenham.

Wolfram, S. (2002). *A New Kind of Science*. Wolfram Media Inc.

Wood, S. N. (2010). Statistical inference for noisy nonlinear ecological dynamic systems. *Nature*, 466:1102–1107.

Yaari, M. (1987). A dual theory of choice under risk. *Econometrica*, 55:95–115.

Index